To Maggie
Star of this book and of my life

ABOUT THE AUTHOR

Derek Taylor grew up amid the coalfields of Nottinghamshire in a house just round the corner from where D. H. Lawrence had lived. His first big shock came when he won a place at Oxford's most aristocratic college, Christ Church. Baffled by the Wooster-like behaviour of his fellow students, he took refuge in university journalism, and that led to a job with Independent Television News.

As a TV correspondent, he discovered that failure can be just as spectacular as success. In Rome, he was wrestled to the Pope's feet by papal bodyguards in front of 5,000 pilgrims. And surviving was often enough – he reported five wars and spent seven months in Iran covering the Islamic revolution.

His later career, in broadcast management, held its own terrors. As chief executive of a large American news company, he often felt that dodging bullets and kidnappers in Lebanon had been preferable to the ritual humiliation of a New York board meeting.

Derek now leads a peaceful life with his wife, Maggie, in Stow-on-the-Wold. He occasionally does consultancy work for arts and media organisations, and otherwise walks, travels and writes. He has one son by a previous marriage, Dan, who has a doctorate in aesthetics and lectures in philosophy. This is Derek's first book.

www.derekjtaylorbooks.com

CONTENTS

AUTHOR'S NOTE

In what follows, I've sometimes swapped around the sequence of events in order to help the narrative along. I've also changed some names, as well as identifiable detail about their owners, in order to protect their privacy. Some place names have been changed too to avoid causing offence. Oh, and in case you do recognise your village and you think I've been unduly mean or even too kind about it, I'll share with you something I've discovered while writing *A Horse in the Bathroom*: there are as many opinions about the English village as there are village-dwellers in England. So my view is one in roughly twelve million, and should be given no more weight than that.

CHAPTER 1

THE SQUATTER
AND THE LANDLADY

My bare feet peel away from the flagstones like sticky-tape from a refrigerator door. I must have spilt some milk by the bed. But it's the same in the bathroom. So I unlatch the bedroom door and, trying not to wake Maggie, sticky-tape my way into the kitchen, then execute a leaden-footed slalom around packing cases and upturned chairs in the living room. It's like paint half an hour after you've put the brushes away. And it's everywhere.

Stow-on-the-Wold church clock strikes and I count. Three a.m. The numbness of sleep is wearing off and I feel the panic rising. It wasn't like this when we went to bed.

It's our first night in The Old Stables, and here it is, going wrong already! Just when we thought it was safe to say, 'Phew, thank God no more guerrilla warfare with the Planning Office, or night terrors brought on by collapsing walls, poison gas and dozy apprentices. No more snow-blocked, wind-torn, flood-sodden delay.' Just when we thought our over-worked bank account could have a bit of a lie-in.

I spy a plastic bowl on the sofa and fill it with warm water. The mop's on the sideboard. And I start to swab a test patch between the back of the TV and some boxes marked 'Precious'. My feet are getting warm, stuck on one spot.

Of course, that's it. We put the underfloor heating on to take the chill off before we turned in. We always thought these so-called scratchproof, non-stainable floor slabs were too good to be true. The heat must be sweating something nasty out of them. Gawd, don't tell me we've got to hack the whole lot up. And there below are the heating pipes, waiting to puncture at the merest tap from a pickaxe.

As the church clock tinkles out quarter past, I flop onto a packing case to watch the bit I've just swilled, willing it to behave itself. I calm myself with the thought that everything looks grim at 3.15 a.m. And I suppose we all get fretful and self-absorbed when a single project takes over our lives.

It could be me, of course. Maybe I've not got the right temperament for it – a bit late to decide that now. We must have been deranged to think of converting a beat-up old stable. Too many TV home makeover shows, that's what it is. How come we didn't just buy one, ready-made?

It had all begun hopefully enough, two years before.

After a career as a TV news reporter, I was working as a consultant and living with Maggie at her house on the outskirts of Stow-on-the-Wold in the Cotswolds. But we wanted to move to somewhere we could call 'ours' without me feeling like a squatter and she a landlady. Maggie came home one day – she has a women's fashion boutique in Stow – and mentioned that a friend of hers, optimistically named Sunny, had put her Grade II-listed cottage up for sale. She was moving to India. The cottage was right in the middle of Stow.

'She's splitting the property in two,' explains Maggie. 'The cottage is one lot, and then she's selling off the rest of the land separately for development. Apparently, it's got full planning permission to build a new Cotswold stone house. Architect's plans thrown in, Sunny says.'

'Well, her cottage is worth a once-over,' I reply. 'Did you know it's got the biggest inglenook chimney in the whole of Gloucestershire? And there's a little window in the kitchen that's supposed to date from the twelfth century.'

Maggie groans.

'No way.' She shakes her head. 'It's so dark. It's got minuscule holes for windows. We'd both go white and shrivel up if we lived in a pokey little place like that.'

This is the same argument we've been having for the past six years.

Maggie wants a house with lots of light.

I need one with character.

We've already rejected scores of 'gloomy' (quote Maggie) Cotswold cottages and 'soulless' (quote me) airy bungalows. It's not that Maggie hates character, nor that I loathe light. It's just that we have different priorities. And what we do have in common doesn't help either – we're both stubborn. So we need a place with both. They do exist of course. Peer into any Cotswolds estate agent and you'll see them, usually called 'Regency mansion with many original features'. They come with those big, square-paned windows that nearly reach the ground, and usually start at around £2.5 million – about £2.15 million more than we can drum up.

'What I was thinking,' Maggie continues, 'was why don't we go for the bit of land, not the cottage? We could maybe build a home on it ourselves, something that's exactly what we're both looking for. I don't mean you and me actually laying the bricks and doing the plumbing. But get one built to our design.'

'Well it's hardly going to have much history to it, is it, if it's a new build?'

'Humour me. Let's look.'

So that's what we do the next day. Me dragging my heels and getting my nose ready for some turning-up.

Sunny leaves us to wander about on our own. The land is overgrown with privet hedges as wide as a bus, unpruned rhododendrons, the odd fruit tree, knee-high grass, and there's a weedy bit of gravel at the far end where Sunny keeps her VW.

On the far corner by the road is a bunch of old garages, a bit like the ones you see round the back of every 1950s block of south London council flats. Admittedly, Sunny's version doesn't have chipped blue paint on up-and-over doors sprayed with 'Kylie is a… whatever'. Sunny's doors are old style, creosote-daubed swing-openers. And Stow-on-the-Wold doesn't do graffiti, unless you count the mason's mark scratched on its church porch.

We have a poke around inside. Behind the end garage door there's a carpet, a couch and a little sink.

'Sunny works as a chiropractor,' Maggie explains. 'She must use this bit as her consulting room.'

The inside of the rest of the building though looks like a place that giant spiders and rats might call home. We can make out a back wall, 4 or 5 metres high, fashioned from irregular Cotswold stones. They're supposed to be honey-coloured but are as grubby as a Victorian factory chimney. With a bit of struggling over heaps of broken roof slates and shifting of rusty wheelbarrows, we also see behind the grime and cobwebs that the two end-walls are built the same way.

'They look solid enough,' says Maggie.

'Hmm,' I add. 'I tell you what, they look pretty old to me.' We stumble back out into the daylight. 'And what's more this bit of land is a burgage,' I say. Maggie's used to my pseudo-academic burblings, so she ignores me. 'Some burgages in the north Cotswolds,' I persist, 'go back over a thousand years. They had a cottage at one end – like Sunny's – then vegetables and a few chickens and pigs down here where we're standing.'

Leaving Maggie working out the direction of the rising sun, I start to stride through the undergrowth to pace out the length of the land, scraping my forehead on a damson tree almost before I've started.

The burgage is a classic length. It measures two perches wide by twelve long. That's a perch as in a 'rod, pole or perch' found in lists of antique units of measurement, a perch being the length from the back of the plough to the nose of the ox. To save you nipping out with a tape measure to check, that's about 5 metres (apparently medieval ploughs and oxen came in standard sizes). So Sunny's burgage is roughly 10 metres by 60.

I wade round the bindweed, duck under the damson, and go back and find Maggie.

'What I'm thinking,' she says, 'is what if – instead of knocking down this old building where the garages are now – we converted it? We'd get the morning sun. And we could have a courtyard here that would be warm and sheltered all day long.'

'OK, OK, I'm starting to see it,' I chip in. 'If we keep these old walls at the back and the side, we could get them cleaned up, and have the stones exposed in a big high-ceilinged main room – maybe with some oak beams. Then you could have six-foot-high windows all along the front.' There's a tinge of triumph oozing into my voice.

Maggie nods and 'Hmms' a bit. It's enough for me.

'You know, this is it,' I say. 'We just need a good builder, that's all. Let's go for it!'

So that's how it all started. My little eyes went wide. And all I could see was a vision of how it would end up, in a perfect home for both of us. Without the slightest thought for the two years of hand-wringing by day and sheet-twisting by night which was on the cards before that.

'Hang on, hang on,' says Maggie. 'There's loads of stuff we've got to find out about first.'

'Well, yes, I know that, of course,' I insist. 'But I'm just saying, can't you see it? A dazzling facade of glass for you and a tall, exposed wall of mellow stone for me. And there should be just about enough room to hold all our clothes and books as well!'

'I reckon it could be.' She's getting keen. I can hear it in her voice.

Now I don't want you to get me wrong. We don't go about drooling our way into adventures like fourteen-year-olds having a first crush and singing 'Love Will Find a Way'. No. We can be quite organised. And back home that night, we make a list of questions. They boil down to two big ones. 1) Can we afford it? And 2) Would we get planning permission?

'I can handle the money,' I say to Maggie. 'I'm good with numbers.'

She gives one of those smiles where her lips are clamped together. I'm affronted at her lack of enthusiasm for my suggestion. After all, I've got more financial credentials on my CV than just filling in expense claims as a reporter.

'You know, I did used to manage a company with a $150 million-a-year turnover,' I protest. This is what I went on to do after I stopped working in front of camera.

But Maggie knows that the American owners of the TV news company I found myself 'in charge of' insisted on putting in their own twenty-five person accounts department to track every dollar and cent of their investment. And they appointed their own finance director to ask me questions, such as, 'So, do you want to start a new service in Latin America, or would you rather fire a hundred people?' My job as chief executive was to guess, from the way he phrased the questions, what the right answer was.

'Well maybe we could do it together,' Maggie adds. She doesn't need to mention her hands-on ownership of a successful retail business for me to get the point.

'Sure,' I say. And I pull up an Excel spreadsheet on my laptop.

We look at the two sides of the equation. Sunny wants £125,000 for the burgage. And if we can get the asking price for Maggie's house, where we live now, after paying off the mortgage, we'd have about £170,000 for the building work. Sounds plenty when you consider the new house isn't going to be that big. Still, I put my name alongside an action point to find an architect who'll give us a rough costing. My other task is to phone the Cotswold District Council Planning Department in Cirencester.

Before I can get round to these jobs, I'm due in London the following day for a meeting with a client (I'm doing a bit of consultancy for a small media company), and I've arranged to have lunch afterwards with an old friend, Ralph.

CHAPTER 2

LARK RISE TO MARXISM

'What you wanna do that for?' asks Ralph. I've just told him about our plans in Stow. He licks beer froth from the moustache that rounds off his pointy beard, then screws up the left side of his face. 'You looking to back out of life and sit in a hole waiting for a quiet death?'

Ralph lives in east London, not in one of the snappy flats around Canary Wharf, but in a mid-terrace house on one of the seedier back streets near West Ham Football Club. It's a source of pride to Ralph that you have to push through wheelie bins to travel the 8 feet from the front gate to his door.

'Well, it's where Maggie's got her business,' I reply, 'and we like it there.' As the flabby words slouch past my lips, I realise I'm showing him an ill-prepared defence against his inevitable attack.

He shakes his head. 'It's *Lark-Rise-to-Candleford* syndrome,' he pronounces.

'Careful Ralph,' I say, getting my thoughts in some sort of battle order, 'You read Russian at Cambridge, not English. You're wandering outside your comfort zone, and I've no idea what you're talking about.'

'Not literature. Sunday night television,' he corrects me.

'Sunday night telly!' I squeak. I've got him here. 'Let me get this right. Sunday nights, you slip into your dressing gown, microwave the cocoa and settle down in front of *Lark Rise to Candleford*.'

'Hardly, old son. My mother wanted a box set for Christmas, and she insisted I watch the first episode with her.'

'Hoh.' It's the sound of my sails as he steals their wind. 'But you're suggesting *I* watch it, are you?' I say, and taking another tack, add, 'I'm all for Jane Austen delivered to the living room of the masses, but endless nights of Dawn French and Julia Sawalha is... is a bonnet too far.' I indulge him with a smile, and lean back to rest on my wit.

'You may not watch it, but that doesn't mean to say you're not a closet fellow-traveller. It's like homosexuality in the fifties,' Ralph presses on. 'You can't admit it to yourself, but just like all the other *Lark Rise* addicts, you harbour a burning desire for life in rural England where men doff their hats, "ladies"...' – he pauses long enough to raise both hands, each bobbing two apostrophising fingers up and down – '... curtsy, jolly red-faced cooks bake apple turnover like they don't make any more, and anyone who is nasty gets their fair dues and turns out to be nice after all just in time for the end credits.'

'You're trying to say that I'm moving to Stow-on-the-Wold out of a need to exist in some pastoral golden age?'

'There, see, doesn't it feel better now you've come out and said the words? You're a romantic, in fact the most sentimental sort of romantic.'

'Is this a defence of life in Whitechapel surrounded by drug-crazed muggers and ASBO-breaching kids?' I've been through this sort of sparring with Ralph before so I know it's best to give as good as you get.

'Hackney Marshes,' he corrects me again. 'Life in east London is what it is.'

'Very profound, Ralph.'

'It doesn't pretend to be something it isn't,' he insists. 'Living in a chocolate-box village like Stow-on-the-Wold – all morris dancers and ye oldie tea shoppes – is a sugary lie. It's like setting up home in a theme park for old-aged pensioners. It's not the real world. It's an invention to feed the perverted desires of the middle classes.'

'Ah, ah, that's it,' I cry, wagging a triumphant finger towards the pub ceiling. 'I see now, these are the lunatic ramblings of a disillusioned Marxist.' I shake my head with a knowing twinkle. 'I see your evil plan, to turn me into a Cotswold cell of the Fourth Communist International.'

But Ralph's not to be bantered off course. 'It probably all stems from your childhood. Brought up in a Midlands mining village, you saw at first hand the oppression of the workers and now yearn for some utopian alternative.'

'Ralph, I admire your ingenuity. But mixing Freud with Trotsky is like... like... like dissecting a football with a scalpel.' It's hard work debating with Ralph. 'Anyway, by the time I was born, the coal mines were nationalised.'

'Only just. The legacy of exploitation was still there. People react in one of two ways to that kind of exposure to social injustice: they either fight it or flee it. You're doing the latter. Spurning your roots.'

'So now I'm a snob, as well!'

'Don't be too hard on yourself, Derek. I expect you'll be quite happy in Stow-on-the-Wold.' He pronounced the four words as though they're in an unfamiliar foreign language. 'We're all victims of society in our own way.'

'Well, that's a consolation.'

The haddock and chips arrive.

'I bet they don't sell many copies of *The Guardian* in Stow,' Ralph adds, biting the end off a ketchup sachet. And we declare a truce.

I usually enjoy the journey back on the train. The threatening grot of west London's trackside houses viewed from a pre-booked window seat gives way to the reassuring safety of fields with cows in. But today the graffiti speeding past outside, I'd swear, says '*Lark Rise* addict' and 'morris dancer junkie'. And the cows, when they finally arrive, look like mock-ups on a low-budget film set.

So by the time I join Maggie on the sofa with my mug of Red Bush tea, my mind's not on our usual news exchange. Well, not on Maggie's turn anyway. I gather there was some sort of drama at the shop today, something about a male transvestite, or a Dior frock being shoplifted, or a woman from Leicestershire who was going to buy twenty-eight pairs of designer jeans and then changed her mind. Something like that, because throughout I'm staring at the eucalyptus through the French windows and then at the Cotswold stone fireplace we had put in two years ago without seeing them.

'So that was my day at the shop,' she finishes. 'It was pretty boring.' And when I just grunt, she goes on, 'Anyway, I'm starving. What are we having for supper? Are we going to do it together? You can tell me about your lunch with Ralph while we get on with it.' This is too many questions and propositions for my distracted brain to cope with, so I just follow her into the kitchen.

Now you may be thinking, 'Oh isn't that nice that they cook together. I wish we did things like that.' Well, think again, because with Maggie and me, the kitchen is a battleground. We both like cooking. But we have completely different styles. She's an 'I'll put in a pinch of this and a dash of that and taste it and see what else it needs' sort of person, while I'm a 'stick strictly to the recipe until the hallowed words of Nigella or Rick are proved to be erroneous' type of bloke. We also each know that our system is the correct one. It is therefore highly dangerous for both of us to be within elbow-range of the oven at the same time.

Over the years we have thus developed a set of culinary rules, roughly equivalent to the Geneva Convention, designed to hold our relationship firm.

- Rule 1: if Maggie's been working that day, Derek does supper, and if Derek's been working, Maggie does it.
- Rule 2: if both have been working, supper preparation is shared.

Then come two important sub-rules.

- Rule 2A: in the event that both are in the kitchen together, neither shall be permitted to wear the head chef's big hat; instead separate and sovereign tasks shall be allocated to each of us.

And finally,

- Rule 2B: neither shall claim to know better than the other what the other should do.

It's here that the treaty starts to break down. Neither of us is capable of upholding Rule 2B.

Tonight we're doing Zardalu Polo. 'What in the name of the blessed Delia is that?' I hear you say. Well, you should have guessed that we're a mite obsessive about what we eat. Not for us a frozen pizza or an M & S shepherd's pie. We do the hand-crafted goods every night regardless of what stresses the day has brought us. If we really can't be faffed, we might go out for a meal. Don't get me wrong though. We're not food snobs. We run a mile at the sight of a bizarrely shaped loaf being sold for £6 by a snotty eighteen-year-old with a posh accent (something which is all too common in the Cotswolds). Nor at the other extreme are we the sort of people who think a cabbage is not a cabbage unless it drops a poached baby slug onto your plate. No, we just like tasty food. And we like doing it ourselves.

And tonight, it's that good old Persian favourite, Zardalu Polo. So while I prepare the rice, lamb, apricots, onion, turmeric and cinnamon, Maggie – in a separate part of the kitchen – is doing something with aubergines and cauliflower. After I've brushed aside Maggie's suggestion about the need to sauté the meat a little longer, and she's ignored my comment about the standard way to cut aubergine being in quarter-inch-thick disks rather than three dimensional jigsaw pieces, Maggie says, 'Go on, then, tell me about Ralph.'

'I think it might have to wait till we're sitting down,' I reply, trying to scrape off the excess cinnamon which I've accidentally spilt on the lamb.

So once the ladybird-shaped kitchen timer has rung 'time up', and we've both got two mouthfuls of the excellent Near-Eastern cuisine inside us, it's time for the unwritten Rule

3. And here you may be permitted a brief 'Ah, that's nice.' Once the food is on the table, we always compliment each other's cooking. The most severe criticism that's ever heard across our dining table might be something along the lines of: 'This sauce is delicious. Perhaps next time it might take a smidgeon less cumin. But it is lovely as it is.' So when we've got that stuff out of the way, I start to recount the detail of what Ralph said about *Lark-Rise-to-Candleford* syndrome and how, in moving to Stow, I was craving a childhood paradise I never had, all of which I deliver with what seems to me minimal outrage and maximum objectivity.

Maggie laughs. 'I like Ralph,' she says, 'in small doses anyway. He's a caricature.'

'Yes, he's a funny guy. So why do you like living in Stow?' I ask.

'Obviously because the shop's here…'

'… and?'

'Well, the countryside's lovely, and I couldn't bear the filthy traffic in a city.'

'Is that enough?'

She puts down her knife and fork and stares at me. 'You know something? I think Ralph's got to you.'

'No, he hasn't, no. It's not personal. I'm just interested to understand what makes rural living in the second decade of the twenty-first century attractive. Academically speaking. It's nothing personal.'

'You're trying to say, is village life all it's cracked up to be?'

'Sort of. I mean villages are misfits, aren't they? The village – little houses, an inn and a church surrounded by fields – is a medieval idea. Let's face it, the English village – as such – is an anachronism. Why would anyone want to live in an anachronism?'

'Now you sound like Ralph. You'll be telling me next that Stow Parish Council should be a step towards the dictatorship of the proletariat.' And with that she helps herself to half a dozen more cubic inches of ZP and a scoop of aubergine.

'Stow-on-the-Wold. I suppose it does have a *Lark-Rise-ish to Candleford-y* sound to it,' I muse, leaning back to stare at the ceiling.

Maggie seizes the moment to attack me while I'm vulnerable. 'What's that?' she cries, poking the bottom button of my shirt. But it's not that innocent little fastening device she's referring to, but the flesh beneath.

'What do you mean?' I reply, quickly leaning forwards again.

'You know, your tummy's a lot bigger than when we first met,' she says.

'I don't think it is at all,' I say, 'I'm very careful about what I eat.'

'You probably need more exercise. Have you been to the gym lately?'

'I haven't had time, what with this burgage project and Ralph and one thing and another.'

Maggie can do a very effective sceptical expression that requires no words. She's right, of course.

Or is she justifying her capture of the last morsel of spicy lamb?

CHAPTER 3

THE NICE HAM SYNDROME

It doesn't take me long next morning to come up with an architectural partnership in our area with a prestigious oriental name and a website showing lots of pictures of oak and glass constructions set on the side of Gloucestershire hills. The designs look exactly like what we're after, and lots of them have won awards in Sweden and California.

OK, so our job falls short of their £2 million minimum assignment, but I don't think there was any need for the receptionist who picked up the phone to be quite so offhand.

The next one Google throws up is Jackson Architects. That sounds more our speed.

The number rings out for about a minute before a female voice delivers a breathless 'Hello.' I'm guessing a wrong number.

'Is that Jackson Architects?'

'Well, not really.'

'Oh, sorry.'

And I'm about to hang up when she says, 'That's OK. We're divorced. He's Jackson Architects. I'm AJ Architects, A for Anthea. I can give you his number.'

It seems a waste not to pick her brains while I've got an actual architect on the line, so I explain our needs.

'You don't want an architect,' she says. 'You want a builder. I can design it for you. But the builder's the one who'll build it for you. He'll give you a quote.'

I make a mental note to try in future not to give away that I'm learning on the job, and ask, 'So, do you know any builders?'

'I've come across one or two,' she replies, 'in the course of my work. In fact there's one sitting in my kitchen now. He lives here. Do you want to speak to him?'

I'm having second thoughts. 'Well actually,' I sidestep, 'we're a bit wary about talking to a builder at this stage. He might grab this bit of land from under our noses and develop it himself. It's a real find.'

'I shouldn't worry about that,' says Anthea. 'This one's got no money.' And before I can respond, I hear her yell, 'Nik!' And I arrange to meet him two days later, that's Saturday morning, at the market cross in Stow to take him to the burgage.

Next, I tap out the number for the Cotswold District Council Planning Office, and begin to explain to the voice at the other end about the burgage and Sunny and how we want to buy it but only if... when she interrupts.

'Name and address?'

I tell her and she shoots back, '10 a.m. Thursday on-site,' followed by a bell-like but dismissive, 'Thank you.'

Saturday comes, and Nik the builder arrives at the market cross clutching Co-op bags in each hand.

'Sorry I'm late,' he says, 'I got here early, so I went to pick up some stuff for the kids' dinner, and there was a queue.' It's an endearing start.

As we walk across the Square, I ask him if he's got any experience of converting historic buildings. He explains that he used to be lead foreman for a company that specialised in restoration work. Then a year ago, he and his partner, Simon set up their own business.

At the site, he doesn't need long.

'To be frank,' he says, 'it's not so much restoration, as a rebuild in an old style. Everything'll have to come down except the back wall and probably the two side walls.'

I feel I can be direct with him, 'How much?'

'I can't give you a real quote till you've got the plans approved and we know exactly what's involved,' he replies. 'But for a rough idea, assume a thousand quid per square metre of ground area. Then add around ten grand for demolition and allow ten more for underpinning the old walls – just in case.'

He shuffles the Co-op bags into one hand, shakes mine with the other, and we agree to talk again once purchase of the plot has gone through.

The pieces are starting to fit together as easily as tiles on a bathroom wall. Those with experience of such matters (or of house purchase) will have noticed no mention of the tricky bits round the basin or at the back of the loo.

First, we have to find the money to pay Sunny. Ultimately, the whole project is going to be funded by the sale of Maggie's house where we live now plus the pay-off I got when I resigned from the American news company. But until the house is sold, we need a bridging loan. One phone call and two signatures later, that box gets a simple, if costly, tick.

Next, tax.

When did you ever have good news about tax? I have a vague memory of some advice on a TV programme that we may be able to pay only 5 per cent instead of the full VAT rate on the builder's services. So I phone the tax office to check. And a jolly woman there says that's correct, and did I know that with a self-build we can claim all, yes all, the tax back on the materials? 'But not fitted wardrobes,' she emphasises.

'Crikey,' I blurt. 'But we're not actually building it ourselves.'

'Oh no, you don't have to get your hands dirty. It's a "self-build" if you contract the builder, buy the materials yourself, and then live in it afterwards.'

'Crikey,' I repeat, 'but that's worth thousands.'

'I know,' she chirrups. 'Brilliant, isn't it? I'll send you the forms.'

'What a very nice woman,' I keep saying to myself. 'I'll never complain about government bureaucracy ever again.'

We're on a roll with banks and tax collectors throwing cash at us. So there must be more good news to come. For instance, we need to get the architect moving. It's got to be Anthea. But first Maggie and I need to sort out our own ideas. Sunny's given us a key to the gate, so we can go and look at it any time we want. And on a cold, bright September afternoon, we spend an hour wandering round the buildings, pacing out exactly how big it is.

Now it's nearly ours, we've pocketed our rose-tinted specs. It's small. There's no avoiding it. But the way things are going for us right now, we know there's an answer, with a bit of imagination. All we need is a small south-facing extension at one end. And we could raise the roof level a little so there's space for a small mezzanine gallery along the back wall.

We recalculate the finances, and find that M minus C (where M is the money available, and C is the cost, according to Nik's formula, of demolishing, converting, roof-raising and extension-erecting) = AN (i.e. Approximately Nothing). So that's all right, though there's now no room for M to shrink or C to swell.

The next morning, I'm standing in Back Walls – that'll be our road when it's all done – on the lookout for Anthea's four-by-four. She's agreed to pop in to have a quick look at the job en route to a meeting with one of her established clients. I see a likely looking vehicle turn in off the Fosse Way, and flag it down when I see a friendly wave through the windscreen. She bumps up onto the curb and a moment later we're shaking hands. I'd vaguely expected a strapping Amazon, for no other reason than that people involved in building work should look like weightlifters. But Anthea's dress size must be what Maggie would classify as 'petite'. She looks overwhelmed by her quilted anorak and wellies. As she slams the car door I ask, 'Don't you need a clipboard or something?'

'Bit soon for that,' she replies. 'I just want to get a general idea of what we might be getting up to.'

When she catches sight for the first time of the old garages crouching shamefaced in the corner of the plot, I think I detect a slight upward movement of her eyebrows. So, once I've explained what we want to do, and she's walked around, poked about inside, and done a bit of rough pacing out of lengths and widths, I take advantage of a long pause in the conversation to ask, 'So do you think it'll work? Or do you think we're daft?' then await her pronouncement.

'I've seen worse,' she says, shakes my hand again, adds, 'Talk soon,' and she's gone.

That evening, with Maggie in full swing moulding pastry for our chicken cobbler, I'm lurking on the edge of the kitchen, a glass of cranberry juice in my hand, giving her a word by word account, anxious to know if she thinks Anthea's opinion is encouraging.

'Well,' Maggie replies, mixing the butter and flour for the topping, 'yours was a silly question to start with. It's like asking the deli if their ham's nice.' (A low blow, as this is a crime I've been guilty of.)

'You know,' I say, 'Hugh Fearnley-Whittingstall puts four tablespoons of flour into his mix. I reckon that's no more than three and a half.'

She wafts me away with the back of her hand. 'Isn't it time for you to watch the *Six O'clock News*?' she suggests.

'Sure,' I reply, 'but what do you mean about the nice ham and Anthea?'

'All I'm saying,' she says, 'is that we're Anthea's potential clients, so she's hardly likely to slag off what we want to do, is she?'

I ponder this as I wander out of the kitchen. Incisive as Maggie's judgement may be, 'I've seen worse' doesn't exactly sound like the kind of endorsement you hear Lewis Hamilton give Hugo Boss shoes.

CHAPTER 4

CAVALIERS AND GASWORKS

'So what's the name of the house going to be?' my sister Anne asks. She and my brother-in-law David have stopped by and I've dragged them off to look at the burgage with outbuilding. I give her credit for assuming we'll manage to buy it and build it.

'Well,' I play for time. 'Maybe, "The Old Barn"?'

'But it's not a barn' she objects, 'and it doesn't look anything like one. It's long and thin, not tall and wide.'

She's right. It's like calling a bungalow *Chateau Magnifique*. People either assume you've got an unsubtle sense of irony or they just snigger.

'How about "The Old Chiropractor's Consulting Room?"' she offers. I'm starting to think she's not taking it seriously after all, though the suggestion may not be quite as daft as it sounds. Just up the road, there's a row of cottages called 'The Old Vet's Surgery 1', 'The Old Vet's Surgery 2, and 3', and nobody seems to giggle. 'Or,' she adds, pointing over at a 3-foot-wide wheel with rusty iron rims and crumbly wooden spokes, half-hidden behind some junky sacks of rubble, 'What about "The Old Cart Shed?"'

Well, at least we can agree on the first two words. And once she and my brother-in-law have left, I head off to do some research, pausing only in Fleece Alley to return the full-throated 'Lovely afternoon,' issued by the vicar, a man of muscular stature and a bountiful beard, who's walking his dog, Black Beauty (this is my name for the animal, reflecting its colour and near equine proportions, though its face is, I admit, more butch than belle). My destination is the glowering gothic St. Edward's Hall in the middle of Stow's Market Square. This is where local records might help me find a name that combines historical precision with... with what? Well, I'll know when I see it.

My first discovery seems to back the cart shed theory. In 1862, the railway came to Stow-on-the-Wold. Or rather, not quite. It couldn't get up the hill. So they plonked a single platform with sidings in a field one mile to the south. This station was a godsend to the folk of Stow. Not as a means of rushing them off to Oxford or Worcester. Stowites have always known that such places will disappoint, without the need to visit them. No. The railway brought regular supplies of coal from Wolverhampton and this was not just to burn in Stow's hundreds of inglenook fireplaces.

Just as the station opened, The Stow-on-the-Wold Gas and Coke Company was putting the finishing flourishes to the town's gasworks. And this, I note, was only a couple of hundred yards from our nameless home-to-be. The fuel for this marvel of industrial development had to get from the sidings at Stow station up Stow Hill to the gas furnace.

All of a sudden, coal merchants and hauliers sprang up everywhere, and the smart money went into cart horses and drays. Though not certain, it looks possible that our old building housed both. Fifteen-love to Anne.

So if we're going to be sticklers for historical accuracy, I guess our prospective home might be called 'The Old Coal Carter's Yard', or even 'The Old Gas Works Supply Sub-Depot'. Now, I do know people – men mostly – who're only happy when breathing in fumes from a steam-driven canal-boat lift, or grazing their knees on a pedal-powered cobbler's lathe, and for whom such names would be bliss. And I suppose, given that both my granddads and their fathers before them were coal-miners, I ought to be relishing these echoes of my own history. I guess too, some sort of industrial name would at least stand out from all the rural idyll addresses in Stow, which, by the way, has no fewer than four 'Rose Cottages'. On the other hand, would we be lynched for bringing down house prices? I decide to compromise, and put the 'Coal Carter's Yard' and the 'Gas Works Sub-Depot' on the 'Possibles' list.

My second thread of research goes back several centuries earlier. The nearest point to us on Sheep Street is where The Crown Inn used to stand. It was built sometime in the 1400s, but came into its own 200 years later. During the 1600s, Cavaliers and Roundheads were constantly marching into Stow, declaring it for King or for Parliament, then promptly losing it to the other side.

In fact, it was in Stow in 1646 that a decisive nail was hammered into the monarch's coffin. After being defeated just north of the town, the Royalist infantry were chased into Stow's Market Square. The thousand or so who surrendered were banged up inside the church for several days without food or other relief. Nasty, but healthier than the fate of the two hundred who resisted. They were slaughtered till the blood ran down Digbeth Street and formed a sinister pool at the bottom outside Maggie's dress shop. Legend has it that ducks swam in the gore.

Records do not show whether the owners of The Crown Inn kept a sign hidden ready behind the bar saying 'The Cromwell Arms' which they could quickly hang up outside whenever the Parliamentarians came to town. The landlord must have done something similar because business at the inn was so brisk during Civil War times that the owners needed to expand. They acquired all the surrounding dwellings and their associated land. And – here's the exciting bit I stumble on – this specifically included our burgage and Sunny's cottage. This latter was turned into lodgings for coachmen and ostlers downstairs, with hay stored above on the first floor. (Would not any management consultancy division worth its salt recommend re-organising these functions the other way round? Improved productivity without having to heave fodder up and down a ladder; fitter employees with sleep no longer disturbed by showers of nose-tickling hay.)

However, what I read next makes my heart pound and I can't help muttering a stifled, 'Shi...!' The chap opposite, who's been studying a single page of his leather-bound volume for the past forty minutes, raises his dark Dennis Healy eyebrows and glares. I make a face like Wallace apologising to Gromit, and re-read the entry before me. On 29 May 1690, an advert in the *London Gazette* stated that The Crown Inn at Stow-on-the-Wold had 'stabling for above a hundred horses'! Now, even on the assumption that the landlord was stretching it a bit before the Advertising Standards Authority got its act together, the early evening scene behind The Crown must have been a circus of steaming, snorting animals being unharnessed, rubbed down and led off to feed and doze for the night. Our building would have been able to take about twenty of them, I reckon. The question is: does it date back that far?

I scamper out of the records library, across the Square, round Church Street and over Sheep Street to look for evidence. The most obvious sign is that our building's the right shape for stables. A bit tall maybe, but then we know from the account of Sunny's cottage that they used to keep fodder up above. Then there's the stonework on the big back wall. The pieces are all shapes, laid hotchpotch, clearly not cut by machine. Not proof of course that it was built 350 years ago.

Short of finding a Roundhead's helmet crushed in the foundations, I can't think what else would clinch it. I wander about inside and out, shifting the odd pile of firewood, pulling aside the occasional climbing rose, and am about to resign myself to an inconclusive result when I realise I've never seen the other side of the big wall. It forms the boundary of the burgage, and so looks onto the neighbour's land. I manage to part-roll, part-drag a mouldy barrel to the garden wall at the end of the building, and heave myself onto it. I immediately see something I'd not known before. The land over there is about 3 feet higher than on this side. I can also see the broken remains of a classical balustrade on the ground.

'So what?' you might ask.

Well, I've just acquired a useful bit of new knowledge from the town records. Some of the three and four hundred year-old houses on Sheep Street are a couple of feet lower than the road, which itself has risen as it's been repaired and rebuilt over the years. So the general rule is that 'lower' means 'older'. A quick check back inside our building shows that its big back wall has no join halfway up, which would have indicated that it was a garden wall that had been extended upwards at a later date. The wall looks like it was built all of a piece, and, I reckon, much earlier than the classical balustrading now scattered in ruins on the far side.

The other thing that's struck me in my afternoon's research is how often buildings in Stow have been used for different purposes as the town's needs came and went. The Crown Inn hasn't had a London-to-Hereford coach clattering over its cobbles since 1814, when it was turned into a private house. It's now part rectory, part antiques emporium. The gasworks and the railway were both dismantled at the same time in 1954. So obviously our building could have housed horses for The Crown, then later been turned over to the coal hauliers.

Pleased with this historical sleuthing, I report back to Maggie.

'How does "The Old Stables" grab you?' I ask with a triumphant beam.

'You don't think we might be jumping ahead of ourselves, do you?' she queries.

'No. Where things come from is important. And the fact that this matters to me, I think, proves something: the reason I like Stow is because of its history.'

'Ah, it's back to Ralph again.'

'Well, he's got me thinking. That can't be bad.'

'What about less thinking and more doing. Like, when are you going to talk to the council planning office about getting permission to build?'

'I'm glad you asked that,' I reply. 'It's all in hand. I'm meeting her tomorrow.'

It's well known that getting planning permission in the middle of Stow – whether for a cute cottage or a public lavatory – is more difficult than being accepted as an MI6 operative, and can be just as arcane. As well as the ordinary planning restrictions you get in the rest of the country, buildings in Stow also have to conform to Conservation Area rules, which means architectural or historic features must be protected. We're also within the boundaries of the medieval town. If we ever manage to live in Sunny's garages, our address will be 'Back Walls', the street that marks the limit of thirteenth-century Stow, and we'll be on the townside of the street. So there may be archaeological evidence that mustn't be damaged. Then, finally, the building stands in the curtilage – 'grounds' to us mortals – of a listed building, i.e. Sunny's cottage. So any historic structures in the garden will have to be preserved. I'm ready for complicated arguments.

The planner is waiting outside the burgage gate when I arrive. She looks at her watch and introduces herself at the same time. She has one of those double-barrelled first names like Marie Antoinette or Violet Elizabeth. Hers is Bella Donna, or something equally botanical. We shall call her Bella to save on typing.

Bella is in her twenties, very tall, slim, in tight-fitting jeans. She has a small turned-up nose. I don't mean like Noddy. More like Becky Sharp in *Vanity Fair*.

'So,' she says, striding through the rampant crocosmia, unfolding a metre-square architect's plan and thrusting one end of it into my hands. 'You've got permission to demolish, and put up a three bedroom cottage here in the middle.' She points in the general direction of Sunny's VW.

'Ah, we don't want to do that,' I say, pausing for effect. 'We want to convert the old outbuilding.' I make an expansive gesture with my free hand along the line of brown garage doors, waiting for her effusive approval of our conservation-focussed aspirations (or whatever consultants working for local authorities call them).

She pokes her head briefly inside the nearest garage, leaving me in sole charge of the architect's drawing.

'We want it demolished,' she states, looking down her nineteenth-century nose at the twentieth-century aluminium door frames. The metre-square sheet of plans is poised in front of my face, around which the wind is threatening to wrap it like a slapstick custard pie. 'It's an eyesore,' she adds. 'The area will be improved by getting rid of it, and by putting up a cottage. In Cotswold stone, of course.'

I'm shocked. But if I'd ever been curious to know what it feels like to be a Cotswold planning officer dealing with an obstinate citizen intent on wrecking the village's heritage, now is the moment for a role reversal.

'Researches show,' I say, confident that weighty tomes of history sit like a bulwark at my back. 'Researches show that this building dates from at least the seventeenth century when it provided stabling for The Crown Inn. It then became a domestic agricultural building.' (As I say these words, I realise I don't know what they mean.) 'Later, during the Industrial Revolution, it was at the forefront of the economic transformation of Stow with the building of the gas manufactory and the arrival of the railway. My wife and I place the highest value on the preservation of Stow's history as embodied in its ancient buildings. We feel we have a duty to restore this old treasure to its former glory.' All this has been accompanied by my scuffle with the drawings which are flapping in my arms like a duck trying to regain its freedom.

'Looks like a bunch of old garages to me,' observes Bella, seizing the architect's plans and folding them with a single movement. 'OK,' she concedes. 'But you'd have to put in glass and oak all down the front.' I'm about to say, 'That's just what we want to do,' when she continues, 'And remember, this is only general guidance. You'd still have to go through the application process.'

And before I can thank her, she's disappeared through the buddleias.

I recall what Mike, who's known me for the best part of a lifetime and who's from an army family, often reminds me: time spent on reconnaissance is rarely wasted.

CHAPTER 5

STRANGE ENCOUNTERS AT THE BURGAGE

'They've got a mouthful of gimme and a handful of much obliged,' sings Ella into both my ears at once.

The good thing about going to the gym (and Lord knows there has to be something good, apart from the doubtful promise of a longer life with a smaller belt size) is that I get time to listen to Ella Fitzgerald on my iPod. And it's not just the sweet sound of her lilting voice. It's the lyrics as well. Who wrote them, I wonder? Take this one. 'A mouthful of gimme and a handful of much obliged.' It describes every American hotel doorman you'll ever come across.

So here I am biking up the hill on the screenette in front of me, level four and ten minutes set on the timer, at the leisure centre in Bourton-on-the-Water, five minutes down the Fosse Way from Stow, with Ella for company.

About four and a half minutes in, my attention starts to drift away from her, and I notice on the counter by my left hand that I've burned nine calories. Nine calories. That must be a piece of cheddar with the total volume of a pinhead. Still I'm over the first digital hill and onto the flat bit in the digital middle. I once heard someone say that for every ten minutes you jog you add six minutes to your lifespan, so the logic is if you find jogging a pain, by not doing it you're adding a net four minutes to your life that could be spent in bed instead. I wonder if it's the same with gym exercises. It must be, I think, as I move on to the treadmill. This is after all just jogging without the excitement of trees and cars and people going by.

I nod and smile to the bloke on the next machine. He's about my age and he's here every day. Well, I say 'every day'. I mean every day that I'm here – which admittedly isn't often. His face is screwed up. He obviously hates it. Like me.

Ella is by now busy out on dates with a duke or possibly a caddie, though she insists that her heart still belongs to daddy. My heart nearly didn't even belong to me. I don't mean a heart attack or a stroke. But back in the days when I used to drink too much, my heart rate suddenly started to go haywire. Instead of the steady beat of the drummer while Ms Fitzgerald sings the blues, it switched to the chaotic taps of someone learning Morse code. But the message was clear. Cut out the booze and get fit. I managed to do both. With some help. The heart still goes nuts occasionally, but it's getting better, under the care of a medical genius called Dr Jaswinder Gill.

The treadmill screen shows 'Cool down' which means my ten minutes are up, so I move over to the cross-trainer, catching sight of myself in the mirror en route. My T-shirt is wet down the front. It's a badge of determination, so I assume a gritty expression for the benefit of my fellow gym rats. But I also catch sight of my middle, pushing that same T-shirt out in a less than athletic bulge. Maggie's right.

I pump my arms back and forth and my legs forth and back with extra effort, as though I can get rid of the spare tyre in the next ten minutes on the cross-trainer. Apart from the many obvious health advantages I gained from quitting the drink, it was also what got me to take up proper cooking. Not just sticking a joint in the oven on a Sunday and loading frozen peas into the microwave any more. And so occurred one of life's sneaky ironies. The calories I saved from all those glasses of wine (and similar) not consumed, I then made up by developing a great love of food. And not just of the stuff I cook myself.

As Ella advises me that the ol' rockin' chair ain't never gonna get her, I step off the machine. The pain-faced jogger is still at it. I give him another smile, and he nods back. A few stretching exercises and that's my lot. I take a couple of deep breaths. Feels good. I swig from my water bottle, then with what I fancy is a swagger, raise my hand in a cheery farewell to the gym attendant. Hmm, I think I'll come back tomorrow. Or soon anyway.

So down to business. I phone Anthea to report on the Bella skirmish. She reckons we should get the planners to commit firmly to giving us consent to build before we shell out the cash to buy the place. So we should put in a planning application pronto. Sounds sensible and she agrees to come over to Maggie's house the next afternoon.

That session with Bella has left me feeling uncomfortable. On the one hand, I'd won the argument about whether we can convert the old outbuilding rather than knock it down. After all, without that, we wouldn't be getting off the starting blocks. On the other hand, she looked miffed when she stalked off. Still, what does seem obvious is that since she'd been happy for us to demolish the old building, in fact positively wanted us to tear it down, she's presumably not going to bother about us changing it round a bit.

I put this thought to Anthea when she arrives.

'Ye-es,' she says with a joyless smile, stretching the word out in a way that makes me think it'll be followed by the sort of drawling 'I can see what you mean' which people use when they want to be polite instead of saying, 'You must be joking, sunshine.'

'And,' I continue, 'it's not as if this is going to come down to her personal whim. Presumably, there are regulations and rules and laws that'll decide the planning consent at the end of the day.'

'Ye-e-es.'

And we move on speedily to agree to submit an application for a 3-metre extension at right angles to the length of the building, as well as a roof raised 2 metres higher than the present old asbestos eyesore so that we can put in a mezzanine floor across the back of the main room.

That evening, Maggie and I do Cajun chicken, braised cabbage and sautéed polenta – one of my specialities – the preparation of which has prompted me to raise the need for a kitchen at the new place in which she can open wine or make tea without getting entangled in my fancy wristwork with the wok.

'The new house will stand or fall by the layout of its kitchen,' I say as we sit down to eat.

'Seems a bit strong,' she comments. 'But I know what you mean. We have to have chopping space on either side of the hob. That's the main thing.'

'Agreed. But there's a lot more to it than that. We need a double sink with drainer on the right, then enough room for the food-mixer and toaster in the corner...' I've plonked a sketch on the table and opened it out next to the polenta dish.

'Wow, you've been busy today,' says Maggie.

'... then the oven would just fit here. But really important is the siting of the cutlery drawer...' and on I go for several minutes, almost letting my chicken go cold.

'Do we really need this amount of detail at this stage?' she asks, when the call of the food finally gets too much for me and she can get a word in.

'Sure we do,' I reply after savouring a mouthful. 'This is not going to be a huge kitchen. So we've got to work out exactly where everything will fit. We should probably have done this even before Anthea submitted the plans. But it's OK; I've been reading on the Internet about culinary workflows...'

'Culinary whats?'

'You know, designing the kitchen like a factory production line, so you're not for ever bobbing about from one end to the next. This plan...' I wave it in the air, '... has an optimal culinary workflow...' She still looks blank. 'Get it right,' I insist, 'and marital harmony could be ours for ever.'

'OK, OK, I take the point,' she says, and ponders the plan for a couple of seconds. 'I think the oven could move over a fraction.'

'No, no!' I protest. And for the next half hour we wrestle over everything from the colander shelf size to whether the fridge door should be left or right opening.

By the time I've restacked the plates in the dishwasher where Maggie's inexpertly positioned them and we've put our feet up, we've pretty much agreed on everything but the location of the kettle plug. So a sense of satisfaction settles over the pair of us. And I seize the opportunity.

'Why don't we crack in a bid now?' I say.

'Shouldn't we wait,' replies Maggie, 'till we know whether the plan's a flyer with your Bella?'

Denying any relationship, I add, 'I'm just worried that somebody else will nip in and collar the place before we've got our act together. After all, there's loads of legal stuff that has to happen between having your bid accepted and signing the contract. Plenty of time for us to pull out if we get the thumbs down from the planners.'

Maggie nods thoughtfully and says, 'We'd better go over the finances. Just to be sure.' So that's what we do, for the fourteenth time. We agree to ask Nik to come back to the burgage to double-check our measurements, then both spend a semi-sleepless night, before offering £120,000 at 9 a.m. the next day while the estate agent is still taking his coat off.

He gets us to sit down, puts on the coffee maker, fishes a blue folder out of his drawer, leafs through it, then tells us that Sunny already has a higher figure on the table from another purchaser, and he advises us to put in our best bid straight away. We go into a huddle and up it to £125,000.

He'll get back to us.

Now that our application for planning consent has been submitted, the moment has arrived when details of what we're up to are made public, and any of our fellow citizens who don't like it will come out of their Jacobean woodwork.

Anthea has warned us to be prepared for rows with touchy neighbours. But she doesn't prepare us for what follows. We receive a handwritten letter on a vellum sheet adorned at its head with the trade address of one of Stow's leading business people, who as it happens has a reputation for touchiness, though he's not a neighbour in the strict sense. The letter is encouraging and complimentary. It says that he is delighted that we've rejected the former plan to build a reproduction cottage and that he supports our proposal to restore the old outbuilding. The author of this treasured missive is regarded by some in Stow as the *éminence grise* of the retail trade, though others might dispute the title. Nobody in Stow is quite sure about his background. I'm told that if you broach the subject, he cunningly diverts the conversation away from himself. But legend has it that he spent most of his working life in the City of London and ended up as a director of a well-known financial institution. Then a few years ago he arrived in Stow, apparently now retired, quickly got bored and so opened up a shop. It seemed to me a strange thing to do. But according to local rumour, he felt he had a point to prove. That he wasn't just a theoretical economist, only good for dishing out strategic advice at a level where everyone has their head in the clouds. He wanted to show that he was capable of doing the business himself, hacking out the profits on a daily basis down at the coalface.

I always find it difficult to describe exactly what sort of shop he's got. It sells upmarket suitcases, champagne flutes, men's straw hats, the sort of mirrors you put on a garden wall and are supposed to look like windows, and crocheted oriental lampshades on top of gigantic, highly glazed, bottle-shaped stands. That kind of stuff. Maggie says it's a 'lifestyle' shop. I suppose he knows what he's doing.

He's also on every committee, parish, municipal, political and voluntary it's possible to be a member of. So the arrival of this letter with the *éminence grise* squiggle across the bottom could be our passport to planning consent. I have a feeling that with him on our side, battles with officialdom could be, if not a walkover, at least as smooth as a three-set match. So I call him up, and arrange to meet him that very afternoon to show him our ideas on the ground.

When I arrive on-site, there's Nik doing the measurements double-check we've requested, plus a young guy who I guess must be one of the Grise's minions, waiting for his boss. And the crowd is massing because there are also two others in blazers and ties. Neither is our man. They introduce themselves as the chairman and deputy chairman of the Stow Planning Committee.

I shake their hands like they've just made it back from a moon landing, and gush on about how we're determined that our conversion will be sympathetic – it's a useful word I've picked up from Anthea – to its historic origins.

'I can't see any problem,' they both say almost simultaneously.

The chairman adds, 'You've got to understand, though, that we're only in an advisory capacity.' He glares at the young minion. 'Cirencester often ignores our recommendations. But I think I can fairly say that you can count on the support of the Stow-on-the-Wold council.' I grab their hands in a repeat of the Apollo 11 crew greeting, and while I'm wondering if a couple of man hugs would be de trop, they back off and disappear up the burgage.

I'm just about to crow to Nik when he seizes my elbow and nodding towards the young guy, says, 'This is Gilbert Gradfram-Polly.' Something like that. My journalistic skill with names deserts me on this occasion. 'He's the Cotswold District Council conservation officer.' I was glad he'd heard my speech.

'I understand,' says Glibpert, 'that you intend to demolish the boundary wall on the corner there, in order to make an entry to the driveway.' I nod. 'It's a problem, I'm afraid,' he adds, 'That's an old wall. And this, as you know, is the curtilage of a listed building, so all such historic features must be preserved.'

'But, the Highways Department in Cirencester are insisting...' I'm trying to give it a note of incredulity.

'They're concerned with road safety, not with conservation,' replies Glueprod.

Nik by this time has started to snap branches off the straggling privet that's covering much of the offending piece of wall, and is pulling away tangles of ivy in 3-metre lengths. Growlpod and I watch entranced, as Nik produces a screwdriver from his trenchcoat pocket and scrapes the wall's blackened surface.

'Breeze blocks,' he pronounces. 'It's Cotswold stone on the outside, stuck onto concrete breeze blocks.'

I can see it would be counterproductive to suggest they might be Elizabethan breeze blocks. Doesn't look to me like Grimsniff is a fan of *Comedy Roadshow*. So I limit myself to, 'I hope we can count on your support for our proposal.'

'I shall be making my recommendations direct to the case officer,' he answers, and exits through the flowering bindweed.

'Good one, Nik,' I say when our visitor's safely out of ear range.

Nik raises his eyebrows and jerks his head towards a point over my shoulder. I turn, to see Mr Grise battling his way through the undergrowth.

His specs bob in greeting. I've only ever seen him before polishing an inlaid poker chip box or adjusting the hour hand of a reproduction carriage clock in the window of his shop. Out of context now, knee-deep in couch grass and leggy rosemary, he looks vulnerable, like a king who's mislaid his horse and wandered off from his courtiers. We make introductions and seem to be on first name terms. He speaks softly, as though I should know what he's thinking without him needing to say it. He's brought a gift.

'It is as you will see,' he whispers, 'an aerial photo, taken thirty years ago, that shows Back Walls, this building...' He motions towards the garages, '... and the burgage.' Aha, he's a man who speaks my language.

'That's very kind of you,' I hear myself say in the same sotto voce tone he uses. And we go on like this, murmuring to each other like a couple of conspirators, for about ten minutes. I tell him about my researches into The Crown Inn and the gasworks. This produces on his distinguished visage what is, without doubt, a sign of approval or even enjoyment. He agrees that the place probably dates back to coaching inn days. We have a bond.

I explain the detail of our building plans. His reaction is hard to detect. But anyway his only counter-comment concerns the idea of leaving the stone wall exposed in the living room. 'That would be more appropriate to an agricultural rather than a residential building,' he says. I reply that it'll be a memento of the building's history. He nods this time, thanks me, I thank him, and before I know it, off he's popped back to his emporium. So that's another ace to us. We've got the Grise in the bag. Touchy he may be, but it just shows, if you treat people the right way…

I wait on for Nik while he finishes measuring out the ground.

'How long do you reckon,' I ask, 'to do the whole job?'

'Twenty weeks, minimum. Maybe more, with the demolition, putting up garden walls at the end. Then there are always delays for something or other. Better say six or seven months to be safe.'

Not bad. In fact not a bad day at all. We've got all the ducks in a row ready for a good shot at planning consent. The leader of the great and the good has added The Old Stables to his Christmas card address list. The builder is on his starting blocks. And all that remains is to sign the purchase contract. I can now admit it. Underneath the bravado, I'd been a bit daunted at first by the idea of 'building it ourselves' but you've just got to be systematic about it. That's all.

At 9.15 the next morning, my mobile rings. It's the estate agent. Sunny has agreed a sale with the other buyer, and the property is now off the market. We've lost it.

CHAPTER 6

POPPING OUT FOR A TUB OF OLIVES AND A MATISSE

Maggie is stoic, declaring, 'Well, perhaps it means there's something even better waiting for us,' then, grabbing her bag and her mobile phone, adds, 'I'm late already opening up the shop. I've got two suppliers coming in today, as well as three women from Bath on a girls' day out. That's always good for sales.' And she rushes off.

I mope.

I make a Red Bush tea and leave it on the desk in the office to go cold, while I slump in the armchair by the back window. I leave messages for Anthea and Nik, standing them down, then can't think what else to do. I spend two hours regretting we didn't bid that bit more. I even do a calculation on an old bit of paper and work out that we could have offered ten grand more than we did. That really bucks me up.

Next, I pass to the stage of wondering whether this setback is telling us we shouldn't be in Stow at all. Perhaps I've got a distorted idea about the wonders of the place.

This reverie is interrupted by my laptop, which has been sleeping next to the cold tea, and now gives a sudden burp. It's delivered an email. From Mike. This is the guy who's known me the best part of a lifetime, and has an uncanny ability to read my moods, even at a distance of 80 miles.

Subject: Worst place in the world
From Michael Morris Date: 26/10 2.48
To:<derekjtayl@internet.co.uk>
Cc:

Hi Derek,
   Just been reading latest book by A. A. Gill – you know, *The Sunday Times* restaurant critic who seems to have a view on everything from fried bread to social psychology. It's called *The Angry Island*. He says he can't think what would induce anybody to visit Stow for pleasure, which he reckons is 'the worst place in the world'.

[If you're of a delicate disposition when it comes to the use of language, you might want to skip the rest of Mike's email.]

   Gill seems to be quite worked up about it. He says your beloved Stow is 'catastrophically ghastly' because of its 'steepling piss-yellow vanity.' His final condemnation of the place is that you Stowites think it's the 'honey-dipped bollocks'.

Best as ever
Mike

I read it twice, then look up the word 'steepling' in the *Oxford English Dictionary* and it doesn't exist. Nor does the verb 'to steeple'. Of course I've no objection to people inventing new words. A. A. Gill might be trying to say that vanity in Stow reaches the same heights as the steeples on its buildings. But there aren't any steeples in Stow. The nearest we've got are some little knobbly turrets on each corner of the church tower, and a grubby, elongated dovecote affair on the roof of St Edward's Hall in the Square.

I'm wondering if he's got us mixed up with some other Stow. There are several scattered around rural England. Still he does say 'Stow-on-the-Wold'. That's pretty definitive. On the other hand, it could be a misprint. Perhaps he meant 'stippling', like that kind of dotty paint effect. Or maybe he intended to say 'stripping', meaning we're all so vain we show off our bodies at the drop of a hat (less likely, probably, since 40 per cent of Stow's population is retired).

But who am I to object to an occasional linguistic imprecision? It doesn't undermine the main thrust of Mr Gill's argument. Because the idea that Stow is a world leader in something – the worst place in the world – is cheering. It means that Stowites can hold their heads high alongside the citizens of Jericho on the West Bank of the Jordan (the most low-lying city in the world), of Tromsø in Norway (the world's most northerly town), and of Vanuatu (the alleged happiest country on the planet). And these superlatives are not to be dismissed lightly.

When Maggie gets home, she's full of what a busy day she's had cladding the more fashionable bodies of the over-forties women of north Gloucestershire. 'Life moves on,' she says, 'Life moves on,' sipping her Pinot Grigio and tucking her feet under her.

'You're right,' I say. 'How about I line up some other places for us to go and look at?'

'Good thinking,' she says and turns on the *Six O'clock News*.

What the bid for Sunny's burgage has taught us is that one way to get a home filled with characterful sunshine is to find a derelict old building and do it up. What hours of googling that evening also tell us is that we're turning up late at this particular party. Everybody else who wants to create their own grand design has already snapped up all the tumbled down barns and crumbly old chapels with a Cotswold address. But we do stumble on an estate agent's ad for a plot of land for sale with building permission in the middle of Shipston-on-Stour, over the border into Warwickshire. It's the planning consent that makes land like this as rare as rabbits' eggs. And you never know, it might have some abandoned architectural treasure lurking in a corner like Sunny's burgage did. Shipston also has far fewer planning restrictions than Stow and we could just about build whatever we wanted there.

Maggie has a day off the next day, so, eager-eyed, we drive north up the Fosse Way till 10 miles on from Stow we turn right at ANTIQUE PINE AND LOVELY THINGS closely followed by SHIPSTON-ON-STOUR HISTORIC MARKET TOWN.

'Ah, Shipston's not a village then,' I observe.

'Well, Stow probably isn't either,' replies Maggie, 'if you're going by size.'

'That's not right,' I insist. 'Stow's a village by two definitions. In the first place, government grants to villages are only given to places with populations less than 3,000. Chris told me that.' Chris is an old school friend of mine who's doing a late-career doctoral thesis on rural government. 'Stow's population is 2,800. And as well, I reckon that a place feels like a village if agriculture straggles into its middle. And there's that working farmhouse and barn with chickens clucking about at the top end of Parson's Corner.'

There's no time for further debate because we're hitting the outskirts of Shipston. We pass through an estate of red-brick houses that, quite frankly, could just as well be in Wigan or Wembley as rural Warwickshire. Still, once we've parked, the middle of the town comes over quite quaint (*Lark Rise* alert!): V♛R 1872 POLICE STATION and 1715 ORIGINAL BELL INN say the house plaques. Maggie spots a Georgian mansion on the edge of the Square, or rather she says, 'Look at those eight-foot-high windows.' But it's not for sale and we know it'd say 'Reserved for multi-millionaires' if it were, so we move on to look at the plot for sale, up the top of Sheep Street.

Well, it's a bit of land. What more can you say? Smallish, and an inconvenient triangular shape. It appears to be a spare piece of next door's garden. Its location is outside the quaint zone, on the edge of the Wigan-Wembley housing estate.

'Plan B?' Maggie suggests.

'Or maybe around Plan X,' I reply. She nods, and we head back to the car and the chase for our next quarry.

This is 5 miles away, across the other side of the Fosse Way, in the village of Aston Magna. The house we're going to look at is advertised on the estate agent's website as a converted forge, which would 'benefit from some investment in restoration.' We turn off just north of Moreton-in-Marsh and after a few hundred yards, the zigzaggy road becomes single track with a bony-looking thorn hedge on each side that's been scalped to a uniform height by a tractor-mounted cutter.

I've just spotted what looks like a chunky, square water tower a few hundred yards beyond the approaching curve, when suddenly my windscreen's filled with the front of an oncoming Land Rover. I swerve left, shout a word beginning with 'F' or 'S' – I can't remember which – while our front wheel skids on the muddy grass, and hawthorn branches make that dreaded scratchy noise on the car's side as the Land Rover's trailer rattles past, its speed undiminished.

The good news is that the car and the two of us are in much the same state of repair as before. Less heartening is the sight of the rear wheels, one of which is up to its rim in a hole.

Maggie moves over to the driving seat while I heave at the back bumper, until after fifteen minutes of whining (from the wheel, not me), of dirt being fired at my jeans, and of ripe country language, we jolt forward (me and the car). I leap into the passenger seat, and we're soon parking by the water tower.

It's still half an hour till we're due to meet the estate agent, so we decide to explore the village. The water tower is surrounded by huge leylandii trees (the sort that provoke neighbours to shoot each other in Norfolk). But through the thin bits at the bottom we can make out half a dozen grey-green tombstones.

We've just started to put on puzzled looks, when we hear a voice say, 'It's a church.' We turn to see a woman across the road grabbing the collar of her Labrador as it tries to climb over somebody's front gate. 'Or rather it used to be,' she adds, as the dog, tongue-lolloping, gives up on the gate and tugs her towards us. 'It's been a private house for the past fifteen years.'

'Gosh,' says Maggie. 'I don't think I'd go much on dead bodies buried under my azaleas.'

The woman pulls an ambiguous face, and says, 'They've got nice views from the top of the tower.'

'So is there another church in the village?' I ask.

'Not any more,' she replies and drags the panting Lab off towards a nearby stile. Neither Maggie nor I are church-goers. Well, not for the religion anyway. I love them as pieces of living history. This one's obviously Victorian, of the waterworks school of architecture. Hence my mistake.

Aston Magna, it turns out, is set on the side of a hill. We walk up through new houses – posh yellow stone ones on the left, brick affordables on the right. We cross a bridge, and as we lean over the parapet expecting to see a little river bubbling past beneath, there's a sudden roar and a loud drumming, as a train races through the cutting below us.

The railway divides the village in two, and we now enter the part where lots of biggish houses are called 'The Old Something'. A terrace of cottages then fronts straight onto the street. There's no post office. No shop. The only concession to convenience is a bus shelter, made chiefly of dark blue plywood. A brass plaque inside announces:

Parish Council

A reward of one hundred pounds will be offered
to any person giving information resulting in a
conviction for damage to Council property.

The Council will hold parents responsible
for the actions of their children. April 2002.

The bus shelter is undamaged. Is that because:

a)   £100 is enough to lure the majority of Aston-
     Magnians into spying on their neighbours?
b)   Parents here, unlike in the rest of the Western
     world, exercise total control over their children?

Or

c)   The bus shelter is not smart enough to be worth
     vandalising anyway?

Next to the plaque is a timetable. There are two buses
a week to Cheltenham, and another two a week, on the
Hedgehog Community Service, to Moreton.

The Old Forge, the place we've come to look at, is at the
top of a little lane next to a farm. The agent is standing by
his car, clipboard with safety catch off. We immediately see
that the building has three floor-to-ceiling windows. 'It has
three floor-to-ceiling windows,' says the agent, reading from
his brief. So Maggie's interested. It's also got a couple of oak
beams. 'It's got oak beams,' says the agent pointing at the
oak beams.

It's run-down. Plaster peeling. Beat-up Formica kitchen. We remain silent on these matters, not wishing to challenge the descriptive powers of the agent further, until we're in the car home.

'I don't mind the state it's in,' says Maggie, 'because we'd want to do things to the inside anyway. The kitchen for instance's totally in the wrong place.' Maggie has a thing about the one who's cooking – which can be either of us – not being isolated from guests who might be having a pre-lunch chat for instance about fiscal deficits or whether Danish bacon beats Gloucestershire Old Spot. And she's convinced me on this score.

'Hmm,' I reply, 'I agree. It's more the village that I'm wondering about.'

'Yes,' Maggie agrees. 'It's peaceful enough, but...' She pauses.

And I leap in, '... you could drive through it and not notice it was there.'

That night, I lie awake, getting all worked up again about A. A. Gill's rant against Stow, and wondering whether I'm biased against Shipston-on-Stour and Aston Magna. I suppose they're nice enough places – in their own way. But they've not got Stow's uniqueness. What can Shipston boast that no other place on the planet has got? And you can search the *Guinness Book of Records* all you like, and you won't find the name 'Aston Magna' in its pages. No, Stow has caché – as well as four bookshops, two delis, two bakeries, an organic food store, a butcher's, a shop that sells signed lithographs by Picasso and Matisse, not to mention some of the best women's fashion boutiques in the south Midlands. I suppose this could just be the basis of a list of my favourite things. But these, plus the ability to go to a party and tell people, 'We live in the worst place in the world,' (you won't see their eyes glaze over, I promise) finally sends me off to sleep in a contented frame of mind.

CHAPTER 7

HOGSTHORPE — TWINNED WITH PARIS

'**I**'ve been thinking about what Ralph said,' I announce. 'This thing about me being denied any sort of childhood paradise.' Nothing's turning up in Stow to tempt us to consider it as the future Taylor-Cox abode, and I'm getting unsettled again.

'I'd love to know what's happening deep inside your head,' says Maggie. 'Ralph's obviously stirred up some bit of grit that's disturbing your dreams.'

'Well, here's the thing,' I say. 'There *was* a little paradise in my childhood. Did I ever tell you...' (Maggie and I have been together for only seven years so there are often bits of our lives that remain undescribed) '... that when I was a kid, my grandma and granddad owned a tiny little cottage up near the coast in Lincolnshire, and we used to go there every summer for a couple of weeks.'

'Ah, a property-owning, trade union mine-workers' leader,' she jests.

'No, no. Not my dad's father. This was my mum's dad, the musician.'

Grandpa Jo Kirkham had in fact also started out as a miner. He went down the pit at the age of ten. It was illegal to employ children until they were thirteen, but with a nod and a wink on both sides, the law was widely flouted. Then, when he was in his twenties, at the end of nine hours hewing coal, he started to go to night school, and to take piano lessons, and somehow by the time he was twenty-seven he got himself a job above ground. In his thirties, he became an Associate of the London College of Music. A hundred years ago, for an ill-educated coal miner, this was an achievement that would rank these days alongside... well it's difficult to imagine what it would rank alongside now. Today we're taught to believe anybody can become Prime Minister or win the Nobel Peace Prize, even if we don't manage it ourselves. In Granddad's day, to leave school at ten, work seventeen years down the pit and then do what he did, was out of the question, an impossibility. But he did it.

'Oh, yes,' says Maggie. 'I remember now. It's an incredible story.'

'Well, that's right. He and my grandma somehow managed to find enough money to buy this little house in Lincolnshire, as a summer holiday getaway for the family, before holiday getaways were invented for ordinary people. Family legend was that they paid £100 for the place. I remember it and the village like it was last week. It was paradise. I used to look forward to it so much that I used to start packing my suitcase weeks and weeks before we set off.'

'Ahhh,' said Maggie in the soppy tone grannies use when their newborn grandchild throws up for the first time.

I harrumph and continue. 'I was thinking we might go and take a look at the old place. I've not been back there since I was about eleven.'

She jerks her head back with a theatrical startle. 'You're not suggesting we find a place to live two hundred miles away in the frozen wastes of Lincolnshire, are you?'

'No, no. We've been promising ourselves a weekend away, and I'm curious.'

'About what exactly?'

'About what makes this village so idyllic.'

'But it'll have changed. And you've changed since you were eleven. A bit anyway.'

'I know. But, look on it as a piece of psychological and social research. How have we both – me and the village – altered?' I pride myself on knowing how to hook Maggie in. Before she became a fashion retailer, she took a Master's degree in social science.

She shrugs her eyebrows. 'OK, why not. So what is this little haven of peace and perfection called?'

'Hogsthorpe.'

'What!?'

'Hogsthorpe.'

'Well, it's certainly not *Lark Rise* or *Candleford*.'

'Exactly. Now you see my point.'

Five days later, as we drone along in a speeding convoy of Eddie Stobart artics and whizzy, lane-swapping Minis, M1

northbound with Hogsthorpe in our sights, Maggie asks, 'So tell me what you remember about Hogsthorn.'

'Hogsthorpe. Hogsthorpe,' I twitch, irritated that its name is not now as fixed as Athens or Tokyo. '"Thorpe" is Old Danish for village. You'll see when we get up there, lots of the villages end either in "-thorpe" or "-by".'

'What do you mean "BI"?' she asks.

'"-by" like in Grimsby. This is Viking territory where we're going. Hogsthorpe is a tiny village with one little main street with a fourteenth-century church – I remember its stubby tower looked like a castle to me as a kid. A pub – or was it two pubs? And there was a little village shop, all brown paint and dusty cereal boxes in the window.'

'What did people do there? To get money to buy the cornflakes in the dusty boxes?'

'Agriculture. It was fields all around us, and the local farmer – he was called Freeman – used to give me rides on his tractor. Up and down the field next door and alongside the dike.'

'Dike. Dike,' Maggie muses, as I turn away for a second from the coach that's just cut in and filled my vision with LEEDS TO HEATHROW SIX TIMES DAILY ONLY £14, to see her face take on an ultra-proper look. 'I'm assuming that this is "dike",' she continues, 'such as the Dutch boy put his finger into to stop Amsterdam getting flooded.'

'Ah, caught you! Wrong. In Lincolnshire, a dike is not something that's built up like an embankment. It's something you dig out to drain the water away from the fields.'

'So it's a ditch.'

'Yes. They're everywhere. In fact at my grandparents' house there's a wooden bridge over the dike to get from the road into the garden. Some of the dikes are bigger, like canals. Dad used to take me fishing in one just up the road.'

'You ever catch anything?'

'Only a cold. Dad's joke. He told it every year. The countryside was so flat you could see for ever. Fields of corn, or potatoes, and not many hedges or fences because the dikes divided the land up. From the house, we could see the bus coming down the lane ages before it arrived. And we'd just go down the path into the road and the driver would pull up for us. There were no bus stops. And off we'd go to the sea. It was about a mile away.'

'OK, downsides then. I'm trying to prepare you.'

'Well, the house was minuscule. There were only two tiny little rooms. No more than about 8-feet square. One was a bedroom, the other a living room with fold-out bed.'

'How about the kitchen and bathroom?'

'Ooh no. There was no running water. There was a pump that must have gone straight down to a well under the house. Do you know I can still hear the noise of that pump? Judder, splosh. Judder, splosh. That was for washing and cooking.'

'Now you're going to tell me something horrible about the sanitation.'

'Yup. It was a wooden bench with a hole in it, inside a hut in the back garden.'

'Oh my God! So was it like that for everyone in the village?'

'Well, I suppose it must have been. You know, I said the English village is an anachronism. Well Hogsthorpe was literally medieval.'

'That must have been horrible, wasn't it?'

'No! I loved everything the way it was. No electricity of course. Oil lamps for lighting. The one concession to semi-modernity was a single gas ring powered from a bottle. But none of that mattered. What I looked forward to was waking in the morning to see rabbits playing on the grass out front, then we'd go and hunt in the field next to us for mushrooms as big as kitchen plates that my mother fried for breakfast.'

'This must say something about expectations,' observes Maggie.

I dart a quizzical sideways look at her.

'Today, if anybody lived like that, it would be denounced as a national scandal and disgrace... because we expect much better now.'

'I guess you're right. And it's worth remembering that kings and queens in the Middle Ages used lavatories pretty much like the one we had at Hogsthorpe.'

Two hours later, we're getting close, and the village names are starting to ring some rusty bells down my less-frequented neural pathways: SKENDLEBY, CLAXBY, MUMBY, CANDLESBY, FARLESTHORPE.

'See,' I point to the road signs. 'Old Danish, the lot of them.' And I realise there's a flutter of butterflies just below my ribcage. I don't know why.

Then all of a sudden, a female voice says, 'Turn left. Then. After. 200. Yards. You have reached. Your destination.' A white van driver behind leans on his horn, as I slow down to peer around at the roadside bungalows. The satnav intervenes to assure me there's no mistake: 'You have reached. Your destination.' It's always right so there's no point in tapping it. So I tap it. But it's had its say, and it maintains a confident silence.

I'm flummoxed. It seems as if we've just flowed into Hogsthorpe from... well, from wherever we were before.

'Ah,' I exclaim at last, 'there's the pub. Oh, and the church on the other side of the road.'

Maggie says nothing.

The place looks as confused as I am. I edge the car forwards along the main street. There are cars and vans everywhere, parked or struggling to get through. A few little shabby terraced houses, higgledy-piggledy, sit on the edge of the street and seem to be in the way. Everywhere here looks untidy. I catch sight of a brick barn-like building on the corner, its roof tiles broken or missing. Then I have a sudden image in my mind of horses. It used to be the blacksmith's. A battered sign on it says DUNKLEYS. It's nothing now.

'Let's start by looking for my grandparents' place,' I say, 'It's on the edge of the village.' The ill-disciplined line of terraced cottages quickly gives way to ranks of bungalows, all a uniform 4 metres from the road, a uniform 4 metres apart, the triangles of their identical gable ends diminishing into the distance.

After five minutes we're out among open fields with deep dikes running along each side of us. This makes me feel better. But we've obviously gone right away from the village and still no sign of the old house. We turn round and drive through the village three times. At last, I recognise a signpost, SEA LANE.

'Right,' I say. 'Where we are now is called "Three ways". Both these roads lead back to the village, and that one goes to the sea. I was thrown because it's all built up with bungalows. Granddad's place is just down here.'

A minute later, I slam on the brakes.

'Crikey!' I exclaim.

Maggie, who's been patient and quiet for the past fifteen minutes, touches my elbow; 'Is everything all right? What's the matter?'

'That must be it.' We've stopped by two large caravans and a couple of cars in the front garden of a rambling house. 'It's been extended,' I say. 'Quite a lot, in fact. And there's no dike at the front any more.'

'Are you sure?' asks Maggie.

'Yes, this is definitely the road. And it was the end one in a line of similar little houses. Let's go in.'

There's a chap bending inside the bonnet of one of the cars on the concrete that used to be the rabbits' playground, and he looks up as we approach.

'Hello,' I say, 'I'm sorry to disturb you. My grandfather bought this house in the mid 1920s. He owned it for about forty years till he died, and I used to come here every summer.'

It's a mouthful of an introduction, but we're in luck.

'Oh aye,' says the man with an encouraging lilt to his voice, and lifting his baseball cap to scratch his forehead, adds, 'I bet it's nowt like it was when you were 'ere last.'

'Too right,' I say, and we're away.

His name's Jerry and he shows us round. The house has had bits added to it on at least eight occasions as far as I can make out, and its total size now must be five or six times what it was in Granddad and Grandma's day. We can detect the original part from its old roof end which is still visible on both sides of the house. But inside it seems a warren and nothing relates to what I remember.

I ask Jerry what Hogsthorpe's like now to live in.

'Me and the wife are both outdoors people,' he says. 'And you get the sea air here, straight off of the North Sea.'

He looks like he's in his fifties. Is he retired? I ask.

'Unemployed,' he answers. 'I'm a skilled motorbike mechanic. I had a good job in Chesterfield, in Derbyshire, then got made redundant. That were two years ago, so we moved to Hogsthorpe. But there's hardly anything going for mechanics round here. I applied for a maintenance job at Butlins in Skegness, and I'm still waiting to hear.' But he's not sounding bitter.

'So what do people do in the village?'

'Well. A lot of 'um's retired. In all these bungalows. They've moved from Nottingham, Derby or Leicester.'

'Do you mix with them much?'

'Some of 'um comes into the pub.'

Jerry then explains that he's in dispute with the local farmer about the tractor access way that goes alongside his garden.

'You can maybe do me a favour,' he says. 'The farmer claims the border's actually back against the side of the house. We've had solicitors on to each other and all sorts of legal punch-ups going on.' He asks, 'Can you remember from years back a hedge along there?'

'As a matter of fact I can, Jerry. I used to play "Chase", running all round the outside of the house including between that side wall and the hedge.'

'Champion,' says Jerry. And I agree to write him a letter that he can use in his case. So we all shake hands and part, with me glowing inside because my memories of a Hogsthorpe childhood are of practical use in the twenty-first century.

Next, Maggie and I decide to go and take some sea air ourselves. The village of Chapel St Leonards is only a mile away. Back in those far-off summers, Mum, Dad, my sister Anne and I often used to walk there or back if we missed the bus or simply because it was a balmy evening. But it's no surprise now that, instead of open fields, much of the still-winding road between the two villages is lined with yet more bungalows, as far as I can tell, uniform with the ones that that have infested Hogsthorpe.

A welcome sign reads: CHAPEL SAINT LEONARDS TWINNED WITH CERANS-FOULLETOURTE.

'I know where that is,' exclaims Maggie. 'I've been there. It's in the Loire Valley. Cerans-Foulletourte has got one of the most magnificent baroque chateaux in the whole region, surrounded by beautiful gardens, alongside the River Loire. It's stunning.'

We enter the heart of Chapel St Leonards past GREENS AMUSEMENTS, I E CR AMS COF EE BAR AND GRILL, POUND SAVER and CRUMBS FILLED COBS TAKE-AWAY. You can't actually see the sea from the village centre. It's hidden behind a sea-defence embankment which rises higher than the shop roofs and separates the village from the beach.

We try to imagine the first visit by the burghers of Cerans-Foulletourte to their new twinning partner. Had the French drawn a name out of a hat? Or does this little seaside village have a particularly persuasive publicity department: 'Chapel Saint Leonards [French accent]: this elegant coastal settlement of Norman origin, as its name suggests, boasts international cuisine (GOLDEN DRAGON CHINESE AND ENGLISH TAKEAWAY), many reminders of a colourful history (HISPANIOLA BEACH BAR), year-round sunshine (DEETRE'S VERTICAL TANNING BOOTH) and breathtaking views of the ocean.'

To be fair, Chapel St Leonards does have the last of these items. Maggie and I walk up the pull-over, which – in my day at least – was what the little road going up the sea wall was called. And from there you see mile upon mile of sands, to left, to right and down below before you. The tide's out and it's a quarter of a mile over grass-tufted dunes to where the waves lap in. It's a sunny autumn day and with the village's garishness hidden behind the sea bank at your back, a desolate beauty stretches in every direction.

It's too cold for sandcastles or paddling, but dogs chase sticks as one or two walkers keep up a stiff pace in the chill wind, and a single fishing boat slides silently out to sea. On the far horizon we can just make out the stretched white arms of wind turbines. We count fifty of them before they merge into the mist to the far right somewhere off Skegness.

We walk for half an hour till we come to a set of steps leading to the top of the sea-defence wall that separates our little promenade from the villages and countryside inland. For no particular reason, we climb up.

There's a shock waiting at the top. No fields to be seen on the other side. No villages. Just row after row, rank after rank of identical rectangular, shiny roofs. Mobile homes. Mobile homes that probably never move and are home to no one except holidaymakers for a week or two each in August. There may be a thousand. Or five thousand. It's impossible to count them.

We climb back down to the cheery desolation of the sand and sea. And as we walk back past The Hispaniola, a couple in their sixties are slipping into yellow reflective jackets. He stoops to fix his bike clips, and says to her, 'That was a grand five minutes.'

'Five minutes!' she replies. 'More like an hour, yer daft old codger. When you get up here looking at the sea, you've no more idea of time than my elbow.' And they cycle off, laughing.

Back down on the village pavement, we weave around a clutch of mobility scooters, their drivers grim-faced and stooped, then through pink and yellow buckets, spades and kiddies' bathing rings piled high outside an open-fronted shop. The owner jumps from his seat to attend to us, then flops back when we ask, 'Do you sell newspapers?' He directs us to the Co-op, where we buy a copy of the latest *Mablethorpe Leader*.

It's two o'clock and we decide to head back to Hogsthorpe and Jerry's favourite pub for a spot of refreshment.

Inside, the place has old beams and a firegrate in one bar, and a pool table in the other, and shows no sign of the ravages of a brewery tarting-up department. Both rooms are empty apart from a half-blind old golden retriever who walks into my leg, and a young guy reading the *Daily Mail*.

'Hello there, what can I get you?' he asks, rising from the window seat. For those involved in village research, he turns out to be a treasure. After he's supplied us with drinks, he perches on a bar stool and chats to us about twenty-first-century living in Hogsthorpe.

'I love it here,' he explains. 'I'm all for a quiet life. I don't think I could stand all that rushing about in a city.' He brushes his shoulder length hair back from his eyes.

'The trouble with Hogsthorpe is people don't muck in with community life. They'll give money for the church fete or the primary school, but they're stingy when it comes to an hour of their time. All these bungalows you'll have seen. The people in 'em come out once a week to go to the supermarket in Skeggy' – that's what locals call Skegness – 'then they shut themselves back up inside their little houses again.'

'Are they mainly retired people?' I ask.

'Yes mostly. They've come here to die.' He grins. 'That's what we say. Let's hope they don't take Hogsthorpe with 'em.' Like Jerry, he doesn't seem sour about this; regretful but cheerful at his own lot. 'I'll give you something that tells a big story,' he goes on. 'For the first time since the 1930s, Hogsthorpe doesn't have a football team.'

'Why's that?'

'Well partly it's because they can't find anybody willing to organise the club and coach the team. But it's more than that. When the lads get to the age when they're just coming through with talent on the pitch, they up and leave. There's nothing for them to do here.'

'You mean no social life?'

'That, but more important, there's no jobs. There's not even an industrial estate or a business park for miles. There's one in Skeggy, but they can't fill the units. And there's no work in farming any more. It's either mechanised, or the fields are full of caravans.'

'But what about the holiday trade? There must be lots of work in that, isn't there?'

'Well, this isn't the Costa del Sol. Holiday work's seasonal. Only a few months in the summer. And anyway, young families who come and stay in the mobile homes, they don't have much money to spend.'

The old retriever waddles over and pokes a nose into my knee.

'Sorry,' says our host, 'come here old girl. She likes to have her chin scratched.'

'No problem,' I say and oblige her. 'So are you set up with a job at the pub?'

'No, I'm just filling in.' He balances a beer mat on the edge of the bar and flicks it with the back of his fingers. 'My girlfriend comes from Essex originally,' he continues, studying the beer mat. 'She wants to go back there. So I don't know what I'm going to do.' He looks back at us. 'You see,' he goes on, 'there's no motorways or fast roads round here, so industry and business aren't interested. Mind you,' he laughs, 'I always reckon if we did have good roads, that'd bring crime in here as well. It's very peaceful in Hogsthorpe. This pub's only once had anything stolen in twenty-five years.' He nods with what could be satisfaction, and goes off to serve a customer who's just turned up in the other bar.

Maggie picks up the *Mablethorpe Leader* – Mablethorpe is a little seaside town just up the coast – and, as if to bear out our young host's judgement, we read, '18 Months Jail For Bungalow Burglar'. 'Bungalow burglary' must be the most heinous crime imaginable round here. The *Leader*'s editor clearly knows the burning interests of his readers because the first inside page headline (next to an ad for 'Seacroft Motability') is 'Councillor Hits Out At Cemetery Vandals', with a picture of a couple standing by an undamaged gravestone and looking like they may have just risen from it. My eye next happens on what I assume is a review of the latest horror movie to be a box-office hit: 'Farrow And Son Have The Top Grossing Louth Beast'. But it turns out to be written by the *Leader*'s agricultural correspondent, and concerns the biggest cow at the Cattle Market in the town of Louth the previous Thursday. It's on page twenty-four and is the only farming story in the paper.

An hour and a half later, after winding our way homeward via SCREMBY and SAUSTHORPE, we coast down a southbound slip road to be welcomed back into the arms of Eddie Stobart and the rest of the industrialised world.

'So, what about the Ralph question?' asks Maggie, pushing her seat back four notches and putting her stockinged feet on the dashboard. 'Are you any nearer to finding out if you're fulfilling a sentimental dream by wanting to live in Stow?'

'Hard to tell,' I reply, 'since there's nothing left of my childhood paradise in Hogsthorpe any more. Before we went there, I was sure Stow and Hogsthorpe would have a lot in common. Both surrounded by lovely countryside – one hilly, one flat but near the seaside, both places attractive in their own way. And both of them, I thought, would be thriving because they're a Mecca for visitors.'

'But I did warn you Hogsthorpe would have changed since you fished in dikes and rode on tractors.'

'Well… I thought, "Sure, it'll be different, but it'll still be recognisable." I suppose I wasn't listening to you properly.'

Maggie is silent.

'Are you trying to upset me,' I demand, 'by not saying, "You never listen to me"?'

'Call it pity.'

My brain's racing on now. 'The really upsetting thing is that young people are being driven out of Hogsthorpe.'

'Because there are no jobs for them.'

'Yes, and it makes you wonder if this is happening to lots of other villages in the rest of the country. And not only young people leaving, but oldies flooding in. What sort of place is that to live in?'

'One with good viewing figures for *Lark Rise to Candleford*?'

'I think you might be stereotyping and getting ageist – I must make a note to throw that accusation at Ralph, by the way. Isn't the real question: are villages coping with all the changes over the past few years? If you think about it, these changes are driven by cities: technology, globalisation, people working in tall, gleaming offices, telling villagers what to do, or just forgetting about them. Villages are left on the sidelines, feeling the world is passing them by.'

'And, they can't just be places where agriculture happens any more.'

'That's right. The days are long gone of a farm needing twenty milkmaids and thirty ditch-diggers – or "dike-diggers" as we say in Hogsthorpe.'

'So villages are having to find themselves a new role.'

'Exactly. And some of them are clearly struggling. Like Hogsthorpe. It's as though the place got made redundant and has drifted into a job it hates, and so has been left with a twisted personality.'

'So what's all this got to do with Ralph's point about your warped golden-age psychology?'

'I think I might be getting a bit bored with Ralph and his question.'

The satnav woman seems to agree: 'After. 800 yards. Take the exit.'

I chuck in a last thought. 'Hogsthorpe has given us one way to measure whether a village is working or not.'

'What's that?'

'The football team test.'

CHAPTER 8

NUCLEAR WINTER IN CHIPPING NORTON

It turns out that our bid for The Old Stables had been a poor second. Maggie makes a point of bumping into Sunny one day in Stow-on-the-Wold's Market Square. Sunny reveals that the winning bid was £15,000 better than ours. It came from a builder, who's simply going to knock down what was going to be The Old Stables and put up the cottage that came with the existing planning consent. Maggie tells Sunny how disappointed we were. And Sunny says how she would have preferred us to get it, but she needs every penny she can get for her new life in Goa. No excuses needed. It's a business deal. So that's that.

Or isn't, as it turns out.

Two months later, on a wet morning in the Yorkshire Dales, I'm walking with another old school friend of mine. Or rather, I'm walking behind him – Geoff's a lot fitter than me. And we're just coming down off the moors in the direction of some steak and mushroom pie in front of a pub fire, when my phone rings.

'I've been trying to get hold of you all morning,' says Maggie. I start to explain about signal strength in remote hilly areas when she interrupts, 'Never mind that. Sunny's plot of land is back on the market. She phoned a couple of hours ago. Apparently the builder who was going to buy came back to her and said he could only pay her half now, and could she wait for the other half till he'd built the house? She's hopping mad and fed up with the whole thing. She says if we put in a fair offer now, it's ours. That's "now" as in this minute at twenty to one on a Thursday morning.'

'Crumbs,' I exclaim. 'What's a "fair offer"?'

'She says it would have to be more than the 125K we put in before, but it doesn't have to be the 140K the builder was going to put up. So I suggested we split the difference. And she said, "Yes," provided we make it formal with the estate agent straight away.'

'So do we go for it?'

'I'm on my way,' says Maggie, and before I can explain again that phone reception's not perfect here and ask if she'd heard what I'd said, she hangs up.

'I'll put draft number fourteen in the post to you tomorrow,' promises Mr Joshua Hurley. He's our solicitor.

We've been at it for a month, trying to get all the sales contract documents agreed. The problem is there are going to have to be some shared bits of property. We'll have to lay down a parking area and a driveway to be used both by us and by Sunny or – more important – by whoever buys her house when she moves to India next year. And what if she sells to a collector of vintage ambulances, or to a mail-order supplier of drum kits? The ways in which our tranquillity could be shattered are countless.

The consequent backwards-and-forwards-ing between solicitors is getting us nowhere, other than to the bank for a second mortgage to pay their fees. The other thing is, Christmas is only a few days away and then Sunny's going away for two weeks. I'm getting the feeling that it's her solicitor that's the problem. I can't imagine that it's Sunny who keeps slipping in all these fiddling little words that would tie us up in legal knots in the event of a dispute about testing aircraft engines on the front lawn.

So Maggie suggests that we have a go at breaking the deadlock face to face over a cup of tea at Sunny's place. Reason must surely prevail before a gentle fire warming the most massive stone chimney piece in Gloucestershire (this being one of several features that earn Sunny's cottage a Grade II listing). And that's what we do. As foretold, Sunny is the soul of common sense. She wants it all settled too, and is happy to agree that no noisy commercial business can be run from either house. It all takes about three minutes, and the meeting glides on to talk of whether they sell mince pies in Goa, or whether Sunny will have to get the ingredients shipped in specially when she's settled there. We then kiss each other's cheeks and agree to instruct our respective lawyers to draw up the documents for signing the following day.

Back home, among the Christmas cards, I find an envelope from my sister Anne containing two copies of a photograph. It's of our grandparents' little house in Hogsthorpe, with Granddad standing in front alongside Chummy, a dog he had before the war. I've reported to her by phone on our Hogsthorpe expedition and mentioned Jerry's dispute with the farmer over the boundary line. She's written a note with the pictures, 'Clearly shows wide gap between side of house and hedge.' Very satisfying, and I write a letter to Jerry enclosing one of the photos.

At the gym that morning, my attention wanders away from 'Holiday in Harlem', 'I Got It Bad (and That Ain't Good)' and other of Ella's masterpieces. The plight of Hogsthorpe is on my mind. It seems to have just slid into a regimented oldie-land. Did anybody decide that's what it was going to be? Did somebody say one day, 'We'll never manage to keep the kids here in the potato fields, so let's go for the grey vote'? I guess not, though I suppose, sometime in the 1970s, a few developers bagged some cheap land, wheedled the district council to agree, and started to throw up two-bed bungalows, twenty to the acre.

So back home after my shower, I google 'Hogsthorpe' and it coughs up something called 'A Parish Plan for Hogsthorpe'. I know about these. My old school friend, Chris, the one who's doing a late-career doctorate, told me there have been hundreds of them written over the past few years, all trying to breathe new life into their own village.

'They're researched and written by villagers themselves,' said Chris. 'They set out problems, hopes and demands for help and action. The trouble with them is they're biased. They're written by well-educated middle-class retirees who have a particular view of the rural world.'

'What kind of bias is that?' I asked him.

'You won't find any of them that, for instance, deal with rural poverty. The Parish Plans see villages as middle-class havens.'

'And what happens to them when they're finished? Do the villagers get any money to implement the plans?'

'Not as such. The plans are used to try to persuade the local authority to divert existing funds to do what the Parish Plan recommends.'

'Hmm,' I said, 'So it's more talk than do.'

'There are some Parish Plans that have managed to achieve things. I'm sure,' said Chris.

The Hogsthorpe Parish Plan is a sad affair. It's not even 'talk', never mind 'do.' It consists of sixteen bullet points, half a dozen words each one, filling one narrow column of a single sheet of A4 paper. It starts with a puzzling:

- 'Improvement to the village bus visibility at corner near service.'

Before moving on to an earth-shattering:
- 'Additional gritting on Thames Street and road to Chapel St Leonards.'

Then managing to dig up five words for the fate of the next generation:
- 'More facilities for young people.'

Finally hitting us with the longest entry in the whole plan:
- 'Identify potential growth in Hogsthorpe (75 per cent of those answering the question said that the village had growth enough).'

Seventy-five per cent sounds a bit suspicious to me, as though it was the result of a straw poll of four regulars in the snug bar of the pub. Still let's say it wasn't, that would at least mean that the overwhelming majority of bungalow-loving retirees in Hogsthorpe are themselves fed up with looking at endless lines of identical bungalows. So there's hope, though hope for what, I don't know.

'It's her bloody solicitor who's behind this, isn't it?' I scream across Mr Joshua Hurley's office.

'She's just doing her job,' he replies.

I want to say, 'So being an idiot is in the Law Society's job description, is it?' but just stop myself in time. It would only spark a tedious lecture on the maintenance of professional standards in rural legal practices.

What's happened is that before I arrived at his office in Moreton-in-Marsh 3 miles away, he'd already had a call from Sunny's solicitor to say that following a discussion that morning with her client, her position remains that there can be no restriction on the commercial activities of her client or her successors in title.

'So is she saying this is a bloody deal-breaker?' I shout.

He sighs and looks to the ceiling, placing the tips of his fingers together. 'If you would like to calm yourself, Mr Taylor, I will telephone her now to ascertain the importance of this matter to her client.'

I sit down again. He leaves the room. He's not risking my hearing even one side of the conversation.

Ten minutes later, he re-enters. 'Her position is unchanged with regard to the conduct of a business at the premises, and she cannot foresee any circumstances in which she would be able to modify this posture.'

'Right, that's it,' I bellow. 'You can call her back and tell her we withdraw!' And I mutter the word 'Ridiculous!' to the door frame on my way out.

It's Christmas Eve.

Not a busy one, as it happens, for us. Because all our relatives are away, visiting other relatives. Normally, Maggie and I don't mind a Christmas on our own. We eat well, go for a long walk, and pity all those people who're stressed by bitter rows with their in-laws. But as Christmas Day worms on its dreary way this year, there's not much smug superiority about in Maggie's house.

I sit looking out of the back window at a fine drizzle from a menacing sky, thinking this must be the most miserable festive season I've ever had. And I can tell you, I've had some depressing ones back in my days as a television journalist.

In the TV news business, you often have to work at Christmas. The hospitality suite would be thrown open in a misplaced and often disastrous attempt to compensate the staff for having to come into the office rather than be with their cherished family members. Somebody who spent too long at the drinks cupboard and not enough in the newsroom usually got fired. One year, it was a studio director for making a computer-generated mouse sit on the newscaster's shoulder during a report on the Archbishop of Canterbury's Yuletide sermon. Or else there was an ugly row. Like the time a production assistant, after lunch, was held up by her ankles from a sixth-floor balcony.

Someone would say, 'Do you remember that Christmas when a young freelance reporter had too many vodkas and forgot to breathe while reading his commentary live on air?'

Nobody actually did remember it. But they all heard the story last year so thought they were there, and so someone would go on, 'God, yes. He was supposed to read, "Prince Charles is an enthusiastic hunt supporter," but he gulped for air just before the end of "enthusiastic," and the "c" got attached to the next word. It wouldn't have been so bad but the poor bugger was so shocked by how it came out that he stopped in his tracks without saying the rest of the sentence.'

It was something like this most Christmases. Then the arrival in the newsroom by mid afternoon of a senior manager, ready to carry out the suspension of this year's guilty member of staff preparatory to dismissal, would usually kill off any residual amusement. And a cynical gloom would settle back in.

In Stow-on-the-Wold this Christmas, Maggie and I survive by a strategy of conflict avoidance, i.e. we keep silent (for want of anything to say) other than emitting routine enquiries about the state of the turkey gravy or the meaning of life, replies being limited to three words of no more than two syllables.

On Boxing Day, Maggie – inspired no doubt by the televised sight of Sir Alex Ferguson screaming words of good cheer at a shame-faced linesman – decides that action is needed.

'Look,' she says, 'we've got to pull ourselves together. We must be able to do better for our money. After all, Sunny's old garages are hardly the architectural cat's pyjamas.'

Still staring out of the window, I muse on Maggie's refined style of phrase. I might myself have said it was well short of A. A. Gill's criterion of the honey-dipped things dogs like to lick.

'Derek, are you listening? Are we pulling ourselves together?'

So we drag ourselves over to Shipston-on-Stour to look again at the empty plot of building land we'd rejected. It's one of those winter days that never gets properly light. Everything's shut of course, so all we can do is peer over the 5-foot-high fence. It's not changed. It's still a small triangular piece of garden remnant with weeds on it.

'You see those trees,' says Maggie on tip-toes pointing to the other side of the plot. 'That's the south side. On a summer's day, it'll be as dark as the mouth of hell.'

I nod. 'And it's got no history.'

So we get back in the car, and head across country to where, according to an estate agent's ad we've seen on the Internet, there's a barn being sold ready for conversion.

The roads are empty. The shops are darkened. The sky is black. The place could be used as the set for a calamity survival movie.

Chipping Norton's in nuclear winter.

And it's not a barn at all. It's an overlarge shed that fronts directly onto a main road, opposite the delivery yard of Mid-Counties Co-op supermarket.

There's nowhere open for a cup of tea so we drive back home.

After we've sat for an hour – me staring, uncomprehending, at a two-day-old newspaper – Maggie slaps shut her book, throws it on the floor, and says, 'Do we want Sunny's funny old building?'

'Yes.' I hear the word spoken by an alien creature in my throat.

'How serious is the threat that somebody who wants to set up a used car business would buy Sunny's house?'

I scrunch up my nose, 'Probably not very.' The creature has taken over my brain.

'Have we got ourselves into an I'm-not-going-to-back-down stand-off with this solicitor for no good reason?'

Breathing in and pulling my hand down over my face like someone fitting a rubber mask, I say, 'I see the way you're going.'

Maggie grins.

And we agree that we'll go and see Sunny first thing the next morning, and say we withdraw our insistence on a no-commercial-businesses clause.

We exchange contracts and complete on the same day, 5 January.

Now it really is ours.

I reckon a good guide as to whether this is the correct decision or not, is how we feel once there's no going back. We're elated. Not daunted. So it must be the right course. That was my logic at the time. Looking back though, I can see it could have been more of a fairground shooting gallery syndrome: after six attempts, hitting a tin duck is what makes you chuffed, not winning the plastic penguin.

CHAPTER 9

THE CRASH OF A DOOR
NOT BEING SLAMMED

So, now there's no more flouncing about, fantasising about what we *might* do with Sunny's burgage and old building. We've signed the transfer document, paid over a substantial amount of money, and now Maggie and I own the bottom of a garden and some old garages on Back Walls, a minute's walk from Stow-on-the-Wold's Market Square.

First thing is to get that planning permission approved. So I leave a message on Anthea's mobile to get in touch with Bella and chase up our application.

The official reply comes two days later in a phone call to Anthea who relates it to me in an early morning email: 'Hi Derek, B just phoned. No extension. No roof-raising. Sorry – Anth.'

'But this planner had already told you an extension would be OK,' says Maggie when I break it to her as she's pulling on her brown suede boots.

'Well… not exactly,' I hedge.

'How do you mean? I thought she approved it in principle when you met her on-site before we bought the land.'

'Well… not exactly. She marched off before I could ask her specifically about any extension.'

'But, I thought we only bought the place because we could extend it, didn't we?'

'Well… yes.'

'It's too small as it is.'

'I know, I know.'

'So, we're lumbered with a stack of old garages that are no use for anything except keeping half a dozen cars in. That is if you're yearning to get asbestos poisoning.'

'We could always knock it down and put up the new cottage. As in the existing permission.'

'Derek!'

'Well… Perhaps we could sell it.'

Maggie groans. 'I'm late opening the shop.' And as she leaves, I hear her *not* slamming the front door.

I phone Anthea to see if she's got any other hints from the conversation with Bella, on what's gone wrong. I get voicemail. At the very least this planning official owes us a meeting. We ought to have a crack at getting her to change her mind. I phone again. Still voicemail.

Have you ever noticed how people you know in everyday life are much more complicated than even the richest characters in books? Take me, for example. I could never exist in a novel. The readers just wouldn't believe in me. Inside me are a pair of traits that seem to belong to two different people.

One, I'm dogged. Won't take 'No' for an answer. It ain't over till it's over. Never say die. While there's a cliché there's hope.

Two, I get anxious. In a crisis I can't bear the wait. It's not that I'm impatient. Uncertainty makes me so stressed I start to hallucinate and fall on the floor with my legs in the air.

So while waiting for Anthea to call back, I become, on the one hand, strong and determined, and on the other, demented and physically sick. All at the same time. I keep pressing the redial button on the phone in between the resulting fits.

After sixteen and a half hours, the phone rings. Actually, it's about twenty minutes, it just seems that long. It's Anthea. Bella has refused to give any reasons for turning down our extension plans. But she will meet us face-to-face, to discuss what we can and can't do.

'I think you should be there,' says Anthea. 'It would be useful to have you there to help make the arguments.'

Maggie's verdict, when I call her with the update, is a variation of this. 'I think we should both go,' she says.

Now I'm fine. Action, I've always found, is the best cure for anxiety, so I spend the next three days searching the Internet for pictures of old buildings which have glass and oak down the front *and* extensions at right-angles to the line of the building *and* roofs at least 8 metres high – *and* that are in the Cotswold district so she can't say, 'Ah well, that's in Leicestershire,' or wherever. 'We do things differently here.' There aren't many. But I do find a couple.

The day comes, and we all turn up at the council offices in Cirencester. As we're shown into one of the meeting rooms, I'm calm. And smiling. Maggie has been coaching me to stay pleasant and even-tempered throughout, no matter how provocative, rude or contradictory this bloody stupid bloody planning officer is.

'What I can't get my head round,' I say as we wait for her to deign to appear, 'is what their underlying philosophy is.'

Anthea splutters, and coughs a 'Sorry,' as she mops up the tea from her plastic cup with her hankie.

'Er, Derek, no,' Maggie warns. 'This is about getting an extension. Not about a sociological dissertation. So focus.'

I nod, and in walks Bella.

I hardly recognise her from that meeting months ago now. She's in a grey formal suit rather than the dressed down, site-visit jeans of last time. She looks even stonier-faced. I try to think of her nose as more Noddy than Becky Sharp.

Anthea gives a business-like introduction, summarising the issues, then whips the ball over to me. Bella sits glassy-eyed through my presentation on our vision of an extension and mezzanine floor, and on how it would be consistent with other similar heritage buildings in Gloucestershire, photographic images of which I display mounted on FIRMBOARD® purchased from Stow Post Office. I talk about how, in wishing to convert this structure into our home, conservation is our guiding principle. I catch her glancing at her watch, and realise this last argument may not be the most productive one given our tiff at the site meeting.

'I don't think,' she replies, having apparently taken no account of what I've been saying, 'that you need all this space,' her nose pointing in turn at all four corners of Anthea's drawing as though it were the detailed plan for a new cathedral. I want to say, 'What are you talking about? All this space! And another thing, don't *you* tell me how much space *we* need,' but Maggie's aiming widened eyes in my direction.

Bella continues, 'For instance, you don't need two bathrooms, and the living room's enormous for a cottage this size.'

I can't bear this any more. But Maggie gets in before me.

'I can see exactly what you mean,' she patters. 'I suppose at the end of the day, it's a matter of personal taste. For us, I'm afraid it just wouldn't work without more room. So, I think what we should probably do is look for somewhere else, and sell this plot to the builder who wants to use the existing planning consent to demolish the structure and put up a new house. I'm sure the Stow Civic Society won't like it. But… I'm afraid I can't see what else we can do.'

Bella doesn't flinch. 'OK,' she says, 'you can have a four-metre right-angled extension. But it'll have to be "No" to raising the roof level.' And she picks up her papers and walks out.

'I thought this was supposed to be a negotiation,' I complain to the other two once the door has snapped shut, 'and since when has it been any business of the planners whether – like any civilised human beings in the Western world – we want two bathrooms?'

'I think she was trying to be helpful,' suggests Anthea.

'Helpful!' I squawk, at which point a woman with a tray comes in and, under the guise of tidying up our debris, herds us out into the fresh air of the car park.

With the words, 'Exercise cools the brain' Maggie sends me off to do two circuits round the lines of municipal employees' vehicles and those of the supplicant citizenry. And by the time I return to where she and Anthea are smiling to each other, my audible muttering has subsided into silent lip movement.

'We were just saying,' chirps up Maggie, 'it could be a lot worse. Sure, it's a shame about the mezzanine, but the more important bit is the extension. And we've got that. Without it, there'd have been no chance of being able to squeeze in.'

'Yeah you're right,' I concede. 'It would have been nice to get the gold medal. But this is an honourable silver.'

'Just let me know how you want to proceed,' says Anthea, chucking her files into the back of her four-by-four, and she gives us a jolly wave as she reverses out.

On our journey home, there's hardly a flicker of bickering between us, as we take stock.

'On the plus side,' says Maggie, 'I've still got my ten metres of sunshine and you've got your yards of exposed oak and stone.'

'Right,' I say. 'We've not had to compromise on those. And the plan for a thirty-five-foot living room has always been a deal-breaker as well. Because that's where we'll spend most of our waking time.'

'And the thing is, there's a bit of sleight of hand to be had there. A main room that big will give the impression that the whole house is on the same scale.'

'You're absolutely right,' I enthuse, holding back to allow an old lady in a hat to steer her Vauxhall Corsa through the narrow gap in the road ahead. 'And what's more, your many-splendoured wall of glass will make it seem even bigger. If we put floodlights in the courtyard outside, even at night it'll look like there are two big adjoining rooms.'

'I know, I know,' says Maggie. 'And the other thing is, so long as we keep our bedroom and its bathroom a decent size, we could chop back on the guest suite.'

'Sure. Who wants visitors to stay more than a couple of days anyway?' And I direct a benign smile at a young chap on a dirt-track motorbike as we drive through the plume of blue smoke he's left behind. We both sigh sighs of contentment and relief.

Over the next few days, however, the ointment turns out to have one little irritating fly in it. A door has to go somewhere on the glass and oak wall. I want a split stable-door into the kitchen. Maggie's keen on double glass doors with oak frames in the middle of the main room, opening on to the terrace.

We racquet the arguments back and forth for ten days, each of us roughing out sketches and plans to show why one works and the other doesn't, till we've run out of paper. Up early on the Sunday morning, I pick up from the floor one of Maggie's old drawings and mark in, for the sixty-eighth time, where the ideal door should be. Leading into the kitchen. Maggie walks in, and gulps back her yawn as she catches me at it, defacing her sketch. Her head makes a vigorous sideways twitch of despair and she shouts, 'That's it!'

'What?' I ask in sulky defiance, imagining she's about to add, 'I've had enough,' or 'You're completely impossible.'

'That's it,' she repeats with slower emphasis.

'That's what?'

'That's it!' She grabs the guilty drawing, and waggles it in front of my nose. 'We need *both* lots of doors!'

I detach the plan from her fingers, and study it.

That is, indeed, it.

'The logic's obvious if we'd thought about it,' she says, flopping onto the armchair. 'Neither of us was actually against the other's idea. But we were both battling for our own. I don't mind a kitchen door. In fact I can see benefits. Just so long as I can have my French windows in the middle.'

'And ditto for me,' I add.

It's a team decision we never regret. For ever after, those two sets of doors become symbols of the unity of our marriage. That's what we tell the more sentimental of our friends, anyway.

So, Anthea turns all our toil into professional drawings and re-submits the planning application.

TWO

CHAPTER 10

HITLER LOVE CHILD IN OXFORDSHIRE VILLAGE

The next big job is to agree a contract with our main builder. Nik is probably our man. But we reckon we've got to be professional about this and should ask to talk to clients he's done similar work for, before we sign him up for definite. After all, one mistake in this department and it could be thousands of pounds down the drain, months or even years of heartache, and enough stress to crack up a wagonload of Buddhists. We arrange to meet him at eleven o'clock on Saturday morning in the Oxfordshire village of Swinbrook, where one of his satisfied customers will be waiting.

We're half an hour early so we go for a wander in the early March sunshine.

Swinbrook is not any old village. It's where the six Mitford sisters lived as children long before they became variously: novelist, wife of fascist leader, communist, Hitler groupie, duchess, and the last one – as described in *The Times* of the day – 'unobtrusive poultry connoisseur'. With five sisters like Nancy, Diana, Jessica, Unity and Deborah, it's not hard to see why Pamela took refuge in a hen coop.

In 1919, the Mitford family moved from Batsford, five minutes down the road from our new home in Stow, to Asthall Manor in Swinbrook. And so the agricultural peace of the place was then constantly disturbed by the comings and goings of celebrities who would have featured in the upper-class edition of *Hello!* magazine had such a publication existed in the 1920s, ranging from the Churchills to the painter Walter Sickert. Life in Swinbrook is described in Jessica's autobiography, *Hons and Rebels*. This includes an account of sister Diana having her appendix out on a table in a spare bedroom, which tells you a lot about the efficiency of the Oxfordshire Ambulance Service pre the introduction of response time targets, as well as about the grandeur of Asthall Manor. How many of us today can boast a spare bedroom big enough to take – in addition to a double bed – a 6-foot-long table and enough elbow room for the performance of major invasive surgery without the medical staff bumping into boxes of old videotapes and an ironing board that should have been chucked out long ago? The Mitfords loved Swinbrook village so much that when they moved away in 1926, it was only as far as nearby Swinbrook House. And that's where they stayed till the girls left one by one and the parents died.

Maggie and I set off, eager-faced in pursuit of Mitford memories, with me holding half an eye alert for any sign that the village is in need of regeneration now that the Mitfords are no longer providing employment for fifty servants, twenty stable lads, several political advisors with extremist views, and a couple of chicken-sexers.

First off, we head for the church. 'It's where Unity's buried,' I explain as we climb the stone steps to get up into the graveyard.

'Is she the one who became Duchess of Devonshire or the one who was a communist and lived in America?' asks Maggie.

'Neither. She was the one who spent five years with Hitler in Berlin then shot herself in the head on the eve of the war.'

'They didn't half live on the edge, those sisters.'

'I know, but they wanted to come back here to this Oxfordshire village when they died,' I say, as we stop in front of three small tombstones. 'Well, these three anyway.' The stone on the right is the cleanest and newest. 'Diana,' I pronounce. 'She married Oswald Mosley, the British fascist. And there's Nancy,' I point to the left, 'who wrote *Love in a Cold Climate*.'

Unity's gravestone, in the middle, is covered with white splodges of lichen. Maggie crouches before it and reads, 'Unity Valkyrie – VALKYRIE! – Mitford. Bloody hell, who'd christen their kid "Valkyrie"?'

'Yes, a sure-fire way to guarantee your child being beaten up behind the bike-sheds on a daily basis. Except of course the Mitford girls didn't do anything so common as go to school. Do you think people live up to their names?'

'You mean like girls called Hillary being sporty?'

'And there aren't many all-in wrestlers called Algernon.'

'So you're saying Unity Valkyrie was marked out as a Germanic fascist from the cradle?'

'Yes, or I suppose if she'd had a good voice, she might have ended up singing Brunhilde at Covent Garden.'

'She probably wasn't beefy enough,' says Maggie.

'There's a cracking mystery about her,' I say. 'She muffed the suicide attempt and survived. Hitler then personally paid for her to be shipped home, but apparently she was treated in a maternity ward. Now why would she be in a maternity ward?'

'You don't mean...'

'Right. There's been a suggestion that she was carrying Hitler's child!'

'I thought he was impotent.'

'Ah. Who knows?' I have another look at the tombstone, and pointing to a half-obliterated epitaph below the name, read '"Say not the struggle naught availeth."'

'And what exactly did Unity Valkyrie's particular struggle avail then?' asks Maggie.

'Well, it's kept us amused for five minutes.'

And with that we have a quick squint inside the church. The main attraction is a three-tier bunk-bed to the side of the altar, where three bearded men are watching us, each reclining on one elbow, heads propped up on their right hands, as you might do on a picnic while you listen to someone tell a funny story. However, the rest of their bodies are as stiff as planks, as though rigor mortis has set in, which in fact it has, about 400 years ago, because their effigies are made of white marble. We read on a little card that they represent three generations of the Fettiplace family, who for several hundred years were lords of Swinbrook before the Mitfords muscled in.

Back outside, we do a tour of the village. It doesn't take long. There appear to be no more than twenty houses in the whole place, and the remarkable thing is that they're nearly all big. The very largest ones, whose spreading complexity can only be glimpsed in the distance through trees, sport gates of wrought iron between 10-foot-high stone salt-cellars, and show no house names. So we can't figure out which ones are the former Mitford mansions. We see not a soul walking in the village to interview on the subject. The not-quite-so-grand residences do have names, like 'Swinbrook Cottage.' But 'cottage' in Swinbrook doesn't have the same diminutive meaning it does elsewhere in England, because Swinbrook Cottage seems from the number of upstairs windows to have at least seven bedrooms.

The centre of the village is a thing of exquisite beauty. A trickling rivulet tinkles between weeping willows, their delicate, swaying branches just showing the first bright green leaves while a million daffodils wave in the grass beneath. I suppose in a place of such opulent perfection as Swinbrook, you need to have some little thing to remind you just how opulent and perfect you really are, and Swinbrook even has this. Two council houses, complete with grubby cement-sprayed walls, identical green doors, satellite dishes plus garden gnomes, jar on the edge of the village.

'I don't think somehow we're going to see Swinbrook competing for rural regeneration Lottery funds,' observes Maggie.

'True,' I reply, 'but does it have a football team?'

It's time to meet Nik. He's already waiting in the car park of a little pub half a mile up the road. He gives us a grin and does a 'Wagons Roll' wave, and we drop in behind his four-by-four as he leads us to a large old farmhouse in several acres of neatly tended grounds. The mistress of the house – all jodhpurs and flowing black hair – is striding down the steps from the portico entrance within seconds of us crunching up the drive. Almost before he's out, she's thrown her arms round him and is kissing him. We get the message.

The house has several oak-framed extensions. One of them looks like a huge barn but actually holds several guest bedrooms. Nik was responsible for building this. Apparently, soon after work started, a stream popped up from nowhere in the middle of the site and proceeded to wash away much of the adjoining hillside, dumping it in the gardens and forming a lake where the new extension was going to be. Surveyors and other experts in such matters, it seems, were left mystified and the owners distraught.

'Nik fixed it!' The woman claps her hands with glee.

'All that happened,' explains Nik, 'is that one day we stumbled on the course of the underground stream over there,' he points beyond the bosom of a garden statue of Aphrodite. 'We unblocked it and the water disappeared. Just like pulling out a bath plug.'

'Oh Nik, Nik, you're too modest,' sings his erstwhile client, kissing him again.

We're soon back in convoy and away to Nik's next work reference. This is half a dozen miles away on the edge of Wychwood Forest. The house we've come to see here is even grander than the Swinbrook ex-farmhouse. It's a Georgian mansion, its giant windows staring at the far horizon and the towering pillars of its porch designed to intimidate anyone who dares to visit. The routine of warm embraces for Nik from the matron of the residence is repeated. The story here is that the family lived for six months in one half while Nik and his team restored the other, then they all swapped over while he did the other half for the next six months. Inside, it looks like the set of *Pride and Prejudice*. I compliment the mistress of the house on her choice of marble floor, saying

that we want stone throughout too, which provokes her
into a long explanation of how it was specially shipped in
from Montepulciano.

'And when you design your drawing room,' she
enthuses, 'I'll introduce you to this simply marvellous
man who's done some splendid work for these friends of
mine.' And she names the castle where they live. I think
I might have gone there on a coach trip with my mum
and dad when I was about ten, but decide to withhold
this information.

'Charming people,' she says, turning to Nik and leaving
me uncertain whether she's referring to the aforementioned
chatelaines or to us. 'Nik, you'll stay for coffee,' she orders/
enquires. By which we gather that our audience is over, so
we effuse our thanks and farewells, and drive off.

In the wrong direction.

We find ourselves speeding through the village of
Leafield. If you wanted to confuse aliens from Galaxy
H218, you could show them a poodle and a whippet and
explain they're both 'dogs'. Or, you could show them
Swinbrook and Leafield and say they're both 'villages'.
Shortly after the LEAFIELD border crossing, we're
presented with a few unprepossessing houses scattered
alongside the road. These gradually get thicker on the
ground till they're in tightly packed clusters but never
losing that unprepossessingness – bungalows, local
authority jobbies, three-bed semis – and this goes on
for about two miles till they start to thin out again and
eventually give way to cow pastures as we pass the back
of the LEAFIELD frontier sign for drivers from the other
direction. During the whole crossing of this rural desert

we've spotted one boarded-up pub, whizzed by the car park of the 'Pearl Chinese Restaurant and Bar', and caught sight of 'The Village Community Shop.' These last words tell us that the people who live here do indeed regard Leafield as a village. It looks like a suburb that's been sliced off from its parent town and tossed down in the middle of the countryside, with its residents now left miles away from all the shopping centres, cinemas, clubs and bus stations they'd been used to.

We pull in to ask the way from a middle-aged woman tugging her dog. When, with a bit of pointing, she's explained the right direction back towards Stow, I say to her, 'I wonder if I could ask you something else.' She looks defensive. 'We were just wondering where most people work in Leafield.'

'Oh,' she replies, 'well, my husband is in the accounts department of a company in Witney. It's about seven miles away. I think you'll find a lot of people in Leafield commute to Witney.'

'OK, thanks,' and I slip in my favourite bland little query that makes Maggie blench, 'Is it a nice place to live, Leafield?'

The woman shrugs, 'As good as anywhere, I suppose. I can walk the dog across the fields.' She smiles, nods bye-bye and is gone.

So, Leafield is exactly what it looks like. That should please Ralph, if nobody else.

As Maggie and I drive home, we decide to award Nik 'Best in Class' for client testimonials. And it seems likely that any snags we hit along the way, he'll have come across before and will know what to do.

That evening, I google 'Leafield Football Club,' and find a pinch of gold glittering in the electronic pay-dirt that tumbles down the screen:

Leafield Athletic Ladies **Football Club**

23 Feb... **Leafield**, Athletic, Ladies, **Football**,
Football Club, Girls, Womens, Female, Soccer.
www.**leafield**athletic.co.uk/ - Similar

... which fields six teams every Saturday including four girls' sides, thus implying that behind the village's dreary exterior beats an adventurous and well-organised heart, worthy of further investigation.

But closer scrutiny reveals that Leafield ALFC is in Solihull, Birmingham. It's nothing to do with our Leafield, which thereby fails the test.

I wonder if Swinbrook has a polo team.

CHAPTER 11

A BOLIVIAN CHINESE PUZZLE

Working out what it's all going to cost turns out to be as simple as modelling a garden gnome from porridge. And there was me thinking it was like baking rock cakes: a bit of delicate finger work with the pastry and a brief spell in the oven, then you could leave the result on the top shelf to get dusty.

Take the cost of the green oak. 'Green oak' is what Anthea told us the columns and beams are called that are going to be supporting the structure of our new home. When we had first heard the phrase, we'd both nodded away like experts. Later when we were alone together, Maggie had been the one to come clean first, 'So what's "green oak"?' she asked. And a discussion ensued. We weren't daft enough to think it meant we had to apply two coats of 'Emerald Emotion' or 'Peppermint Dream'. We assumed it meant the timber would turn a light mossy colour as it was exposed to the weather. But a week or so later, this idea fell on its face when we made that visit to the first of Nik's clients in Swinbrook. We realised that her oak columns and beams, though the shade of milky coffee on the inside, had turned a mucky grey on the outside. So we then plumped for the idea that 'green' was some kind of reference to its supposed energy-saving properties. When I told Nik this, he grinned. 'Not unless you think draughts will cut the gas bill,' he said. 'What happens is, when the wood shrinks, the wind can start to whistle through the cracks.' Could be worrying, but I figure character comes at a price. 'Green,' Nik finally revealed, 'just means no preservative or paint.'

'What's that got to do with "green"?'

He shrugged.

Anyway, it's one of the few things we agree on with Bella. There are going to be 10 metres of glass along the front of the building, in metre-wide panes framed in green oak. But as to the finances: the fact that the wood ends up looking grubby doesn't make it dirt cheap, though the exact cost, as I'm about to find out, is as obscure as its name.

There are scores of questions like this that can cost village stables converters sleepless nights. So when one day, while leafing through *SelfBuild & Design*, one of the magazines aimed at people like us, I give an audible 'Ah-ha,' and point at a half-page glossy ad. I may have found a shortcut to normal slumber. It's a home-builder's trade show at the NEC in Birmingham.

So that's where I find myself ten days later.

It takes no more than thirty-five minutes – the time to get from the NEC car-park to the show hall via a straggling line of fellow self-builders – for me to start to wonder whether 'shortcut' is the most *bon* of *mots*. I'm now wandering with a million or so other demented souls around what appears to be a triple-sized aircraft hangar with 5,000 aisles of little stalls. Young women in super-short skirts and wearing T-shirts that say things like, 'Jenkins Sanitary Wastepipes, fit and forget' or 'We'll make the earth move for you, Darryl's Diggers' jump out at me and thrust pamphlets into my hand. I ask one where the oak sellers' stalls are, and she says, 'I think you've come to wrong show,' then leaps on the unsuspecting woman in a knitted Peruvian beanie hat behind me.

A middle-aged man – whose black bow-tie, evening suit, sideburns and moustache were last seen in a song and dance act at the Liverpool Empire around 1972 – is trying to lure us to watch a theatrical performance of... of grouting. He keeps pointing at a workman in purple overalls, whose floor actions are largely invisible to the audience, and saying, 'You won't believe it, ladies and gentlemen, you won't believe how easy it is to grout your floor with EASYFLOORGROUT®. You won't believe it.' Most of us who've stopped in front of his stage are only pausing to snort uncomprehendingly at the 400-page exhibitor-indexed show guide. And we move on hastily when we realise we might be burdened with a free sample tub of the miracle tile-gap filler which more underdressed young women are trying to palm off on the slower movers among us. I'm getting increasingly vulnerable myself. My pace has slackened to that of a glassy-eyed zombie under a growing load of plumbing, roofing and flooring handouts by the time I stumble on a clutch of oak-frame suppliers somewhere around Section 593 of Aisle ZYF.

Oak-frame companies, I soon discover, operate as a secret society. I spend an hour and a half interviewing a random selection of their sales personnel. You don't want to be bothered with the detail, I'm sure. So here are the headlines.

Their first rule is: units of measurement shall be encoded to protect the mystery of the cult. Some oak companies set their prices according to the length of pieces you buy, which must surely mean you pay over the odds for thin bits. Another firm deals in weight, which means you need an Excel spreadsheet and a PhD in arboriculture to calculate the cost. With a third, it's cubic metres. Try converting all the beams and braces and columns you think you need into cubic volume. It's like pricing ice cream according to its specific gravity.

Next task, track down the flooring companies. I'm in luck. They're in a loose flock only eighteen aisles and fourteen sections distant from the oak lot. Floor slab suppliers, it turns out, are all managed by reverse-arithmetic accountants. This is the only obvious explanation for their pricing policies. As I bounce from one exhibition stand to another, I discover that flagstones vary from £20 to £100 per square metre according to how far they've travelled. If the tiles come a long way, say from China or Peru, they're three times *cheaper* than if they've come from northern Italy. And the priciest come from Snowdonia, an hour and a half from the NEC up the A5.

A breezy gent with rolled-up sleeves and loosened tie in front of a stand decorated with pictures of native Andean women in shawls and brown bowler hats, has the answer... 'Labour costs,' he says. 'They work for two pence a month in Bolivia. But the quality of the stone's miles better than any fancy-pants Eyetie rubble. Just feel that,' and he thrusts a postage stamp of shiny stone where I've no choice but to give it a little fondle.

I thank him and move on, regretting that I'd asked, since we'll now have to factor in the ethical dimension. Can we live with ourselves if we've furthered the oppression of Bolivia's indigenous Quechua-speakers? Or do they need our business to survive? Or, in these straightened times, should we be supporting the slate quarries of Blaenau Ffestiniog? It'll take hours of trawling through past *Panorama* reports on iplayer to decide.

In The Showtime Café over a lunchtime egg sandwich, which has the consistency of an ideal floor tile but at Welsh prices, I report in by phone to Maggie. She wants me to check out underfloor heating suppliers.

'What do we want to do that for?' I stare at the mobile in disbelief. 'If it goes wrong, you have to take a pneumatic drill to the whole floor.'

'I'd have thought you were all for it,' she protests. 'Underfloor heating means no radiators everywhere to wreck your vision of rural tradition.'

'Yeah, maybe.'

'Radiators are where minimalism meets inglenook. They spoil both.'

I agree to find out more. But it's the same impenetrable tale of pricing by whim. And these are only the first layers of confusion. Do we want dry electric heating beneath limestone flags alongside pegged oak columns? Or should we go for hot water piped under travertine marble with ten-year timber in the roof? Or any mix of the above? The flames of conflict look stoked for weeks to come.

So I start the half-hour trudge back from exhibition hall to car park, bent like a bag lady by the weight of brochures in each hand and by the egg-born cramp in my stomach.

Another task then springs to the top of the 'to do' list. We've got to sell Maggie's house where we live now. It's on a road of mainly 1960s houses on the outskirts of Stow. To save money (and to cock a snook at estate agents), I decide to have a shot at doing it myself. There are now all manner of lures to persuade you this is easy. First, we subscribe to a website for £120 which circulates the details of the house to dozens of other property sites, and you get sent a smart-looking 'For Sale' sign complete with wooden post. I borrow a sledgehammer from the chap next door, and view the result with pride.

'Why is it at an angle, pointing up the road?' asks Maggie.

'That shows we're selling it ourselves without a slick and slimy professional in the way,' I reply, picking up the sledgehammer and setting off back to the neighbour's.

I find a company on the Internet that does house nameplates, and for £12 they produce one for us that says 'Fort's Edge'. Along the top of the back garden of Maggie's house – and that of all our neighbours – runs an earth bank faced with Cotswold stone. It's the boundary of an ancient Iron Age fort. So I compliment myself on the historical accuracy of my choice of house name, and screw the plaque onto the wall of the house where it used to say 'No. 3'. This is brand marketing at its best.

Next I take a cunning photo of the house with trees in the foreground that makes it look like it sits in acres of private grounds.

Then I turn out a fancy brochure on my lap-top and print off twenty copies. We also advertise in the *Sunday Times* and the *Daily Mail*. Both are quite pricey, but only a fraction of what the estate agent's fee would be.

Then we sit back and wait.

And… I bet you've guessed wrong here… we get hundreds of enquiries. No exaggeration. It becomes a full-time job printing off the brochures, and the phone doesn't stop ringing for the next couple of weeks, mainly from retired couples. Some drive for hours especially to come and view the place.

We're on constant red alert.

Tuesday 0823 hours. Operations Group convened. Location: the map table, to the edges of which are relegated coffee, muesli, yoghurt and cranberry juice.

'OK, brief me on today's targets.'

'Well…'

'We don't have time for "Wells". We just need to know who's in our sights over the next seventy-two-hour period, what are their weaknesses, our resources and optimum mode of attack.'

'Right. Well, 0900 hours, we've got the Lightfoots, Cedric and Gladys.'

'Intelligence?'

'It was difficult to assess their IQs over the phone but…'

[Snort] '*Intelligence*. As in information on their location, vulnerabilities, combat experience, etcetera.'

'Pensioners. Live in a bungalow in Enfield. Been coming to Stow on and off for years.'

'Right. Darjeeling tea, Jaffa cakes, and the wheelbarrow needs to be moved so they can see the full scope of the front drive.'

'Give me the run-down on *your* schedule.'

'Well...' (Ha!) '... there are the Handsovs (Carl and Marlene) from Burton-on-Trent at 0945 hours, the Longarms (Stell and Wilf) from Milton Keynes at 1015...'

'Stop there. Problem. I've got the Chummy-Headlocks (Cynthia and Auberon) at 1025. Could be dashed tight...'

It's not exactly like this. But Maggie and I agree this is what it feels like.

At about ten past nine, the doorbell rings, and there framed on the welcome mat are Mr and Mrs Lightfoot. He's bald. She's fat. He's smiling too much. She not enough.

'Sorry we're a bit late,' he says, as I shake their hands and herd them through the hall and into the living room. 'We've had a problem with the van,' he explains to Maggie, 'it's been playing up for the past few days. It started with a knocking whenever we went downhill. I thought at first it was the axle, didn't I, Gladys?' She remains impassive. 'So once we arrived at the NUCL site last night...' (Knuckle? They're bare fist-fighting fans?!) '... Oh sorry you'll have to forgive us. We forget not everybody's got a caravan. That's National Union of Caravan Lovers. I'm the assistant regional representative for Hertfordshire. Sorry, I'm wandering off the subject. Anyway I was underneath the van for two hours last night. First I had the cam crank regulator bolt off, but that wasn't it, so then I...' About eight minutes later, I manage to ask them if they'd like a cup of tea. The Jaffa cakes are already arranged on the coffee table in an attractive configuration.

'No thanks,' says Gladys, 'we'd just like to get on with it.'

'Nice back garden,' says Cedric, peering through the French windows.

'Oh, thank you,' says Maggie. It's her department.

'Do you get a lot of noise from the school across the road?' asks Mrs L.

'Oh, that. Good lord, no,' I reply. 'It's not like living in London you know. This is Stow-on-the-Wold.' I give what aims to be an indulgent laugh, but then wonder if it came over as mocking.

'The children here are very well behaved,' chips in Maggie.

'And quiet,' I add.

The Lightfoots look at each other. Then he mumbles something about needing to get to the supermarket before it closes, and thanks us for our time. She says, 'It's not as big as in the photo, is it?' And he adds that they'll be in touch, before doing an embarrassed sidestep to join her as she passes through the front door.

With minor variations to the preliminaries, this conversation is repeated with the Handsovs, Longarms, Chummy-Headlocks and approximately 196 other sets of viewers, the overwhelming majority of whom we never hear from again. The only significant departures from this model come when, through the front window, we see potential purchasers pull up outside, then drive off without even getting out of their cars.

So after two months of this, we surrender, and decide to put it with an agent. Apart from anything else, the planners are getting restless again. In fact there are signs of a full-scale insurgency brewing.

CHAPTER 12

GLIBPERT'S REVENGE

An email has arrived from Anthea.

'I don't believe this!!!!!!!!! Give me a call please so we can discuss this.'

She's forwarded a message from Bella, who says:

'Dear Anthea,

'We have a problem with this application as the conservation team have objected. I have attached a copy of their response.'

Then comes a report, headed 'From Gilbert Gradfram-Polly.'

It's long. I scan it.

'... historic structure... However... relies on an extension... would dominate the existing building... In addition... rear of extension would appear as large expanse of masonry... uncharacteristic element within the setting of the neighbouring cottage.'

Then there are three options with boxes to be ticked: CONSENT /REFUSE /REFER TO SECRETARY OF STATE. The tick's against the middle one.

Maggie says, 'It makes you want to say "Bugger 'em" and demolish it.'

For Maggie to say this, it's dire. I call Anthea, who reckons that our chances of getting anything beyond the existing footprint of the garages and workshop are now counting backwards fast towards zero. 'The problem is,' she points out, 'it's going to be a loss of face for them to go back on what they've put in writing. The only thing I can think of is for you to have a chat direct with this conservation officer. I think he's new, and it's his first job.'

'Yes, he's twelve next birthday,' I say, explaining I've met him.

OK, nothing to lose now I guess. Before I phone him, Maggie spells out some advice on how to handle the encounter, then gives me a good luck pat on the back, and – when he answers his mobile at the second ring — I come out fighting.

My opening moves are designed to get him to lower his guard. I ask if he's happy to talk about his recommendation. He says, 'Yes.' I stress how much we agree with his description of the building as an 'historic structure.' He murmurs, 'OK, good.'

So I move on to Round Two: softening him up. I've got a couple of sharp jabs ready. He's mentioned that the back of our extension would produce a 'large expanse of masonry,' but it won't be seen from anywhere but the car park.

His block is weak, 'Yes, but it *will* be seen.' OK, but has he noticed that the barn just up the road has one side which is also 'an expanse of masonry' – without a single window – roughly five times bigger than what we're proposing? I hear the air expelled from his lungs with the force of the blow.

But he bounces back off the ropes. 'The fundamental point is that this is within the grounds of a listed building, so as an historic structure, the outbuilding must be maintained within its existing footprint.' And he follows up with a straight right, quoting clause and sub-clause from the relevant Act.

But he over-reaches himself and starts to lose his balance. 'An extension,' he says, trying to build on his last hit, 'would be detrimental to the look of the facade.'

He's toppling forward, and it needs only the slightest biff from me to drop him to the canvas. The facade, which he's so keen to protect, I point out, is currently a line of battered garage doors. I can see he knows he's losing now, so I'm on to him before the referee can intervene. We have an existing permission to demolish the whole structure, I point out. Which does he think would spoil the facade more: a small discreet extension, or tearing the whole lot down?

There's a pause while he takes a mandatory count of eight. Then he's struggling to his knees. 'I wasn't asked to decide between competing proposals,' he whines, trying to block my assault.

I can see he's groggy, and he retreats, staggering across the ring. 'I'm only making a recommendation.' It's a weak counter. 'This is not a final decision. I'll discuss it with the case officer.' And that's how it stands at the end of the bout.

The points are mostly mine, I reckon. I look over for approval from Maggie, who's been listening on the other phone.

'I said, "Make sure you *cuddle* him,"' she sighs. 'I didn't say, "Make sure you *clobber* him".'

Oh.

It is at this point that I begin to believe we will not get the planning consent we need, and that we'll have to sell up to the builder who wants to demolish our old stable so he can erect the new repro Cotswold cottage instead.

I'm puzzled as much as morose. I need some fresh air. Maggie's already left for the shop, shaking her head. I wander into the Square, where the vicar gives me a clarion-volumed 'Lovely Morning', which from my side of the words is untrue, but which it would be churlish to reject. So, lying, I smile and agree with him, as Black Beauty lumbers past. My mind is still full of unchristian thoughts about planners and conservation officers. I'm thinking to myself, 'I bet the builders in Hogsthorpe didn't have any of this bother. Presumably all they did was pop into the council offices in Louth [home of the famous large cow] one Friday afternoon and say, "Oh by the way, we thought we'd let you know we've got a couple of our lads starting in Hogsthorpe Monday morning. Going to put up four thousand bungalows. OK?" To which the planner probably retorted, "Spot on, Garry. Much appreciate the tip-off."'

I'm starting to believe that this tale has now acquired definitive villains: the evil masters of the planning process at Westminster and their diabolic minions in Cirencester. Or am I just indulging in self-justification?

I turn into the High Street as the bells in the church tower fill Stow's Market Square. Stow has the heaviest peal of bells of any parish church in Gloucestershire. Have you ever noticed that the genuine sound of bells being rung by half a dozen people pulling hard on bell ropes, rather than some synthesised recording, is one of an arrhythmic jangle? With these monstrous pieces of metal, weighing over a ton each, swinging about over your head, it's almost impossible to achieve the constant beat of a conventional musical instrument. But the power and the beauty of the sound more than make up for the lack of rhythm. I've loved church bells ever since I was at Oxford, where the landlord of The Turl pub complained they were disturbing his drinkers. And one of the things I'm looking forward to at our new house is being able to hear from there the changes rung at St. Edward's.

With my ears filled to brimming, I look around the Square at the mishmash of shops, houses, pubs and cafes on all sides. No two roofs are the same height, none slant at the same angle. No two buildings have the same window frames, and many are bent and warped. One facade sticks out from its neighbour, while another tilts sideways a little. Some have pillars, the next has a porch, some are flat-chested, others have shopfronts that look like joke spectacles on a wrinkled face. The tiles on the rain-stained roofs sag, or poke up and are spattered with knobbles of near-black moss. The walls are all different colours. Forget that nonsense about 'honey-dipped' stonework. That's seeing things as you think they *ought* to be. Take a proper look. The colour of Stow's buildings is more like cheese that's been dropped in mud, then stamped on a few times. Cheddar mostly, but sometimes Double Gloucester, seeping through a grey or even black covering, then topped off with the odd blotch of lichen in mustard or off-white. However mellow Cotswold stone was in the quarry, it soon weathers on the wall. So all this around me is a higgledy-piggledy delight of refusal to conform. I'm not trying to pretend that Stow-on-the-Wold is the Keith Richards of domestic architecture, but it's not the Singing Nun either. It sits somewhere between strutting anarchism and simpering jollity. Holding two arthritic fingers up to the twenty-first century's straight-lined neatness, Stow's buildings come from an age long before planning officers marched in with their regulations and their interpretations.

But then of course, I remember. One of the reasons I can still enjoy this shambolic beauty is because those very same planners now bend over backwards to preserve it for me. OK then. The Planning Office is *not* the arch-villain of the drama. I suppose it's like the rest of us. It gets things a bit wrong sometimes. And with this charitable thought settling into unfamiliar surroundings in my brain, I take a wander round the Square.

It's clear the recession is having an impact. There's more than one empty tea shop with TO LET in the window. And as Maggie knows from her own boutique as well as from chatting to her fellow retailers, Stow this year is getting a busload fewer visitors here and a carful fewer shoppers there. But it's more than the commercial downturn that's affecting Stow. Buyers' tastes have been changing too.

For much of the past thirty years, Stow has been to antiques what Melton Mowbray is to pork pies. But the antiques trade isn't what it was. It used to be that Americans landing at Heathrow would grab a black taxi and snap, 'Take us to your old Brit antique stores.' The cabbies, pausing only to start their taximeters, would shoot up the M40 and, £350 later, deposit the eager collectors in the Square. There they could be heard demanding Crown Derby inkwells, Chippendale tiffin-trolleys or whatever it was they considered to be the prized relics of Britain's once mighty past. Stow could pride itself on having the most authentic supplies and the most expert suppliers.

But nowadays, it's often Japanese and Australians who arrive in coaches or rented Ford KAs, and are more interested in taking photos of themselves outside the New England Coffee Shop or in purchasing tankards that say, „Other way up". There *are* still antique shops in Stow, but they look mournful and bereft of customers. Most of the dealers in the Square itself have gone, and where once stood polished walnut and flowery porcelain, you now find cream teas, or posh anoraks, or Joanna Trollopes and a little white tree with necklaces hanging from its branches in an upmarket charity shop.

But it's a tribute to Stow's commercial resilience that the town has a growing reputation as the supplier of another category of valuable household object. Art. Galleries are springing up all over the place. And there's something for all tastes. For example:

- *A Cheeky Visitor*, squirrel on a windowsill reproduced in photo-realist detail with a single-hair paintbrush (would make a nice eightieth birthday present for Nan in Merthyr Tydfil).
- *The Tuileries from Boulevard Haussmann*, a cityscape with sparkly colours in the style of the Impressionists (could suit newly retired solicitor).
- *Arousal in Crimson*, a square metre of brown acrylic paint with a blue spot in the middle (twenty-five-year-old banker might acquire to show girlfriends he has soul as well as a Ferrari).

Most of the antique dealers have always had on their walls the odd gilt-framed canvas along the lines of *Sir Josiah Spatchcock Astride Winsome Lass* (i.e. a horse). So for some it was a natural progression to phase out the scorned Tudor tables and Edwardian candelabra, and buy in squirrels, boulevards and emotive spots instead. But for many, sales in the Spatchcock department have apparently not been brisk enough to tempt them to leap across to the art bandwagon, so instead they sell up in Stow and 'go online' with a small, rented workshop in Bourton.

As I drift past another darkened window front, it strikes me that Stow's problem isn't a lack of shops. It's got too many. Why aren't they being turned into homes for local people, or else for weekenders? That's a good business. And what would the planners make of that?

CHAPTER 13

£*{],%@@, MORE OR LESS

Sometimes, on this earth, good things happen against all the odds. I'm not undergoing a religious conversion. I'm talking about when you leave a job interview thinking it hadn't gone too badly, and immediately see from the mirror in the lift, a little lump of something that belongs hidden inside a nice white hanky but that's stuck to your nice white shirt collar instead. You swear and with a heavy heart go back to the Appointments pages of the Sunday paper. Then six days later you get a letter offering you the job at your chosen salary. Sound familiar? No? Think I'm exaggerating for comic effect? Well, the year was 1997. Place: the London HQ of a major management consultancy. Job: a directorship. Star of this drama: you guessed it.

Now we're about to get our share of these good things against all the odds.

First, a few days after my boxing bout with Glibpert, Anthea calls. Bella now says that they *will* allow a *linear* extension, that is, one that continues the line of the long building, rather than our proposal, which would have turned it into an L-shape. No reason's given for this latest U-turn. But we know not to demand one.

The big advantage of what we'd wanted originally – the right-angled extension – was that we'd have had a room facing south, which of course would have had a glass- and oak-front like the main part of the building. And for Maggie, as Champion of Light, that had been important.

But we soon realise that we want this house so badly that we'll put up with not having the L-shaped extension. Over the next week, we indulge in what our son Dan, who's an academic philosopher by profession, says is 'post hoc rationalisation.' We get foisted on us an uncomfortable decision, and then afterwards hunt down reasons why it really suits us. We justify it like this:

1. The bedroom will be further away from the noise of the road.
2. From the courtyard garden, we'll have an unobstructed view of the tower of Stow church, which is prettily lit up at night.
3. We'll avoid having to bridge the mains sewer, which – we've conveniently forgotten until now – passes under the garden.

But I'm still cautious. We don't actually have it signed off yet, and Bella has, we know, changed her mind before. 'I think we should make sure we've got the Grise batting for us on this latest plan,' I say.

'True,' replies Maggie. 'We don't want him to revert to touchiness.'

So off I go to consult him. He's behind his desk, in the den of his emporium. He strokes his chin throughout my account of our scrap with the planners. They must figure high on his list of people to disdain because he makes sympathetic murmurings. But he doesn't go so far as to voice his support for our extension. Instead he asks me what kind of roof topping we're going to use. I've not the remotest idea about this. So I just say we haven't decided yet, but of course, we won't now be raising the height of the roof. He then spends half an hour describing six different kinds of coping stone to top it off.

I thank him, and say, 'One thing's certain. We won't just put concrete on it.' I'm trying to lighten the mood. But humour, it seems, is an unwelcome guest among the reproduction Gladstone bags and Puritan-style hat stands of the Grise emporium.

'I know you won't,' he comments, 'because I wouldn't let you.'

I figure he's had plenty of chance by now to object to our latest plan, so I thank him for his continued support, pausing for the phrase to sink in. Getting a nod in response, I wish him good afternoon, and the bell on top of his door clanks me on my way.

Over the next two weeks there's one more spat with Bella. This time it's about skylights. She's agreed to one in the main bathroom. We want a couple more. But she's lost interest by now, and just keeps pressing the F4 key on her computer which she must have programmed to send out a 'NO' to tedious supplicants. By the time the final planning consent comes through a month or so later for a linear extension with *one* skylight, we've moved on to other contests. So there's no national anthem nor raising of the flag. Just a whimper of satisfaction one morning over the figs and yoghurt.

Our other piece of good news is no surprise to me, though I accept it might be to you. I wouldn't want you to think that the whole of this book is about confusion, incompetence and occasional bumbling by accident into the right course. Mostly on my part. Not at all. Because when it comes to selling our existing house, I do something clever. I'm not given to self-congratulation, but I figure by now you may be hungry for something that deserves an out-and-out celebration.

You'll remember that I had a crack at selling the house myself, but without a single nibble. So in the end, I'd had to hang my head in failure before the knowing smirk of an estate agent. Well, at that point there were three lots of potential buyers, who'd set themselves apart from the others by actually phoning back with a question after their viewing. Is the flowering currant bush legally protected? Where's the nearest bread shop? No more than that. So when we signed on with the agent, I insisted that if we happened to sell to any of these three, whom I'd found myself, no commission would be payable to him. He'd agreed, with the kind of look busy adults give children who're insisting they don't want CocoPops but Frosties instead.

So now, after six weeks, a couple from the Home Counties phone to say they'd like a second viewing that same afternoon. We scamper about, scrubbing the place from porch to loft, stuffing all the bright blue, half-opened bags of compost into the shed, and we've just remembered to switch on the coffee machine and the bread-maker, when the doorbell rings.

The couple have brought their mother, who lives in a village just outside Stow. We invite them to wander around on their own, with Mum choosing to settle herself on the sofa, where I chat with her, while Maggie lurks about trying to overhear the conversation upstairs. They seem keenish, and even measure up where a sideboard and a boat trailer might fit. Then off they go to think some more.

The comforting news is that they're on our list of three leftovers. The discouraging bit is that they haven't even put their own house on the market yet. And as every house-seller knows, that's hopeless. So we just enjoy the super-clean house and forget about them.

Two weeks later, the action starts.

Or rather stutters.

Our computer has come down with an infection and emails are being routed through to my mobile. Now you may have an image of my Blackberry or iPhone lighting up every couple of minutes and zipping webpages and videos across its busy screenette. Forget it. I'm too mean to invest in that sort of technology. What happens is, at 9 a.m. one morning, my Nokia 0000001 clangs twice like a ship's bell to announce the arrival of a text in capital letters. As usual, it shows only the first dozen words before it shuts down. I glance at the message and realise it could be life-changing. So, fresh out of the shower, I drop my towel, and scuttle naked down the stairs, calling, 'Maggie, Maggie, look at this, look at this.'

'Not a lot new there,' she says, as I gambol into the kitchen.

'It's an email on the phone, from the Home Counties folk,' I cry, and jabbing a wet finger on the Down button, I read it out. 'THANKS FOR GIVING US THE OPPORTUNITY OF LOOKING AT YOUR HOME AGAIN WERE NOW WAITING FOR OUR PURCHASERS SURVEYOR BUT'

'But, but… what?' she demands.

'It's the phone,' I explain. 'It'll come. Wait a minute.'

'But the Home Counties folk said they hadn't even started to look for a buyer for their place.'

'Well, I suppose things must have moved quick,' I guess. And I've just started to run up the stairs for a bathrobe, when the bell clangs again to announce the arrival of the next batch of words, so I turn in mid flight and sprint back into the kitchen, poking the green button as I go, to bring up the next episode, which is, 'IN VIEW OF THE FACT THAT OUR PURCHASERS HAVE INVOLVED BUILDERS FOR A LOFT CONVERSION WE FEEL CONFIDENT IN MAKING YOU AN'

This time we stand staring at the phone, me rubbing my backside where I scraped it against the oven-door handle on my last entry. It's a reliable old thing, the phone, and after about four minutes, it finishes its sentence: 'OFFER SUBJECT TO CONTRACT OF £*{],%@@ WITH COMPLETION END JULY ALL THE BEST KEITH AND RUTH.'

I jump about and abuse the phone in terms unsuitable for the ears of our prospective buyers' mother in a village just outside Stow.

'You're talking to inanimate objects again,' says Maggie. 'What's it mean?' she asks, looking over my elbow and pointing at the '£*{],%@@'.

I explain between expletives that my mobile does this sometimes. It thinks numbers are some kind of secret message which it has to encode.

'So we'd better speak to them,' Maggie suggests.

'No, no, that'd make us look flaky. It's easy enough to work it out.' And I explain that the symbols are on an alternative keyboard in the phone's memory and if we match them to the numeric keyboard, we can decode the figure. She looks at me as though I'm lecturing on black holes.

It takes about half an hour. Pausing only to drape a kitchen towel round my loins, I draw four grids on separate sheets of paper, insert symbols and figures, place the papers on top of each other, then hold them up to the light so I can see which match what. I then transcribe the resulting numbers onto a fifth sheet, which gives me the Home Counties folk's bid.

It's slightly more than double the asking price, which does seem overgenerous on their part. I'm just about to check that I've got the sheets of paper in the correct order, when Maggie comes back into the room.

'They're offering £55,000 below what we want,' she announces.

'How do you know?'

'I just phoned them.'

So the excitement is short-lived. We text them a polite rejection and it's back to the agent.

A week later they edge up their offer. After a mini-summit, Maggie and I dribble our asking price down a mite. And this edging and dribbling goes on for a fortnight. But the Home Counties folk are still far short of what would make the 'in' and 'out' figures balance on our budget spreadsheet.

Still it does seem clear that both of us want a deal. So we spend an evening extracting average prices from my stack of NEC brochures, double-checking the results against Nik's magic formula, and deciding how much more we need to squeeze out of our buyers. Then we develop a strategy. And the next afternoon, when Maggie comes back from the shop, we put it into action. The phone call is brief. I've got notes in front of me.

'It seems to us,' I start, 'that you like our house, and we're anxious to sell it, now. So why don't we split the difference?

We'd absolutely understand if that doesn't fit your budget and you said "No." In that case, we'd both look elsewhere. If you say "Yes," we'll be out by the end of the month, and you can move in.'

They call back twenty minutes later. It's 'Yes.'

Next morning, I phone the estate agent and tell him we've sold without him. There's silence for about ten seconds, then he just says, 'Crikey.'

It's one of the sweetest moments of my life.

CHAPTER 14

THE WEDDING, A TWO ACT DRAMA

The next three weeks are occupied by the most miserable event that can afflict any of us in the normal run of our lives. It's right down there with divorce (I know, I've had two of them), or discovering your home's been burgled (only one of these for me), being made redundant (one), and getting pneumonia on your eighth birthday (obviously just the one, but it felt like four at the time).

It's... *MOVING HOUSE.*

The Home Counties folk are anxious to take over Maggie's old home and we need their money, so we have to find somewhere temporary to live while The Old Stables is being built.

We've set ourselves a meagerish budget for the monthly rent, on the grounds that it will only be for a few months, so we can rough it. We troop round all the estate agents in the district, carefully avoiding the one who'd been fairly cheated out of the commission on our sale, and get shown scores of identical ten-year-old terraced hovels. They all have lawns that look like motorway verges but a lot smaller, from which you enter a front door that leads straight onto the beer-sploshed carpet of the lounge, half of whose area is under the stairs, which go up to two cupboards and a cracked bath. Even the agents don't bother rehashing standard comment number five, 'It just needs a little TLC. It's very cosy, really.' Instead, they loiter at the door and say nothing. I suppose they're trying to get us to move upmarket and so improve their commission. And it works.

On the fourth day, Maggie says, 'I can't do it any more. I'm going to be sick if I see another one.' Fair point. So we go back into the office of the latest agent and tell her what she's been hoping to hear from us all morning. She goes into instant gush mode: 'I've got the very thing for you. It's in the village of Blockley. It's only come in this morning. I haven't even seen it myself yet. So we could all go off and explore it together, couldn't we?' This is a question that requires a reply only if you're a character in an Enid Blyton adventure.

Mill Cottage is about a hundred yards down a driveway on the outskirts of Blockley. It sits in the several acres of grounds attached to a rambling eighteenth century house which the agent tells us was once a watermill. Mill Cottage has its own private garden with a stream running through it. Ducks come waddling over to greet us as we walk up the path to the oak stable-door. Inside, the rooms are not cottagy at all. They're all spacious. And light. There are big French windows that look out over the brook and across farmland to a tree-topped ridge. There's an inglenook fireplace. You probably think I've gone over to the enemy and done an estate agent's starter-pack course. But if I tell you that neither Maggie nor I turn a hair when the agent says the rent is double our original budget, and if I add that we merely look at each other and nod, then you'll understand that my sugary language is no marketing ploy.

Having signed up without further debate back at the agent's office, we get in the car and Maggie straightaway says, 'Do you think we've done the right thing?'

'Well, we've now bust our budget by several thou,' I reply.

'I know. But I couldn't have lived in any of those student squat places we saw before. I'd have woken up each morning itching all over.'

'I know, I know. I think we're going to need the pleasurable comforts of Mill Cottage, Blockley each evening, if we're going to stay sane over the next few months.' Maggie nods, and I add, 'It's going to be a stressful time.'

What am I talking about? 'Going to be...' What's it been then for the past six months? But it's true. It's about to get worse, by a jumbo-sized bundle.

What makes *MOVING HOUSE* such a down-there miserable event is the *taking-all-the-little-things-in-the-house-and-wrapping-them-in-paper-and-stuffing-them-in-boxes-that-you-then-inadequately-label*, which is followed by *living-for-what-seems-an-age-in-a-small-warehouse-full-of-boxes-not-able-to-find-anything*, and then there's the *all-the-big-things-being-carted-away-till-your-home-is-as-lonely-looking-as-a-prison-release-hostel*. It's not these acts in themselves that are so depressing, it's what they represent. The stability of your life, the ordinariest bits of it that you rely on and that you usually take for granted, are suddenly attacked, beaten up and kidnapped. So over the next few days whenever Maggie says something encouraging or helpful – in the way that women do all the time no matter how awful the world around them becomes – I just snort a 'hhHH' produced by a sharp intake of air at the back of the nose, or snap out a 'What do you mean!'

You see, *MOVING HOUSE* is bringing home to me the true, dreadful scale of the whole stables-conversion project we're undertaking. It's as though we're dismantling our ship from under us while we're sailing on it out at sea, and then expecting to build a new one while we're floating about on the waves. And it's too late to change our minds. We're in mid Atlantic, hundreds of miles from the nearest shipping lanes and the sky up-wind's looking black. My only hope is that the delights of Mill Cottage will make us feel like we've washed up on a pleasant little island, not our ultimate New World destination, but similar enough to a Caribbean holiday resort that I'll feel able to abandon these increasingly tedious seafaring metaphors.

The day comes.

Maggie's house, my house, our house, has been stripped bare the day before by the removal men and we've spent the night squirming about on a double lilo, just the thing you need in mid ocean, after picking at takeaway chicken balti and spicy ladies' fingers in polystyrene trayettes while sitting on the floor.

At 9.04 a.m. we lock the door for the last time. Maggie peels off to the shop, and I sit outside in the car waiting for a phone call from the office of Mr Joshua Hurley, our solicitor, to say the Home Counties folk's money has been transferred across. It comes at 10.05 a.m., and eight minutes later the new owners of Maggie's house arrive, all chirpy and sporting milk cartons and kettles and mugs and packets of tea. I shake Keith's spare hand, give him the keys, wish them both luck, and clear off.

Over at Blockley, the trouble has started early. I arrive to find the giant removals van locking horns with a sturdy beech tree at the start of the drive that leads to Mill Cottage.

The driver winds down his window and passes down his expert judgement, 'We're going to have to unload it all into a littler van that can get underneath the branches, then shuttle up and down to the front door.'

'How long's that going to take?' I ask in plaintive tone.

He shrugs the corners of his mouth, 'Fair few hours, I'd say.'

His mate in the passenger seat leans over, and adds helpfully, 'The boss says he can't get a littler van here before two.' The driver winds up his window and I catch sight of him unscrewing the top to his flask before the steam condenses on the glass and blurs my view.

It's eleven o'clock so I head off into the centre of Blockley in search of refreshment for body and spirit. Alongside the village green – it's an odd affair because it sits up at one end about 8-feet higher than the road – there's a shop-cum-post office, and the woman behind the counter sends me off on my quest for tea and possibly sandwiches, across the road, through the mournful churchyard, and into a tiny square containing two tables with parasols and chairs. It's the home of Murray's, a cafe which I see, as soon as I enter, doubles as a deli.

Blockley is going to be my sort of village.

As soon as I've sat down and picked up the menu, a voice calls out, 'Hello there, how are *you* doing today?' It belongs to a chap in his thirties who's topping off a couple of cappuccinos with chocolate powder alongside a stack of glass cabinets packed with irregular shaped slices of carrot cake, lardy loaf, and extra-thick cream strawberry torte with brownie mix topping. Murray's is the size of place where everybody's within chatting distance of the counter.

'A helluva lot better for being in here,' I reply.

'That's what we like to hear,' he says. 'Be with you in a tick.' And what seems like a second later, he's at my table, having meanwhile delivered the cappuccinos to their destination somewhere behind me.

'What's it to be today?'

'Have you got Red Bush tea?'

'Yup.'

'... and...' I scan the glass cases... 'a slice of lardy cake.' The selection is such that you can feel lardy cake is the slimmer's option.

'Good choice,' he says. 'It's made by a lady just down the road, and popped out of her oven only a couple of hours ago.' He nips back behind the counter and while he's organising the tea bags and lardy, asks, 'You just visiting Blockley?'

I explain that we're renting here for six or eight months while we have the restoration work done in Stow.

'Sounds like *Grand Designs*,' he says, back now at the table.

'Well, more *Modest Little Plans* really.'

'Lots of luck. Let me know if you need anything else. Help yourself to a newspaper if you want. Hi Charlie. Hi

Martha. And what have *you* got?' The bell over the door's just clanged and he's crouching down now beside a grinning little girl who's thrusting Paddington Bear in his face.

Once I've moved on through sea bass fishcakes, salad and fresh baked bread (I figure the cake was elevenses and then it's time for lunch, but I do make a mental note to go to the gym this week), while scanning the *Telegraph* and the *Guardian* (you can't be too careful in a new village home, you don't want to offend political sensibilities before you've even scraped the mud from your boots), I realise it's time to go and supervise the removers.

'That was excellent,' I say, fishing out my wallet.

'Great. My name's Chris by the way.'

'Good to meet you, Chris. I'm Derek. And Maggie and I will be back in here. Often, I'd say.'

'Thanks. I'm afraid the bad news is though that we're going to be shutting in a few weeks' time.'

'Oh really? Not enough business for you here?'

'It's just time to move on.'

'That's a shame. Seems to be that's what's happening in a lot of villages. Places like this shutting down.'

'I know. Well, we'll see what happens.'

Back at Mill Cottage, the littler van's arrived and its first load's being fitted in. This amounts to the sofa and four boxes. My job is to stand about inside the cottage, like those teenage kids you see employed to direct traffic in fields used as temporary car parks on village fete day, waving their arms about meaninglessly, which I do whenever the movers back through the front door with a bedside table or a standard lamp. The task's only three-quarters done by the time Maggie gets back from the shop late afternoon. Removal costs are up by 40 per cent.

The following week sees a repeat, in reverse process, of the misery we went through at the old house. But at least it is a reverse process. We've got a sofa to sit on opposite a TV (which announces 'And now for the news where *you* are' then shows reports of a shopping centre stabbing and a bin men's strike in central Birmingham). We speed things up when we take a decision to nominate about half of the removal boxes 'Not wanted on voyage.' (That's the last ocean-going reference, I promise.) This is stuff we can do without till we get to The Old Stables, stuff that can be stacked up in the third bedroom of Mill Cottage. And by halfway through our second week, our feet are firmly on dry land. (Sorry.)

Blockley's only minor downside stems from the otherwise endearing fact that our watermill – or rather the landlords' – is one of no fewer than twelve such mills, which started to turn around the time of Domesday Book. Over the centuries, these have powered everything from silk-glove factories to a bone-grinding business. Each one, of course, needed somewhere for the miller and his clan to live, and we discover over the next few days that the village now has twelve Mill Cottages, more or less. It makes for an entertaining breakfast time, seeing how many letters intended for other Mill Cottage dwellers we've received today, and speculating on how many of our own bills and good luck cards have gone AWOL. Even this mix-up has its benefits, because around ten o'clock a selection of us mill-cottagers often meet up at the village post office to swap mail. Maggie and I start to meet some affable neighbours that way.

Our landlords' converted mill sits just over the other side of our garden stream. He turns out to be a man of fearsome strength and energy. I bump into him just as I'm loading the car with the last lot of empty removal boxes to take to our allotted garage hidden away at the far end of the Mill House grounds. I tell him how much we admire their home.

'I did it all myself,' he says. 'I laid every single stone of Mill House, fitted every window, put on every square inch of roof, landscaped all these grounds, did every last bit of decoration in your cottage as well. It was all a total wreck when we bought it. We didn't use builders. I did the lot myself.'

'Crikey,' I say, not feeling I can mention our little enterprise in Stow. 'How long did it take you?'

'On and off, eighteen years. And by the way, I hope you don't mind a bit of noise. Just for this weekend. Our daughter's getting married on Saturday. Three p.m. in Chipping Camden church. The reception's going to be here. In marquees. Two hundred guests.'

'No bother. Congratulations…' But he's already off.

Saturday turns out to be a warm day. It's the last weekend in August. So I sit outside in my shorts and watch across the stream the white-jacketed waiters, catering vans, a jazz band and a platoon of wedding furniture humpers arriving to get set up throughout the morning. All under the energetic eye of our landlord. It quietens down at about 1.30 p.m., but then suddenly an hour later, he's back out there. There seems to be a problem with the eating arrangements. Next thing, I see him emerge round the edge of Mill House, half-running but bent forward from the waist at right-angles, an eight-seater table upturned on his back. He clunks it down, shouts at a waiter to fetch a cloth for it, then runs back and repeats the exercise three times. The peaked-cap chauffeur who's been shining the door handle of his vintage Rolls, a white-ribbon across its bonnet, pauses to watch.

I reckon there are about twelve minutes for the father of the bride to shower, change and escort his daughter to her big moment.

At six minutes to three, she emerges, tall, white and serene, and heads for the Roller. He catches her up – still fiddling with his collar button, the tails of his morning coat flying – just before she gets there.

I settle back in the sunshine to observe the moorhens forming street gangs to intimidate the squirrels who venture down to our stream. The sun is making wavy patterns on the tree-topped ridge across the cornfields, and a treacherous little idea insinuates itself into my brain. It says to me, 'What are you doing putting yourself through all this stress of converting an old stables? Mill Cottage has got everything that you want, and everything that Maggie wants. Why don't you see if you could buy this place instead? You could sell the burgage with planning permission at a profit, and I bet the couple who own Mill Cottage would sell it to you if you made a good offer. Just think what worry and effort you'd be saving yourself. Think how lovely it would be…'

When Maggie arrives from the shop, I poke this serpent of a thought back under its stone, and she joins me with a glass of chilled white wine in her hand. She turns her chair so she too can see the proceedings across the stream without twisting her neck.

There's something surreal about watching someone else's wedding from the front row of the stalls. We're close enough to see prim aunties in sugar-bowl hats, the lads from the bridegroom's office horsing about, the flower girls falling over and getting mud on their dresses, the best man looking more and more ragged as the evening progresses, and our landlord being *mein host* all over the place. But what with the syncopated rhythm of the Dixieland band, we can't hear what the performers are saying, so Maggie and I write our own script as the play unfolds before us. That night, once the strains of 'My Old Kentucky Home' have subsided, we sleep content.

CHAPTER 15

A SEVENTEENTH-CENTURY CAR PARK

So, now we've got the planning consent, we've got the money (thanks to the sale of Maggie's house), and we've got Nik. So D-Day approaches.

Disentangle Day. Declutter Day. Dump-all-the-rubbish-from-the-site Day

We tell people, 'We're converting an old stables.' And that's technically true. The Tax Office defines it as a conversion. And so does Bella's planning department. So judge for yourself. We'll be knocking down the roof and the whole of the front. We'll be taking down one of the end walls and rebuilding it 4 metres out (though Nik says a lot of the stones won't be reusable, so 'rebuilding' might be fanciful). The whole floor will have to be hacked up and replaced by steel-reinforced concrete. So that'll leave just two walls of the old stables standing: the high one that runs along the boundary for the length of the building, and the thick, end wall next to the road. Oh, and *these* might need to be underpinned, or otherwise tampered with, or – and this is what keeps even Maggie awake at four in the morning – it's just possible they might be so unsafe that they too would have to be pulled down and rebuilt. Where that would leave planning consent, VAT status, diplomatic relations with Mr E. Grise, my craving for tradition, not to mention the state of our finances, are questions we only allude to when we want to terrify ourselves.

Anthea knows a good structural engineer who'll pronounce on the state of our walls (and thus of our future mental health), and she's fixed a site meeting with him for the following Wednesday. That will be Judgement Day.

But first, on Monday, it's D-Day. The paper stage is over. I'm already there, exchanging 'Wonderful Mornings' with the vicar and his dog, when Nik's four-by-four arrives outside the burgage at 8.27 a.m. Three of his lads tip out, and he sets them to work clearing the site of all the trees, bushes, rusty barrows, heaps of shattered tiles and the rest of the detritus that I've never really noticed before. Remember, the burgage is a long, narrow piece of land. And though the house will be long and narrow too, other stuff's got to be squashed in next to it, like a courtyard, but also a driveway leading to parking spaces we share with Sunny (or whoever buys her cottage). So all plant and tree life has to come out.

I'm amazed how fast the area starts to open up. If I were going to get rid of that gnarled damson tree for instance, I'd first have to draw up a plan of action, then trim off the branches, and cut them into small pieces. Next I'd saw the still vertical trunk into manageable slices where it stood, sweeping up the shavings as I went. Then I'd dig out the roots. Finally, I'd cart it all away piece by piece. It would take me two full weekends, at least. And that's assuming, unreasonably, that I hadn't pulled a muscle in my shoulder on the first morning. What Nik's lads do is throw a rope round the redundant tree, give a good heave, and chuck it, roots and all, into the skip, taking approximately two and a half minutes.

At about 9.30 a.m., Sunny appears in her dressing gown, and shows the guys where the electricity supply is. Nik leaves them to it. I stick around for a couple of hours feeling self-important and at the same time redundant, then leave to attend to the other fag-ends of my life.

When Maggie and I go to review progress in the evening, it is with a sense of joyful freedom in our hearts, possibly akin to that felt by the countryman immortalised by Vaughan Williams, heading for 'where, for me, the apple tree / Do lean down low in Linden Lea.' (Hum immortal tune.)

'No more theoretical battles with bureaucrats,' I say to Maggie as we park the car in Back Walls. 'Action. That's the thing!'

'Yes,' she says. 'We ought to just stop and mark this day. We've actually, at last, started to build our new home.'

'Well, knock down the old one, anyway,' I quip, and we giggle like kids let out early on a spring afternoon.

Our euphoria lasts about as long as Vaughan Williams' three-verse song.

The burgage is transformed. Now that much of the Cotswold jungle has been hacked out, the plot of land looks wider than we'd thought.

'We'll be able to have a nice-sized courtyard to look out on,' says Maggie, doing metre-long strides from the glass and oak facade (battered garage doors) across the terrace, bedecked with potted bay trees and primulas (chopped white roots, mud and shattered tiles), then looks up.

'Bloody hell!' she cries. Maggie is occasionally given to utter this expletive, but only when she suffers a life-threatening shock, so I rush out of the old building, where I've been trying to discover if there are any original beams in the roof, stumbling over a rusty upturned wheelbarrow handle, and land on one knee behind her.

'What is it? What's wrong?' I ask the back of her thighs.

'I never realised before, when all this was trees and hedges,' she says, 'but now anybody walking along the alley...' (Fleece Alley, an old sheep-run, goes along the side of our property allowing the residents of Back Walls to cut through to Sheep Street and the Market Square) '... will be able to see straight into our living room!' I struggle to my feet, and before I can judge for myself, she adds, 'And what about the neighbours in that house!' She points to a three-storey cottage a few yards along on the other side of the alley. 'If they decide to peer over as they get out of bed, they'll be able to see everything, from what I'm eating for breakfast to the colour of your nightshirt! It wouldn't matter if we were having tiny, lace-curtained windows. But the house is going to be like one of those aquariums you see in dentists' waiting rooms!'

I try to find some reassurance for Maggie by walking back and forth along the alley several times, crouching progressively lower, with my head bent sideways peering towards her. A young woman picks up her small child when she sees me, and holds it in a protective hug as she hurries past. Back in the burgage, I tell Maggie, 'I reckon there's no problem. Except for people going past who're taller than five feet six.'

'So approximately fifty per cent of the adult population.'

We try various positional experiments to test the full extent of the difficulty, and, concluding that we are comprehensively doomed, withdraw in anxious silence.

That evening we discuss whether a 1.8-metre-high wall would give enough cover. Or bamboo shrubs. Or tall, sun-seeking eucalyptus trees. At 3 a.m. these options are still fighting each other in my fevered brain. So the next evening, after Maggie's finished at the shop and Nik's lads have left for the day, we go back to see if any one of these solutions would do the trick. But it's clear that now the decluttering job is complete, we're even more exposed.

Three o'clock that night, it's the same routine inside my head. So by the next morning – which is J-Day – I'm tense and tired.

It turns out J is not only for Judgement, but also for Jeremy, the structural engineer who'll be the one delivering verdict and sentence on the issue that's even more critical than protection from passing voyeurs: are the two main walls unsafe and going to have to be rebuilt?

Jeremy arrives on-site to find three of us in two camps. Nik and Anthea are in a jolly mood in one corner. Yeah, well, it's not the whole of their lives at stake. I'm in hunched silence in the other. I wouldn't say Maggie and I are falling out of love with the place. It's just that our desire for it no longer burns like Wordsworth's 'sacred flame'. Our feelings for The Old Stables have come down to earth. The honeymoon boarding passes have turned up crinkled in the bottom of the washing machine.

But I'm still loyal. So when I see the bits of asbestos flaking from the roof, hear the battered aluminium door frames rattle in the breeze, and smell the inside like a disused dockside warehouse, I feel the need to defend the place and our marriage to it. So I start to tell Jeremy about my researches.

'It doesn't look much today, but in the seventeenth century,' I boast, 'this place was one of the stables for The Crown Inn. According to the *London Gazette* of 1690, a hundred coaching horses could be kept here overnight.'

'A sort of early NCP franchise', he quips. And without waiting for any uproar of laughter to subside, he darts behind me, banging a wall here, measuring a width there, kicking a stone where he presumably thinks it matters.

Nik's dug out a couple of deep holes next to the tall back wall. Jeremy shines his torch down inside.

'That's brash,' he says, making what I assume is another witticism, and though I don't quite understand it, I ho-ho anyway. The faces of the other three remain unmoved, still staring into the hole. 'Brash,' says Nik, looking at me as if I'm a slow child, 'brash,' he repeats, 'crushed limestone.'

'Ah, yes,' I say. 'Brash, yes, brash.' Then, 'Is that bad?'

'No, it's good,' explains Jeremy. 'It's solid, like a natural foundation. No need for underpinning. In fact you'd need a pneumatic drill to shift it.' I peer down. Now I can see it, looking like a mini cliff-face glinting in the torchlight. We've allowed £10,000 in the budget for making these walls safe and my heart starts to dance. But it's soon clear it's not all saving. There's much talk, largely unintelligible to me, of the need for columns, piers and curly tail-ties. Jeremy talks of the risk that the Big Back Wall could 'bulge and wave.' Is this technical, as in 'brash'? Or is it jocular, as in 'seventeenth-century car park'? The impression I'm getting is that while the wall might not sink like a Coke can in quicksand, it could fall over. Finally, unable to bear the strain, I ask Jeremy what he really thinks of the wall.

He walks along it, places his eye next to it, strokes it a little and says, 'It's a damn good wall!'

I don't quite kiss him.

As the meeting breaks up, Maggie arrives. It's her lunch break, and for once I'm able to give her a bit of heart-lifting news. 'With the five grand or so we've saved,' I say, 'we can upgrade the kitchen.'

'Possibly,' she replies. 'I know you fancy yourself as an amateur Raymond Blanc, but I thought you were supposed to be an amateur Eric Braithewaite as well.' (He used to be my accountant).

'Yes of course,' I reply, 'I mean so long as the budget allows.'

'Oh, by the way,' Maggie chips in, 'I think I've got the answer to the people-peering-in-the-windows problem,'

'Really,' I marvel. 'What's that?'

'It's like the doors argument we had.'

'What do you mean?'

'It's not a case of either/or. It's both. Or in this case, all three or four. Bamboos, eucalyptus trees, a higher wall and maybe a trellis with clematis on top of the wall as well. All of them together should block the view.'

'You don't think it's going to feel like Colditz, do you?'

'Prisons aren't the only places with walls, you know. Remember when we went to the Alhambra Palace in Granada? The Spanish have these beautiful courtyard gardens. Leave it to me.'

'It's all yours,' I say, as we wander out into Back Walls. I'm delighted to have any item crossed off my worry schedule, which has a habit of lengthening if I take my eye off it for a minute.

'Good morning,' a voice calls from behind us, and we turn to see a figure in a dark blue skirt and jacket smiling from the doorway of the house just below The Old Stables. 'You must be the people who've bought the old bit of land,' she continues. 'I'm Joanna.' And almost before we've managed to return her smile, she asks, 'Would you like to come in for a glass of sherry or a cup of coffee?'

We accept, introduce ourselves, shake hands, meet her husband John, and settle ourselves in their living room.

When I opt for tea rather than the sherry, Joanna asks, 'You're not in need of a stiff shot then after your morning with the builders?'

'I don't drink,' I explain.

'That's very virtuous,' she says.

'Not really. I finished my lifetime's quota of alcohol fifteen years ago.'

'That's being a journalist for you,' says Maggie.

'A journalist, eh,' says John. 'Who did you write for?'

'I was ITN's first Middle East correspondent,' I explain.

'Ahha,' says Joanna. 'I lived in Jerusalem till I was eighteen years old. My father was head of the Palestine police.'

'Wow, you must have had quite a childhood,' I say.

'I did,' she replies. 'I was with my father inside the King David Hotel when it was bombed by Jewish guerrillas.'

'Goodness!' I say. 'Ninety-odd killed, if I remember right.'

Joanna nods. 'My father was hurt. He was blinded for three months. I was fine but we were both very lucky,' and she sips her sherry.

'It was a good few years later that I lived out there of course,' I say.

'It's still the same old quarrel today, though,' she observes, and we compare notes on what's changed and what's not.

Joanna, it turns out has had a colourful life. Somerville College Oxford, then later she became a hospital matron, in an age when – as is often fondly recalled today – hospital matrons ruled with an iron rod. Next she married John, who with his business partner set up a farm to protect rare breeds of cattle and sheep. So she became a farmer's wife. Though she and John are now retired, the business is still going strong as Cotswold Farm Park, made famous by the BBC's Adam Henson of *Countryfile*.

'John was amazing with the animals,' says Joanna. 'I remember once a particularly aggressive bull got loose. Everybody was terrified. But John just went straight up to it, and said, "Come on, you silly old thing," and it followed him like a lamb back into its field.'

'It was a big, soft creature, really,' says John.

Half an hour later we're back out in the road, the richer by a book on the Palestine campaign in World War One, half a dozen homemade scones, and two new friends.

'Now you see,' I say, 'these are the kind of neighbours you get in a place like Stow.'

'They're excellent people,' says Maggie, then adds, 'You're not suggesting though are you, that you only get good neighbours in a village?'

'No, though I have lived in flats in London where the people in the same building might as well have been the inhabitants of Number 23 Tiananmen Square, Beijing for all I ever saw of them.'

'So you reckon villages are friendlier than cities, by and large?'

'I guess so. And I tell you what, I can't say I ever had a neighbour in London who could charm the socks off a ton and a half of ferocious animal. You never know when that could be useful.'

I spend my next days chasing quotes for cement, bedroom window frames and drainage pipes. Nik gives me a list. To get the tax break, we have to buy them all direct ourselves. Every spare minute Maggie and I have together, we devote to viewing roof tiles and flagstones, and to evaluating the benefits of competing styles of bathroom basin soap trays and of kitchen unit door handles.

Some problems of course are predictable. Take utilities for instance. Sunny has decided to go to India for six months with her sister to start to plan her new life there. So we're going to need our own power supply earlier than expected. We'll have to get npower to put in an electricity meter. Just a meter. The supply's there already, waiting to drive everything from the concrete mixer to the ten o'clock brew-up kettle.

The first number I phone for meter installation isn't the right one. No surprise there of course. But when I dial the fourth one and again reach the wrong department, I decide to keep a log. The seventh customer services operative tells me (when, exasperated, I ask, 'How hard can this be?!') that the number *he's* giving me is absolutely, without any doubt, the guaranteed correct one. Nevertheless, I'm still repeating the same conversation – my voice now soprano – with the eighth and ninth departments. At number ten, I'm starting to guess the woman at the other end can hear my pathetic sobs, because she says she herself will phone the next number, and call me back. Remarkably she does so, and reports that this number, too, of course, was wrong, but she does now have the correct one, which God himself has vouchsafed her. He must have done because it works. They will send me a form to fill in.

I lie down for the rest of the day.

CHAPTER 16

FOURTH APOCALYPSE HORSEMAN IN REDUNDANCY SHOCK!

Any idea, now Nik and his lads are in full swing, that it's just a question of head down and get on with it till the job's done, is as naive as pitching your tent on the side of a volcano and hoping the smoke will be clear by tomorrow. Things start to go wrong straight off. Badly wrong.

First, there's the 6-foot-high garden wall, which should have come down in a couple of hours. It's the one Glibpert the conservation officer thought was an historic monument. It's got to be demolished so the lorries can get in to cart off what Nik estimates is eighteen to twenty loads of junk which will be left once the burgage has been levelled to a bomb site. Getting the wall down is Jason's job.

If I say Jason is a skinhead, you'll think he starts riots at football matches and marches with the BNP. And you'd be wrong. Jason's got a chubby baby face and an innocent smile, so his hairlessness puts you more in mind of a bald newborn than a rampaging thug. He's emerging as the constant in the shifting fortunes of the Old Stables. The other 'lads' come and go as required. Jason's there at 8.30 every morning, and whatever's needed that day, he knows how to do it – and to do it with tireless good humour. That is until he meets Glibpert's historic wall.

The trouble is that its breeze blocks are stuffed with solid concrete. Pickaxes snap against it. So Nik rents a pneumatic drill, which Jason battles to hold in a horizontal position, his whole body juddering in perfect sync with the hammering chisel end. The result is a pathetic little line of scratches. For the first time, I see a scowl trace its way across Jason's normally contented visage.

'This is rather a difficult task,' he says to me between bouts of attempted drilling (His actual words cannot be reported in a respectable book, but you could probably write that bit yourself). He can keep it up only for a minute or two at a time – which is no bad thing from one point of view, because people who live several doors away are complaining about the racket, with undeniable justice.

Each day when I call in at the site, I find Jason either banging away with the drill like one of those Libyan rebels you see on the news manning an anti-aircraft gun, or taking a pause to massage his wrists and check how many teeth he's got left. Finally, after almost a week, I arrive to be greeted by his old smile.

He says, 'It was difficult, but the task is now complete,' (time for your authorial skills again), and he plants his boot on the ankle-level rampart which is all that's left of the cursed wall. It's just about low enough for a lorry to bounce over.

The first one turns up three o'clock Friday afternoon. The driver stays in his cab shouting at his girlfriend on his mobile ('No, I've told you... I've told you before... What do you mean the dog's got to go?') while Jason scoops up assorted loads of rubble with the mini-dozer and clatters them into the back of the lorry. When he's finished, he walks round to the front to give an 'All done' thumbs up to the driver, who clunk-bangs off, still shouting into the phone now trapped against his cheek, without ever having acknowledged our existence.

So we're all set for this routine to be repeated a dozen and a half times.

It is not to be.

Nik calls early on Monday morning to report that a nearby road is shut for repairs. The council says it could be closed for weeks. Jason gets on with a bit of pushing and smashing, carefully avoiding any damage to the asbestos roof which will need special treatment if any of us are ever to see our grandchildren. But of course the results of his labours have now got nowhere to go. So when I arrive at 4 p.m. Monday, the broken masonry, rotting timbers and assorted rusty debris have piled up and filled every square inch of burgage around the mini-dozer, which is wheezing like a sickly parent beset by hungry children.

The next morning, on-site at 8.15 I'm taking in the scene of now silent devastation, when Nik arrives, and announces he's having to call off all further work till the site can be cleared. My heart sinks.

'It's just bad luck,' he says. 'Sorry.'

I can't help thinking it's an omen. Two setbacks. First the stubborn wall. Now the blocked road. There's bound to be a third. The big one. I regard myself as a rational person. I don't just mean that I'm not given to outbursts of lunacy (though at least one of my previous wives accused me of that, unjustly of course). What I'm trying to say is I think I'm fairly logical in my beliefs. But I have to confess I've got a thing about the number three. Mike – you remember, he's the chap who's known me the best part of a lifetime – reckons it's my brain in desperation trying to regain control by making a pattern out of life's chaos.

'In my experience, bad news comes in packets of three,' I say to Nik, shaking my head. 'So what's going to come round the corner next and smack us in the face?'

'Look, Derek,' he replies. 'I've been in this game for twenty-five years. And in *my* experience, troubles on a building site don't come in threes. They more like come in big economy-sized packets. They come in hundreds.' He pats me on the shoulder, and climbs into his pick-up. 'Get used to it. And don't worry.'

As I watch the dust rise in his tracks down Back Walls, I know why when we tell people we're building a grand design, or in our case a modest set of drawings, they marvel. That's because it's an unusual thing to do. And brave. And foolhardy. And completely unnecessary in a world where umpteen million customers of Barratts and Wimpey can't be wrong.

The vicar has paused this morning on the corner of Fleece Alley, and I can't help thinking – uncharitably perhaps – that Black Beauty may have been up to no good on the bottom of our wall. Nevertheless, once we've exchanged assessments of the miraculous beauty of the first falling leaves, I wander along the alley and down Sheep Street, drifting towards my own personal consolation zone. Retail therapy. Specialised retail therapy. I speed up as I get close to one of the four bookshops in Stow. This one's housed in a square flint-faced building that looks like a stranger from Sussex among Stow's blocks of oolitic limestone. It had started life as the office of the old brewery. Yes, as well as making our own gas, we also used to brew our own beer. Or rather Messrs Beman, Charles and Fletcher did once they'd built the Victoria Brewery here in 1837, Mr Fletcher apparently seeing no conflict of interest with his other job as 'Overseer to the Poor.' (Which way was the traffic? Alcoholism driving drinkers to the workhouse? Or the redeemed poor expanding the market for the beer?)

One of the things that strikes me about Stow is that it's always had lots of different cards up its sleeve. It was never just an agricultural settlement. And in the early nineteenth century, lots of villages all over the country, like Stow, had their own brewery. Jobs, relaxation, a source of local pride and the temptations of the devil all in one glass. What's happened since is that the big brewing companies have driven these little local ones into oblivion. Yes, I know there are still independent brewers around, given a new burst of life by CAMRA and the real ale movement. But they're the exception to the brewing giants' rule. The Victoria Brewery shut for good in 1914.

You could say it was a symbol of the English village's story, or at least part of it. When the world consisted of a million little places where things were made, villages could just as well be those little places as towns and cities. But once efficiency demanded centralisation (i.e. in cities) in order to achieve economies of scale, then village industry collapsed. But don't get me wrong. I'm not trying to turn the clock back. Life's moved on. And villages that win – in a world that'll sideline them given half a chance – are the ones that have found little new businesses to replace the little old redundant ones. Stow's Brewery Yard is a triumphant example. It's now a circle of small-scale commerce from posh hairdresser on the left to Persian carpet vendor on the right. And of course an antiquarian bookseller in the old brewery office.

The inside of The Book Box gives the impression that people come a poor second to books, the latter occupying 90 per cent of the cubic footage of the place, with humans restricted to small passageways one sideways person wide. The shop stocks lots of old guidebooks to the Cotswolds, so it doesn't take me long to find what I'm after: something to tell me what the villages hereabouts were like a hundred years or so ago. Rejecting *A New History of Gloucestershire* by Samuel Rudder, 1779 (too old and too expensive at £699) and *A Cotswold Book* by H. W. Timperley (too vague and too recent at 1931), I settle for *Highways and Byways in Oxford and the Cotswolds* by Herbert A. Evans, 1905 and *The Changing English Village 1066–1914* by Ms M. K. Ashby, which is a history of the nearby village of Bledington. I pass over two £20 notes to the shop's proprietor, who is busy explaining the English Civil War to two confused American tourists, and make for the Square and its several tea shops.

Over a pot of camomile, I delve into my rucksack and pull out *Highways and Byways*. Its author, Herb Evans, it turns out, was an aficionado of that newly popular Edwardian pastime, bicycling. So what's he got to say about Stow? In his lead-in, he says that there's something about the names of some villages that 'makes the traveller feel that life is still worth living...' Blimey! It doesn't take much to lift old H. E. out of suicidal depression. He goes on...'Stow-on-the-Wold itself, for instance, suggestive of isolation and defiance.' Hmmm, I wonder if these are tactics the Samaritans have ever tried.

The houses, he says, have a 'quiet, comfortable appearance.' And the place as a whole is 'old-fashioned.' He then goes on about the church, the Battle of Stow, and an incident in 1772 when five soldiers of the Royal East Kent Regiment perished in the snow at the foot of Stow hill. Lest we get the wrong idea, he adds that the village is a 'bright cheerful place enough on a fine spring morning,' which is when he biked there, and is 'unpretentious'. So in 1905 there's not much to offend even A. A. Gill.

I look out through the cafe window at the Market Square and wonder how I might describe its atmosphere today. Quiet? Bright and cheerful? The scene through the window of my chosen tea rooms is not so much a bustle, more a shuffle of the stick-wielding elderly, and a dawdle of buggy-pushing families. They've just got off a bus with 'Jones Tours of Swansea' written on the side. ('Be sure to be back here at 11.30, 'cos we won't wait. Ha ha.')

Comfortable? I suppose Herbert means the buildings are well-maintained, middle class maybe. Stow's certainly stayed up-at-heel, though there are two or three shops with dark and empty windows and an estate agent's sign that gets all the other shopkeepers complaining about sky-rocketing rents. The farmyard over to the left by Parson's Corner boasts rusty corrugated iron and cracked sinks for the dogs to drink from. But I don't mind that. That's what real farms look like. They're not Constable prints, if they ever were. Nor do they all have steel and white concrete warehouses where the old barns once stood.

Old-fashioned? An obvious 'Yes', though I bet Herb couldn't have bought ostrich burgers or Pot Noodles here in 1905.

Unpretentious? What did he mean by that? Modest, not showy, not getting ideas above its station?

As I consider this, I realise there's no simple answer to the question of whether it's like that today. Because this is the place where I live, so I can't form snap judgements about it as a tourist might from North Carolina or South Korea. For them, Stow is a tea-stop, halfway between a quick whizz round an Oxford college and a brief gawp at Shakespeare's second-best bed in Stratford-upon-Avon. But as far as we Stowites are concerned, where we live is a hundred things at once.

Gawd, if I keep on thinking like this, I'll never come to any conclusions about village life and what makes it work. And of course, that's what I've been doing about Stow, avoiding any conclusive judgements – ever since that fish-and-chip lunch with Ralph. I've been fiddling around at the margins with the question of whether Stow works then filing it away again under 'Too Hard For Now'.

So that's what I do again. Slot it back in the drawer.

I flirt briefly with the idea of a lardy cake, see some overseas visitors waddle past, and instead turn back to *Highways and Byways*. What about villages that are less complicated than Stow? Ones that are smaller? How are they faring these days?

One of my favourites is Bledington – hence why I'd chosen Ms Ashby's volume. It's a thickish tome, so I opt first for a glance at Herbert the biker's snap 1905 opinion of the place. It is a village, he says, with 'the deserted melancholy air of one which has seen better days.'

This is too much for my curiosity. I chuck a fiver on the table and decide to head off right now to give it a fresh look. It's only ten minutes away. 'Deserted.' 'Melancholy.' 'Seen

better days.' There must be some clue in today's Bledington
as to what makes the place now the reverse of these three
gloom-ridden qualities.

CHAPTER 17

THE GOLDEN AGE SWINDLE

I park in the gravel patch behind The King's Head. It's supposed to be for patrons only and, although I'm not one this particular day, Maggie and I often are, so I figure that's OK. This is one of the reasons I like Bledington. The King's Head does delicious food (which, as you now know, for me is right up there among books and history). Modern guidebooks call it a gastro-pub, a horrible word, though I'm tickled by the idea of the marketing department that first invented it without realising 'gastro' has undertones of a stomach upset with projectile vomiting.

A couple of chickens are loose on the path and scatter at my approach (what's wrong with the foxes round here?) as I make for the second reason I like Bledington: its village green, at the top end of which I decide to sit and take in the scene, after reading the plaque on my chosen bench:

George Beacham
Died 1ˢᵗ March 1978
Clerk to the Parish Council and Church Warden
For 30 years

From here you hardly notice The King's Head. It's a low old building on the edge of the green. There are no garish signs, and anyone driving along the little road that passes through the centre of the village could easily miss it, unless they're locals in the know (or of course happen to have consulted www.tripadvisor.com where six of whose seven reviewers give it ⦿⦿⦿⦿⦿). At the far side of the green, a small stream trickles under a bridge.

Just beyond it, by the bend in the road is an old stone house that Maggie and I looked at in the days when we still thought we could buy the light-and-character combo off the shelf. I would have snapped up the place on the spot because of its name alone. The house is called 'Waterloo.' It summoned up in my head images of an infantryman returning in 1815 from the horrors of Wellington's famous victory to the bosom of his family and the tranquillity of this village. But, when Maggie suggested it had probably been named by a retired ticket collector who'd worked at the Southern Region's mainline station, that killed it for me.

There are no parked cars visible around the green, and apart from a couple of kids' swings by the pub, an ITV film crew working on *Marple* could set up and start to shoot straight off without touching a thing. Chocolate box or what? Now, of course you may think this looks like it's playing right into Ralph's hands. *Marple, Lark Rise to*

Candleford, they're all one. But you're forgetting, I've got a new shot in my locker, or rather my rucksack, from which I extract Herbert Evans' trusty volume to check again his 1905 judgement on the village: it had, I read, 'the deserted melancholy air of a place which has seen better days.' It's the reverse of that now. But the question is, had it actually ever seen 'better days' before 1905?

My hand digs back into the rucksack and brings out Ms Ashby's history of Bledington, *The Changing English Village 1066–1914*. Deciding that I need sustenance to help me tackle her 425-page study, I rise from George Beecham's bench and make for The King's Head. It's near enough lunchtime. OK, so it's only ten to twelve. You need to get there early to bag a table. And anyway I can taste the game pie already.

At a small oak table next to the today fireless inglenook, I sip my cranberry juice and head straight for the back of Ms Ashby's volume, hoping for, and relieved to find, a comprehensive index. By the time my jugged hare (even better than the pie) and chips arrive half an hour later, the story's taking shape. I'll paraphrase.

Over the past nine centuries, it seems Bledington's drama has been played out by two groups. They are: The 𝕷𝖔𝖗𝖉 𝖆𝖓𝖉 𝕷𝖆𝖉𝖞 𝖁𝖊𝖗𝖕𝖗𝖎𝖈𝖍𝖕𝖊𝖗𝖘𝖔𝖓𝖘 and the poorpeople. I can't say Mr and Mrs poorpeople because that would imply a middle-class title. Oh, and to be fair, I should add that the 𝖁𝖊𝖗𝖕𝖗𝖎𝖈𝖍𝖕𝖊𝖗𝖘𝖔𝖓𝖘 weren't always peers of the realm, some were 𝕬𝖇𝖇𝖔𝖙𝖘 𝖔𝖋 𝖂𝖎𝖓𝖈𝖍𝖈𝖔𝖒𝖇𝖊. During the first few hundred years after the Norman Conquest, Bledington was home to the lower orders. According to Domesday Book, in 1086 there were only twelve families in the village: eight villeins and four bordars. This meant they weren't free to leave the place without the permission of the Abbot, that they had to work on his land without pay and were basically at his mercy, or to be more precise – and to dispel any idea you might have, that a man of the church would personally make sure Bledington's villeins, bordars and their families were fed and cared for – at the mercy of the Abbot's steward who lived it up at the manor house nearby. So no paradise there then.

By the mid 1700s, according to Ms Ashby, 'hardship both grew and took new forms'. The better-off farmers pushed the poor into cottages that had no gardens where vegetables might have been grown and pigs and chickens raised. Nearby woods were cleared so there was less fuel for fires. The word 'starvation' was commonly used at this time to denote both hunger and cold.

With a frisson of guilt, I order The King's Head's home-made apple pie, but feel cleansed when I turn down cream with it, and read that in the nineteenth century there were at least moments of communal jollity. In 1815, the villagers all gathered inside Bledington's Home Farm cart shed and were treated to a dinner of roast beef and plum pudding. Pausing only to pop to the bar and ask for cream to be added to my pie after all, I read on and discover that the motive for the villagers' celebration was the victory at Waterloo! And, as I recall, our almost-home of that name is right next to Home Farm House, and I've noticed an old long building nearby. The cart shed – the very site where the victory was celebrated? We could have been living there now if Maggie hadn't put me off. But she would have rejected it anyway – the windows are too small.

By 1851, the village was overwhelmingly a place for farm labourers. There were sixty of them. 'It may be doubted,' says our author, 'whether any family gained a living without anxiety.' There were periods of famine, and the stealing of food and fuel became more common. After the workhouse opened at Stow in 1836, there were more and more cases of Bledington people who were unable to support themselves and so were sent there. The workhouse regime was apparently as oppressive as that of a prison. One benighted inmate, Jane Waring of Bledington, and her blind common-law husband escaped through a window, leaving 'her two bastard children behind her.' She was eventually tracked down in Woodstock 16 miles away, begging for food, and was dragged back to the workhouse.

By the end of the century, 'voluntary associations for prosecution' were set up in the district, i.e. vigilantes. They kept dogs, including a pack of bloodhounds, to pursue sheep-stealers.

I'm in need of fresh air, so pack my books into the rucksack and go to the bar to pay my bill.

'Oh, you didn't finish all your apple pie,' says the landlady. 'Was it all right?'

'I'm sure it's lovely,' I reply. 'Just lost my appetite.'

I wander out into the sunshine on Bledington's green. So much then for our Edwardian cyclist's 'better days'. Maybe he too expected a village to be an idyll of prosperity and peace. So where did this myth of a pastoral golden age come from? It's been around for a helluva long time. We should probably blame the ancient Greeks for starting it off with all their bucolic stanzas describing youths with pan pipes frolicking in the fields with fanciable demi-goddesses. Later came Spenser and his 'Faerie Queene', Marie Antoinette dressing up as a shepherdess, followed by Wordsworth and the Romantic poets. Today there are the TV companies with

Lark Rise, The Darling Buds of May, All Creatures Great and Small, etc, etc. Then there's me with my childhood memories of rabbits and mushrooms and tractor rides in the eternal sunshine of Hogsthorpe. I'm responsible too. In fact lots of us are. In the globalised economy of the twenty-first century, city-dwellers yearn for clean air, open views, less stress and fewer drive-by shootings. So they retire to a village.

We've come to see the escape into village life as 'Recapturing an Ancestral Peace'. TV programmes, sociologists, me, we talk about RE-generating the English village, as though some past dynamism has been lost. Maybe it has in some places. But not everywhere.

I look around at Bledington with its village green, its little stream running through, its pub and its well-kept, pretty – yes, I'm not going to make an excuse for the word – its pretty houses, set off by neat and imaginative gardens. It's not a question of having lost 'The Good Old Days' at all. It's more: 'You've Never Had It So Good As Right Now In The Twenty-first Century'. This most peaceful and affluent little spot was for hundreds of years a sink of misery and despair for most of its population. How common is that story to the villages of England, I wonder?

So what's happened to bring about such a staggering improvement to life in Bledington since 1905?

I can think of five things straight off:

1. Mains sewerage,
2. Internet shopping,
3. Final salary pension schemes,
4. Monty Don and *Gardeners' World*, and

5. A 4,000 per cent improvement in the purchasing power of the national average wage. (Actually, I'm not sure about this figure, but whatever it is, it's going to be impressive.)

Villages have got swept along with all those benefits which, no doubt, city dwellers would claim *they* devised and produced. My conclusion, therefore, is that some villages at least have not been thrown struggling onto the scrapheap by the rise of the globalised metropolis, but are in fact in mid-season form (though the demise of benefit number three, above, might mean it'll be back to the knacker's yard again in a few years' time).

My deep sigh of satisfaction as I survey the horizon round Bledington Green grows deeper when I spy the tower of the village church, poking up above the cottage roofs. That'll be my next stop.

As I've already said, I'm not religious. But churches, especially village churches, are for me the most exciting buildings imaginable. If someone in the future invents a device which enables us to travel 700 years back in time, you just tell them: 'Sorry, it's been done already!' You or I can do it right now, any day of the week (though there's a degree of overcrowding on a Sunday). Go into a village parish church. Many of them are pieces of England straight out of the Middle Ages which have never stopped functioning as they did then. Of course, to be fair, some don't live up to my hype. The Victorians did their obsessive best to tidy them up and so wrecked a lot of them. But there are plenty they didn't. The best ones for me started life around a thousand years ago, got bits added and altered for the next half-millennium, till the Reformation, and then were largely left alone. I say 'largely' because most of them do lack their medieval stained glass, wall paintings and statues, which Cromwell and the Puritans later smashed, white-washed over and tugged down. Boo.

Bledington Church is one of the best time machines around. But don't worry; you're not going to have to sit through a geekish account of box-pew ends, collar-beam roofs and finial-topped fonts. Let me just say that there's a ramshackle elegance about a good parish church. You can't help taking to the one in Bledington as soon as you catch sight of it, with its huge, square Perpendicular windows that look like they've been stolen from a cathedral and foisted on the reluctant little Norman nave. Someone has slapped a big white label on its tower, or – as we see on slightly closer inspection – a big white clock face, strangely diamond-shaped, announcing 'VR 1897'. Then there's the door, made of cracked, shrunken oak that must pre-date Noah, full of nail holes, some with the dark stain of the nail rust still in them, and two giant black hinges that obviously once supported the Great Gate of Kiev before the village carpenter got his hands on them. Open this door and what hits you is the smell. Musty and rich. Like fourteenth-century armpits. Now go in yourself, hug its fat columns, fear its leaning-over chancel arch, and feel what it was like to be here on 14 September 1371, or whatever date you choose between 1100 and 1525.

I shall be for ever grateful to Bledington's worshippers for keeping this building still doing what it's been doing, without interruption, for the past millennium. The parish church has obviously been part of the glue that's stuck this village together during all those grim times when there wasn't a glorious battle to celebrate. And, though Sunday attendances are down everywhere, the old church must still help stick the village together today. Let's not forget George Beacham, of memorial bench fame, churchwarden for thirty years.

There's a big difference between a city parish church and a village one. In cities, they huddle, half-ashamed at the feet of tall, loutish office blocks or are squashed unnoticed between a mini-mart and a KFC, knowing they don't really belong there any more. In villages, their towers and spires are still the tallest things around and their graveyards let them breathe. Even to those villagers that go to them only on Christmas Eve, or when Great-uncle Donald dies or Gillie gets married, they mark out *this* village as something separate. Something you can belong to.

I make my way back to the car by a different route and am reminded that Bledington is bigger than you first think, and it has a new section. There's even a close of bungalows, which – unlike in Hogsthorpe – have spread only a hundred yards or so. And there's a short row of more affordable houses, looking a bit ashen-faced, it has to be said, alongside the healthy tans of the rest of the village. So that's the other good thing to say about Bledington: it caters for all tastes and incomes.

As I take a wistful glance at 'Waterloo', I notice something about Bledington that's *not* changed for the better. I'm looking at a house name a couple of doors down, 'The Old Post Office'. Bledington no longer has any kind of shop. Nor of course, does it have any jobs for locals, apart from a dozen cooks, waiters and bar staff at The King's Head. But then little villages are not for working or shopping any more. It's a fact of life. There's a clear line between Bledington and the slightly bigger villages like Stow where people can do both. And I suppose it doesn't mean that Bledington and the thousands like it across the country are necessarily in need of regeneration, whatever we think that means.

Back at the green, a mum is showing her wellied toddler the ducks, two blokes in tweed hats are laughing while their dogs wrestle each other and a handful of kids are seeing how high they can go on the swings. A village green does make a difference to a village. Aston Magna, where you're never sure whether you've reached the middle till you're back out in open fields at the far end, didn't have one. No heart. No bit in the middle where you can stand and look around, and feel you're taking in the whole village. Like the church, an open acre of grass in the centre tells you, 'This is it. This is what you belong to.' The Market Square does the same for Stow.

Half an hour later, I pop into Maggie's shop.

'You look pleased with yourself,' she says. 'So has it been a good day with Nik at The Old Stables?'

'Oh. Oh, no,' I say, dropping the corners of my mouth. 'It hasn't. It hasn't at all. Work's had to stop. The lorries can't get through to take all the rubble and stuff away. The council have got no idea when the road's going to reopen.'

'Oh. Why didn't you call me?'

'I didn't want to worry you while you're working,' I say, crossing my fingers inside the pockets of my jeans.

Monday 8.30 a.m. a week and a half later, Nik calls.

'Great news, Derek,' he announces. 'The road's open again. I've just spoken to the lorry firm. We're top of their list. They'll start shifting all the rubble and stuff later this morning.'

'Hurray!' I shout down the phone and share with Maggie the glad update.

O ye of short memory! As if converting The Old Stables were all beer and skittles.

CHAPTER 18

TALES OF THE DEAD

One of the disadvantages of building within the boundaries of medieval Stow, is you have to employ an archaeologist to watch you dig out the foundations and then report back to the council's planning office.

The ground under Stow is apparently chock-full of artefacts. The village's history goes back more than 3,000 years. Bronze Age pottery's been found here. If you were a Midlands-based travelling salesman in the first millennium BC, hawking bags of salt, copper helmets, or antediluvian knick-knacks, you'd be bound to pass through Stow. Three ancient trade routes met and crossed each other on the top of the hill that's now Stow-on-the-Wold: the Jurassic Way, the Salt Way, and the one the Romans adopted and straightened out to make the A429, alias the Fosse Way. It's not hard to see that what must have been lively crossroads would soon turn into a place where people stopped to buy and sell from each other. And this same place is where Stow's long, wide-open Market Square sits today.

What's more puzzling is this. Around 700 BC, Iron Age settlers turned the Stow hilltop into a fortified camp. You can still see its outline in the twenty-first century road pattern and in the occasional, otherwise unexplained 6-foot-high earth banks, like the one you may remember inspired me to market Maggie's old house as 'Fort's Edge.' But this camp had no water supply. The two wells which the Iron-Agers used are several hundred yards down the valley. And again, you can still see them today, just follow the sign that says it's forbidden to use the well water to wash your car.

Now, security was as hot a topic for village folk 2,700 years ago as it is nowadays for inner-city dwellers. Clearly the average Iron Age family was safer on a hilltop where they could see trouble coming, whether in the form of a cutpurse or a cut-throat. But it wouldn't take a Health and Safety Officer, you'd think, to point out that all a mugger or tribal enemy had to do was stake out the water holes outside the safety of the fort's walls, and sooner or later the victims would be lining up for their water and as good as offering you their money or their jugulars.

By the Middle Ages, Stow came at its thirst problem from a different angle. There were at least twenty-one ale houses, and by some accounts every single dwelling in medieval Stow was set up as a pub. To be fair, a lot of these drinking dens were no more than the front rooms of cottages whose occupants had seen a chance to make a quick groat or two on market day. They used to pull up a bush by the roots and hang it outside, which in an illiterate age, and before the development of intuitive street signs, meant 'Ale for sale'. Goodness knows why a bush. The only explanation I've seen is that the Romans used to hang up a sprig of vine leaves to indicate a wine shop, and that the British, not having vines to hand, used a bush instead. Sounds pretty thin to me, given that I'm talking about a thousand years after the last Roman had belted off to beat the barbarians back from the gates of the mother city. Was the fourteenth century landlady so unimaginative that she had to resort to a symbol that ran the risk of deluding thirsty visitors into thinking she was running an early example of a garden centre? Why not hang out a flagon for instance? Admittedly, I can see you might not have a spare one, or probably they didn't have handles in the fourteenth century to fix them up from. But there must be a thousand things more suitable as a makeshift pub sign than a herbaceous shrub. OK, I concede I can't think of any right now that don't involve writing or flashing neon lights. So I suppose if bushes are what you've got to hand, they're as good as anything – once people get used to them.

By the fourteenth century, Stow was in its heyday. Twenty-thousand sheep could be traded in the open space between Huffkins Tea Rooms and the Co-op on market day. And back then there was none of this buying lamb futures, or trading in sheep derivatives. You didn't pay till you could see every last one of the woolly little creatures bleating in front of you. It must have been a logistical nightmare. But the medieval Stowites were well-organised. They designated overspill areas, first in Sheep Street (the name gives it away), and then in fields immediately outside the limits of the little town. These holding zones were all linked to the Market Square by a series of long narrow alleys threaded between the houses. They were known as 'tures' and still are. It's one of these old sheep runs, the one called 'Fleece Alley' that passes alongside our prospective home.

You'll have guessed by now that I love the way bits of history pop up hundreds of years, and sometimes millennia later. So I've got mixed feelings about having to get in an archaeologist. On the one hand, it's expensive. Around £800, would you believe, for a few hours on-site plus a written report. And if anything of historic importance is found, all work has to stop while experts investigate. And that delay would cost us. For example, in Bourton-on-the-Water, just down the road, a company there decided to build itself a second warehouse. The archaeologist was brought in, as per the rules, and soon turned up evidence of an Iron Age settlement right where the new building was due to go up. Word has it that it cost the company £70,000 or more because the landowners have to find the cash to pay for the excavations if they want their building to go ahead. If that happened to us, we'd be bust.

On the other hand, I'd love it if some incredibly precious but very small and easy to dig out artefact turned up in our burgage. I mean, who wouldn't want a Roman Mithraic altar outside the bedroom window? Or I'd even be happy if a pair of fifteenth century wool shears was found mouldering down a drain hole. I don't tell Maggie my fantasy.

Still, one way or another, the archaeologist suddenly becomes an important figure in our lives. And I'm looking forward to an informed discussion with a Simon Schama-type figure on second century BC water supplies and the impact of the plague on Elizabethan lamb yields.

So on the appointed day, I arrive early on-site, though not early enough to catch the vicar and his dog, evidence of whose recent presence I think I detect in the glistening patch at the base of the front wall. As usual, there's not really anything for me to do while I wait, except keep out of Jason's way.

People are fascinated by building sites (I've noticed they even put special little windows in the fencing round giant construction projects in London). And here in Stow, locals now regularly stop for a chat to see how it's going. This makes me look busy and involved rather having to just stand there like the kid with flat feet on sports day. Today there's a young lad peering over at Jason and Nik who're marking out the position of the foundations.

I start up a conversation with the boy, who – I assume from his remarks – must be doing some sort of sixth form course on local history. So with not a little pride, I explain to him that as it happens we're expecting an archaeologist this very morning to investigate the site. I'm just about to tell him that he's welcome to stick around when he says, 'Yup, that's me.'

Jez, it turns out, is in his mid twenties, an archaeology graduate of Winchester College. It was his shorts and Arsenal shirt that threw me.

'There aren't many jobs around for professional archaeologists,' he explains. 'I'm just temping for the research company.'

But will he know a second century Roman baptismal font when he sees one?

'OK. Cool,' he says, taking up a business-like legs-akimbo stance as Jason prepares to dozer out the first foundations. 'What we're looking for here is mainly medieval stuff, or maybe, just maybe Iron Age or Bronze Age. As you'll know,' he adds with what could be a patronising glance, 'the Romans didn't actually settle in Stow.'

'Yes of course,' I laugh, 'everyone knows that.'

'They just scooted by along the old Fosse Way.'

For the next four hours, Jez peers into holes which Jason is delicately scraping out with the JCB's claw. At no point does Jez hold up his hand and shout 'Stop', or point with knowledgeable amazement at some unrecognisable but promising lump on the growing spoil heap.

During the coffee break, he tells me about a recent dig in a large housing estate near Bath.

'You'd never believe it,' he says. 'In the twelfth trench, on the twelfth day of the month, at around twelve noon, they found the first of twelve bodies. It was mental.' He shakes his head in wonderment at the extraordinary nature of an archaeologist's life. 'Freaky,' he adds.

Do archaeologists hallucinate with all that staring into pits? Or has this one watched *Shaun of the Dead* too often? Or maybe he's detected my boyish enthusiasm and doesn't want me to be too disappointed.

Still, Nik, who's just arrived in time to hear this, can beat it – for body count if not the level of juvenile dementia. In Gloucester, a new road was going through an ancient burial ground where it was believed twenty skeletons lay buried. 'Anyway,' says Nik, '250 bodies later...'

Jez taps with a rueful foot against a ginger beer bottle, circa 1930.

Three weeks later, we receive a very nice fourteen-page glossy report saying nothing of historical importance had been found.

Plans for the oak are now top of the worry list. After flirting with several different carpentry companies, we settle on a traditional one-man outfit that Anthea's worked with before. We're still quibbling about prices. And everybody seems to be talking about something different. For Maggie and me, the important things are looks and cost. To Jeremy the structural engineer, it's physical support for the roof and walls. Nigel, Anthea's oaksmith, thinks the place will 'feel incomplete' unless we have a roof with a framework made entirely of oak beams as well.

It's now the beginning of October and the first seeds are whirly-gigging down from the sycamore tree next door. Another site summit meeting is called for. This will be our first face-to-face meeting with Nigel. Now, what would you expect someone to look like who lovingly crafts oak trees and turns them into houses? I think about this the night before, and come up with a vision of a kind of giant hobbit. Cuddly, but strong and determined. I reveal my vision to Maggie over breakfast.

'Now, now,' she chides. 'Just remember Simon Schama in an Arsenal shirt.'

'So you're saying I'm guilty of stereotyping.'

I take her silence as an affirmative.

It's misty and chilly in Stow as Nik, Anthea, Jeremy the surveyor, Maggie and I huddle against the now roofless, frontless, but still-standing Big Back Wall, waiting for Nigel. Nik and his guys have completed the demolition – including all the special safety procedures for the asbestos roof – in half the scheduled time so we're back on track. The space looks open and empty. Big enough, in fact, to take our new home.

A large pickup truck pulls into the road, and a tall, balding, gangly man with a grey beard jumps down.

'There's Nigel,' says Nik.

Nigel smiles, nods, and says in a quiet, but cut-glass accent, 'Sorry to hold you up. The wagon wouldn't start.'

I study him, trying to decide whether he looks more like Bilbo or Samwise, though I have to say that when he reaches under his vast baggy sweater, pulls out a small tin and starts to roll a cigarette, the J. R. R. Tolkien image is somewhat blurred. He nods at Anthea's first explanations while his tongue moves across the Rizla paper.

The plan is that metre-long curved oak braces will support each end of the huge beams spanning the length of the main room.

'I know they may seem intrusive, these braces,' says Nigel. 'They do stick out, I'm afraid, like big wooden brackets, but without them the whole structure of the building would be unstable.'

'Oh, no, I don't think they're intrusive at all,' I say. 'They'll be part of the character of the place.'

'Yes,' says Maggie. 'But what about in the kitchen? I think we might forever be banging our heads on them. We can't have oak braces over the hob and the sink.'

'Hmm,' says Nigel, 'Maybe you could redesign the kitchen.'

I wince. Redesign the kitchen! Does the man know what he's suggesting? Visions of chaotic culinary workflows and shattered marital harmony flash before my eyes. This is like war breaking out between your children. It's a clash between tradition and cooking, both almost as dear to me as the desire for our new home not to fall over. I'm just about to throw my arms up in the air in exasperation at the unfairness of life, when Jeremy comes over the hill on a cavalry horse.

'Well, look here,' he says, marching us over to the Big Back Wall (having metaphorically dismounted first, of course). 'I was just about to say, I've been doing some calculations, and we're going to need to put in steel columns, embedded at the base in the concrete.' He kicks a pebble to indicate the spot. '... to make sure the wooden columns don't shift.'

'Steel!' I protest.

'That's right,' says Jeremy.

'But that's going to look horrible!'

'No, you won't see them,' says Nik. 'We'll plaster over them. All that'll be visible is Nigel's oak.'

My shoulders relax again. 'So where does that leave the kitchen and the braces?'

'With the steels in place, we can probably do without them there,' says Nigel, flicking the butt end of his roll-up onto a heap of rubble left tidy by Jason.

'And does that mean we could also do without oak rafters in the roof as well?' asks Maggie. 'They're terribly expensive, and nobody's going to see them. It'd be like wearing a diamond necklace under a T-shirt.'

'Sure,' says Nigel. 'Fine by me.'

And he looks at Jeremy, who smiles and says, 'Agreed.'

'Great stuff!' I say, 'Team, team, team!' forgetting for a moment that this cinematic quotation was immediately followed by Godfather Robert De Niro beating the brains out of his treacherous fellow *mafioso* with a baseball bat.

Jeremy scratches his chin. For the first time he looks concerned.

'So what are we going to do about that droopy old wall?' he muses. I'm getting mixed up. If Jeremy jokes, does that mean everything's really OK? Or, does he make light of potential catastrophes so that the customer – me – won't keep having heart attacks? But I want him to tell it like it is, now. After all, Maggie and I could be casting nervous glances up at this wall for decades, as we eat our muesli and watch *Newsnight Review* and every minute in between.

'Let's hope the steels stop it falling over,' says Jeremy, patting the wall as you might do Great-auntie Flo on her 103rd birthday.

'*But you said it was a damn good wall,*' I squawk. '*I made a note of it.*'

'It *is*, for what it is,' he says, 'Ha ha.'

'I suppose it's a lot easier to pop in a single piece.'

I knew it was a daft thing to say as soon the words left my mouth.

I'd asked Nik what an OSMADRAIN SOMETHING CHAMBER was, the label half-obscured on a crumpled delivery ticket. He'd explained that it was a large pre-cast concrete cylinder that you put below ground under a manhole cover and over the main drain. He'd added, 'We used to have to build them out of bricks. It was a helluva job, standing in a slimy pit.'

And that's when I said it: 'I suppose it's a lot easier to pop in a single piece.'

'I tell you what,' he says, 'if you're here Monday, you can see us "popping it in."' You'd think I could spot sarcasm at 50 metres by now.

Three days later, I call at the site late afternoon. Simon's head, woolly cap above cigarette, pokes out from the top of the hard grey canister half-buried in the mud. Simon is Nik's business partner. He nods, a hand emerging to flick away the fag, then drops back out of sight.

'It took three of us most of the day to heave it into place,' Nik explains. I mumble something sympathetic, cut my losses and leave.

Nik and Simon are our biggest counter-weight to the bad luck that keeps bobbing up. As well as organising all the work, administering finances and contracts, Nik has another key role: keeping our spirits up. He's also not averse to laying blocks and brushing muck (which we now know to be the technical term for neatening up the edges of recently applied mortar in a wall). Site work however, is mainly Simon's lot. When he's there, as he has been the last couple of weeks, the job rattles along, with drains dug, foundations filled, till we imagine we'll be ahead of schedule.

That is until the Great Radon Barrier Crisis.

At first we were told that our site is not exposed to significant levels of the carcinogenic gas, radon. Then the building control officer – that's the bloke whose job it is to make sure we comply with all the detailed regulations governing how the house is constructed – says it is, after all. In some areas of the country, radon from natural sources can build up in the soil, then seep into houses, and, it's thought, cause cancer. Nik reassures us. The radon count under Stow is low, but building regs are very cautious.

'All you need to do,' he explains, 'is put a bitumen seal over the whole concrete base of the house.'

'Fine, can't see a problem,' I say.

'Then it would need to go up inside the walls to the ceiling.'

'What!' I squeak. 'Up inside the walls to the ceiling! You're kidding.'

'Nope.'

'You don't mean covering the whole of the Cotswold stone wall inside the house with filthy black tar!'

'Well, it's a kind of black fabric. It's not "filthy tar". And you wouldn't see it. It'll be behind the plaster.'

'So what happens to my exposed stone wall along the length of the living room? This is a bloody disaster!'

'Mmm. I see what you mean.'

I scuttle off down to Maggie's shop to pour the poisonous news into her ear. She's advising an American woman on the quirks of French couture, processing a credit card payment from one of her local regulars, and supervising the delivery of some designer jeans, all at the same time.

'This style's called Lauren Vidal... pop your PIN number in please... put the second box in the corner over there... maybe Nik knows some other way of doing it,' she says. I nod and leave.

The other thing I should have mentioned about Nik is, he's not one of those builders who stands there scratching his chin and shaking his head and saying, 'It's a problem. I knew we should have never tried that. I don't know what we'll do about it.' Nik likes to tell you the answer in the same breath as announcing the problem. And if the solution's not obvious, that just makes him more determined to hunt it down and serve it up on a plate. If you're ever going to be silly enough to do this converting an old stables yourself, and you ask me for one piece of advice, I'd say, 'Find yourself a Nik and a Simon.'

So I try to hold fast to this faith for the next couple of days till I'm rewarded by a phone call. And sure enough, he's found a trump card again.

There's a new product, a radon-proof membrane which you fit over the base of the building, and – here's the important bit – in our case, it only needs to be fixed on the inside walls for the first metre above the floor. This bit will be hidden in plaster. Then above that, we'll have our 3 metre's height of exposed, butter-coloured Cotswold stone, once it's been pressure cleaned, that is. Nik's already got the OK from the building regs officer, and the builders' merchant has told him they'll get it in from the factory in south Wales.

The only problem – or what we think is the only problem – is a delay of a week or so till we get our hands on it. So what's become a sad and familiar story is played out again. No other work's possible till the stuff arrives.

I stop by the site that morning just to walk about and picture what it'll look like when this is where we live. I need cheering up. You'd think by now I'd be used to this stop-start rhythm. But, as Maggie will tell you, patience has never been my strong suit. All I see are two stone walls, a hard concrete floor, an idle cement mixer, and slag heaps of muddy rubble. There's a morose silence about the place. It's like a teenager's bedroom at eleven in the morning. It'll be noisy again later, but right now its sulky messiness feels permanent.

CHAPTER 19

ME AND BAIRT LAWRENCE – PART ONE

Subject: Coalmining and capitalism
From Ralph Aardman Date: 23/09 11.24
To:<derekjtayl@internet.co.uk>
Cc:

Hi Derek,

I've just come across an article about your birthplace in researches for my thesis on the death of capitalism in twentieth century rural Britain. I'm right aren't I that you were brought up in the same pit village as D. H. Lawrence? Anyway here's the link: http://www.healeyhero. co.uk/rescue/pits/mooregreen.htm

I thought you might be interested.

How's construction of the retreat from real life going? You still hankering after that childhood paradise you never had?

My love to Maggie.

Best as ever
Ralph

I'm back at Mill Cottage, and for want of anything better to do while The Old Stables lies in its latest coma, I've been catching up on emails. There are loads that need urgent attention, from the builders' merchant (unpaid invoices over thirty days), the scaffolding erector (future contract), the ready-mix supplier (warning of present insurance liability), the bank manager (interest rate rise), etc., etc., which I decide can wait while I look at Ralph's.

I click on his link and there sure enough are pictures of Moorgreen Colliery in the village of Newthorpe in Nottinghamshire. I wasn't actually born there, but it's where I spent much of my childhood. I look up from the laptop screen in time to give a wave to our landlord who's striding past in goggles, swinging his petrol-powered leaf-sucker back and forth, as he's been doing since early morning. In the field behind him, a tractor is pronging up the bales of hay scattered every ten yards. Suddenly a sparrowhawk drops onto the branch of a sycamore tree five or six yards away, hunching its shoulders like an old man in a cloak. I jump up to get my camera from the other room. But by the time I get back, it's gone and the landlord and his chugging leaf-sucker are back in the window frame.

Maybe what Ralph means is that by choosing to live a village life, I'm compensating for a grim childhood of coal-dust-choking poverty. Maybe through his Marxist-filtered specs that's what he sees. I'm going to have to put him right. That's not what it was like at all.

Newthorpe village isn't too far from the little town of Eastwood, which is the birthplace of D. H. Lawrence. And in many of his novels, plays and poems, he paints vivid pictures of the area, especially of Newthorpe and the countryside round about.

We lived on the edge of Eastwood. In summertime, I used to walk across fields to Greasley Beauvale primary school in Newthorpe village. Lawrence himself had been a pupil there. Of the thirty-odd kids in my class there was barely a handful whose dads weren't coal-miners. There were seven pits within four or five miles. Newthorpe was where we kids used to build dens in the earth bank by the old disused railway, scoop up frogspawn with cupped hands to take home in jam jars, and in winter, leap onto icy slides in the school playground where the caretaker had helpfully chucked buckets of water the night before, (which under today's Health and Safety Laws would probably earn him a jail term for reckless endangerment of children's lives). There were old people in Eastwood who could still remember Lawrence.

I was with my dad one day in the early sixties, passing The Three Tuns Inn when out tottered an elderly miner, Edwin Cresswell, white muffler at his throat, a carved walking stick in one hand, dog-lead to fat Staffordshire terrier in the other.

'Ah do, Mesta Teela,' he greeted my father. I should explain that the dialect here in the Erewash Valley owes more to

Old Norse than to the *Ten O'clock News*. For anyone born more than ten miles away, subtitles are required.

'Ah do, Mesta Teela,' *(Good day, Mr Taylor.)* Edwin turned to me. 'Ey up, lad.' *(Hello, my boy.)* Then back to my father. 'Ow insoid a Thray Tuns wor jus gassin abaht Bairt Lawrence.' *(The landlady of The Three Tuns Inn raised the topic of Herbert Lawrence.)* 'Aye, ahh wor a skewl we im. Ey wor a reet mucky bogger, tha knows.' *(Yes, I recall when I was at school with him, his sexual morals were questionable even then; you'll appreciate what I'm saying, I'm sure.)* 'Ey wor awles plyin wi gels, not wi lads.' *(He used to play with the girls rather than with the other boys.)* 'A reet mardy lettle sod, tha' Bairt Lawrence. *(Herbert was a delicate soul, rather prone to tears.)*

I've sometimes wondered whether Edwin was retro-fitting his memories to contemporary public opinion. This encounter between him and my father occurred soon after the *Lady Chatterley* court case, when censorship of Lawrence's novel had just been lifted and the newspapers were full of salacious extracts from it about the gamekeeper's 'John Thomas' and Lady Chatterley's naked cavortings. Edwin was contributing to the national debate.

Newthorpe (locals, the older ones anyway, call it 'Naythrop') is the village my ancestors came from. In 1820 my Great-great grandfather Samuel married Mary and they set up house at her parents' cottage in the village's main street. They earned a living right there in their own home, knitting stockings and other small bits of clothing on a pedal machine, about the size of an upright piano. The whole family – they had eight children – helped out. Most of Sam and Mary's neighbours were also framework knitters. It had been like that in Newthorpe for about two hundred years, ever since the little farms, just big enough to support one family, were killed off when the big landowners enclosed the common land.

But by the time Sam and Mary got married, change was on the way again in the village. In 1819, there'd been riots in Nottingham, 7 miles away. The knitters were being driven out of business by mass production. I don't know whether young Sam was there chucking rocks at the dragoon guards who'd been mustered to keep the peace and kick the poor. I like to think he was. But it was a lost cause.

Work was moving out of the home. And out of Newthorpe. By the 1850s, framework home-knitting was gone for ever. While the women of Newthorpe were trapped at home with up to a dozen kids, the men turned to work in the huge coal mines that were being sunk at places like Moorgreen on the edge of the village.

I say 'men'. I should say, 'and boys.' In 1857, Sam and Mary's youngest, Isaac, my great-grandfather reached the age of ten and followed his four older brothers down the mine.

So Newthorpe had become a pit village. And for the next 130 years, every morning and evening, its streets echoed to the clatter of pit-boots as black-faced men and boys tramped home to wash at the kitchen sink.

The next economic earthquake hit the village in the 1980s. Maggie Thatcher decided coal-mining wasn't economic. 290,000 jobs to go. Rioting again. And worse. In many pit villages of south Yorkshire and Nottinghamshire, families were divided as accusations of 'Scab' dirtied the air. And to this day there are brothers who've never since spoken to each other because one broke the strike while the other picketed.

These sorts of family splits were nothing new. Take my dad's story. What would Ralph make of that? I decide to ask him, so tap out an email.

From Derek Taylor [derekjtayl@internet.co.uk]
Date: 14/11 19.23
To: Ralph Aardman [ralphaardman@internet.com]
Cc:

Hi Ralph,
Thanks for the link to Newthorpe and the pit. Thought you might be interested in a sociological case study.

In 1921, my father, Albert Taylor, won a scholarship to a grammar school in Nottingham. His father, Arthur, who was a leading light in the local branch of the National Union of Mineworkers, had to pay a small daily sum to keep his son at his new school. Only a penny or so. But it was a scrape for my granddad because in 1921, he and his fellow miners were out on strike. The coal-owners had decided to cut their pay and increase the length of the working day. Granddad Arthur was proud of his son's academic achievements, and somehow he found the money to keep him at the grammar school.

Five years later, Albert Taylor left school and got a job in the offices of the local coal company. He'd broken the cycle of son following father down the pit. It was the summer of 1926, the year of the General Strike, and one of the first jobs Albert was given was overnight fire-watch duty at the coal company offices. It was feared the strikers might try to set light to the building. Albert and his two pals, fellow office juniors, were supposed to bike off to the police station for help in the event of trouble.

On their first night on duty, a light midsummer one, the three young blokes passed the time playing cricket on the grass outside. Just before six in the morning, there was a distant noise. Louder and louder came the sound of tramping feet. Rough voices in unison. The strikers, marching like marines, came into view. And there at their head, holding one end of the Union banner was my grandfather, lustily singing with the rest, "Though cowards flinch and traitors sneer, / We'll keep the red flag flying here." My grandfather turned and waved to young Albert, as if for a second a father's pride trumped loyalty to comrades. Then he marched on past with the other men to mount that day's picket at the pit gate.

I once asked my dad whether my grandfather saw it as a betrayal, his son working for the coal-owners against the strikers.

Dad replied, 'Oh no. What was important to him was that *his* son wouldn't have to spend a lifetime down the pit as well. They were strong men, but they knew coal-mining for what it was: dirty, dangerous and badly paid.'

Class treachery? Or an escape from oppression?

Best
Derek

And I hit the SEND button with the high hope, though low expectations of confusing him.

In the mid 1980s, Newthorpe avoided the bitter clashes that split other villages. Miners' jobs there died more slowly. Moorgreen colliery stayed open for a couple of years after the other pits in the area had all closed down, and when it too shut in 1985, there was no point in striking or struggling. Mining was long done for.

By pure fluke, two years later I witnessed the final minutes of the last vestige of coal-mining in Newthorpe.

We were staying with my parents for the weekend at their new bungalow between Newthorpe village and Eastwood. By now I'd moved, to a different planet. A place at Christ Church, Oxford, then work as a TV news correspondent meant a home in London when I wasn't travelling in the Middle East or the United States. On the Sunday morning I got up early to go for a jog. Love of cooking, less often my own back then, was already starting to show in my waistline. I slogged along Main Street, down Mill Road and into Engine Lane. It was not yet eight o'clock but several dozen people were standing outside their houses, arms folded, smoking, chatting quietly. And there across the road was a gigantic bulldozer. The big metal scoop you'd expect to see had been replaced by a huge, fearsome prong. Its target: a concrete tower with two iron wheels on top, the headstocks, which were now all that was left of Moorgreen pit. This last ugly, lonely monument was to be demolished.

I joined the little group to watch. The machine advanced on the headstocks tower and poked it viciously in the chest like a schoolyard bully. The third jab punctured the tower's front then tore back the concrete casing with an agonised yowl. Our faces expressionless, we watched the walls being smashed, the iron wheels bent, and a curtain of dust rise to conceal the final act in a 123-year drama.

A middle-aged woman, hair still in curlers, turned to me, 'Bluddy gud riddance, ah say.'

An older man interrupted, 'That's as mebee. Burr it's bin the life of this place for more 'an a 'undred years.' He took a drag on his cigarette cradled against the wind inside his hand. 'And men 'ave died down there. We munt never forget that.'

CHAPTER 20

ME AND BAIRT LAWRENCE – PART TWO

So what's Newthorpe like today? I went back there last year for an in-the-footsteps-of-Lawrence walk with Geoff and Chris. You've met them already. They're both old school friends. Geoff's the one who hikes a lot and is as fit as a butcher's dog, and Chris is the one doing a late-in-life doctorate. We decided to head off first to where the old pit had been. The path lay downhill by the side of a straggling hedge, and we chattered on together, joking about the old dialect words. I offered 'wittle', as in man with dog saying, 'Dunner wittle thi'sen, eh norrot yuh!' *(Don't worry, he'll not hurt you)*. And Chris, whose dad had been a collier, threw in 'scrozzle', as in miner describing life at the coalface, 'Yo'd aye to scrozzle ower tubs' *(You'd have to struggle over the coal wagons)*.

We were laughing a lot so didn't notice that by the time we reached the bottom, the path – as paths are wont to do if you don't keep them on a tight lead – had wandered off on its own somewhere. Where we wanted to go was on the other side of the thick, high hawthorn hedge, which – as we scoured its length for a way through – suddenly revealed a couple of metres' width of fence. A bit on the high side, but, in the spirit of fifteen-year-old lads out on a lark, I said, 'C'mon, we'll get over it.'

Geoff looked at Chris, and Chris looked at Geoff.

Now, I've never been famous for my sense of balance. But I have been famous for forgetting I've never had one. So I got as far as climbing up the fence like a ladder, and even got my right leg over the top, slotting the toe of my hiking boot into the second rung down. I then noticed my other boot, the one still on Geoff and Chris's side of the barrier, was also slotted over the same rung. The two toe-caps were staring past each other in opposite directions. The obvious solution to this uncomfortable posture was to simply crouch down, grasp the top rail of the fence with both hands, and thus secured, reverse the process which had brought me to this position in the first place.

However, as soon as I attempted this, I realised that because my toes were pointing in towards each other, my knees were locked. This meant I would have to bend from the waist, and because the top rail was down below the level of those same knees, I'd also have to do some tricky shifting of my body weight. For those of us who are equilibrially challenged – and have more than sylphlike midriffs – this would have been hard enough on firm earth. But, of course, my feet were turned inwards so providing none of the stability of the conventional forwards-pointing foot model. The result was I almost toppled head-first into the spiky hawthorn hedge that bordered the section of fence.

I had begun, as Geoff later pointed out, to 'scrozzle', and, as I realised myself at the time, to 'wittle,' as well as wobble.

'Don't bother, Derek, it's not worth it,' said Chris.

In other circumstances I might have been flattered by this advice. It assumed I'd had the foresight to provide myself with a shortlist of options, one of which was 'not bothering'. But bothering now seemed like the only choice open to me. And what's more I was stranded and bothered.

It was at this point that a young woman walking a long-haired mongrel came by on the side we were trying to reach.

'Are yer orlright?' she asked as the dog trotted over, wagging its tail, before attempting to join me on my lofty perch. 'Shouldn't you get down from up there?' she asked. My mind was so busy with the task of staying upright that I didn't even point out to her that we'd gone beyond considering what my objective should be and that she would be better employed developing plans for my recovery.

Geoff said, 'See if you can twist your right foot round so they're both facing in the same direction.' Now this, in theory, was a sound stratagem. And a few seconds earlier it might have seen me make an elegant descent back down to where my two friends were waiting. But in the meantime, the fence, subjected to the mongrel's enthusiastic attentions, had begun to vibrate with a rhythmical sideways motion, like the Millennium Bridge over the Thames, which you'll remember had to be shut for re-strengthening as soon as it had opened to foot traffic.

'Steady!' said Chris, grabbing the woodwork in an attempt to get it to return to its natural state of stasis.

'I've got yer,' said the young woman, rushing over and reaching up to clasp my right ankle in an iron grip, thereby stifling my timid efforts to execute Geoff's plan.

Meanwhile the oscillations of the fence, as though I had become one with it, were spreading upwards, first to my hips, then my torso, before overtaking my neck. Taken together they amounted to a sort of dad dance, an impression which was accentuated by my arms which by now were outstretched, and by my hands which were gyrating at the wrist, as I tried to keep my centre of gravity within a ten-degree angle as measured from the base of the fence.

Within seconds, this performance stepped up several gears till it more resembled the frenetic final stages of the Flamenco. Chris was pushing his shoulder against the swaying woodwork, and the young woman was desperately attempting with her free hand to grab hold of my other ankle, while the dog, in a misguided belief that it was helping, kept leaping up against the lower rails, thereby further accelerating the fence's jiving rhythm. Images of my Newthorpe childhood, Oxford student days and TV reporting adventures all flashed before my eyes.

Clearly this state of affairs couldn't be maintained for more than a few seconds, and it was Geoff who cut through the Gordian knot. With the authority of a man who knows what he's talking about, he called out, 'Jump!' And like a battle-hardened soldier who never questions an order, that's what I did.

Whether it was the ideal solution I shall never be sure. I might have scored a perfect ten for the landing, but for one factor. My right leg and foot were somewhat slowed in their bid to keep up with the rest of my body by the young woman's merciless grip round my ankle. Fortunately, even she had to let go as it scraped over the top rail.

'There,' she laughed, peering down at me, as the dog, tongue at the ready, poked its head through the woodwork, 'that's a lot better, innit?' And, though I could have done without the mirth, I had to admit she was right.

Because, at the moment I reached ground level, I'd had only one leg available to support me rather than the traditional two, I'd ended up crumpled in a humiliating heap in soft mud at the foot of the fence. However, a cursory survey of my limbs and vital organs revealed nothing more serious than a torn hiking sock and a damp backside, which can hardly be compared with the certain and horrible fate that would have befallen me if I'd been pitched head-first into the hawthorn hedge.

The young woman explained where the stile was, I got to my feet, and two minutes and three light-hearted hops later, we were all on the far side of the fence.

I breathed deeply and strode on.

The three of us were now walking where the headstocks of Moorgreen pit had stood up to that Sunday morning when I'd seen them demolished. We immediately discovered that two clever things had meanwhile happened here. Half the area has been turned into a park with trees and curvy paths and benches where you could sit and watch the sparrows bicker. The other half, which, as Chris pointed out, is hidden from the main village road, is now an industrial estate (Unit M22a: TEKNICOLOUR PRINTING LTD, Unit 7: TOUCHABLE LINGERIE AND HOSIERY).

I turned to Chris. 'Who would have been responsible for this?' I asked. 'It seems inspired – putting both somewhere to work and somewhere to enjoy nature on the site of the old pit.'

'A planning office, I guess,' he replied, 'somewhere in the local authority.'

'A planning office that plans. Blimey, there's a novel concept. We could do with a few of those in the Cotswolds.'

We were going to be walking where Lawrence set one of his Nottinghamshire novels, *The White Peacock*.

Herbert Lawrence, whose father was an uneducated collier and his mother a former governess who'd come down in the world, could be just as rude about his origins as the old miner, Edwin Cresswell, was about him. Lawrence said of the squalid Eastwood slum where he was born: 'I hate the damned place.' But from the upstairs window of the little terraced family house, he could see the fields and hills. And when he was older he used to turn his back on the 'ugliness, ugliness, ugliness' – that's what he called Eastwood – and walk over to pay court to Jesse Chambers at her parents' farm just beyond Newthorpe village, right where we are now.

His route would have taken him right past Moorgreen pit, which he renamed Minton Colliery. The sight he described in 1911 in *The White Peacock* has gone now.

'We came near to the ugly row of houses that back up against the pit-hill,' he recorded. 'Everywhere is black and sooty: the houses are back to back, having only one entrance, which is from a square garden where black-speckled weeds grow sulkily, which looks onto a row of evil little ash-pit huts.' The 'ash-pit huts' were lavatories.

Geoff, Chris and I left today's park and industrial estate behind, to cut across the main road and into what Lawrence thought of as 'the country of my heart.'

First we passed the lodge reckoned to be the inspiration for the gamekeeper's cottage in *Lady Chatterley's Lover*, then into woods that border a long lake. Some place names

Lawrence changes, others he doesn't. But you can often fix exactly where he's talking about.

'Nethermere' he writes, 'is the lowest in a chain of three ponds at Strelley: this is the largest and most charming piece of water, a mile long and about a quarter of a mile in width. Our wood runs down to the water's edge.'

Strelley is Felley Mill Farm. Nethermere, Moorgreen reservoir. And on we went, just as Lawrence did, up the hill and across the fields.

'Some of the stuff he wrote at this time could be a bit purple,' said Geoff. He read English at Durham. 'In *The White Peacock*, he describes the 'ears of corn waiting to be *kissed*...' Geoff pronounced the word as Lady Otteline Morell might have done lounging in her boudoir. '... *kissed* by the sun.'

By the time we'd done the full circuit and arrived back at the pub at the Moorgreen end of Newthorpe, it was gone two o'clock. Not a problem because it's the kind of place that serves meals all day. Good old English food of course, like Thai green curry and chicken fajitas.

'Plenty of mementoes of Bert Lawrence in here then,' I said, shaking my head at the widescreen telly, which was showing a repeat of *Escape to the Country* ('In Hampshire with a couple of retired ex-pat house-hunters who have a budget of £650,000 for their new rural home,' read the subtitles).

'A prophet is not without honour except in his own land,' said Geoff.

'I didn't know you were turning religious?' said Chris.

Geoff grinned and took a healthy swallow of his pint.

'Well, consider the irony,' I went on. 'Millions of people – from Japan to Argentina, Germany to the USA – are familiar with the village of Newthorpe and the countryside we've been walking through this morning. They may not know the place by name, but if they've read about these places in *Women in Love*, *Lady Chatterley's Lover*, *Sons and Lovers*, *The White Peacock*, they'll know it all right. And out of all these millions of people in the world who've come to know Newthorpe, one small group seems as blind as a garden gnome to the place's importance in English literature. Who do I mean? The people of Newthorpe itself, that's who.'

'Yes, you're right,' said Chris. 'You'd think at least there might be the odd photo of him on the wall.'

'So why do you think that is?' I asked.

'Setting up a Bert Lawrence memorial, I suppose, isn't top of your To Do list in a recession,' suggested Geoff.

'Could be a money-maker though,' said Chris. 'A tourist attraction for all those Japanese and Germans you were talking about.'

'So whose is the fadge-eat-us?' It was the pub manager who'd arrived with our meals. None of us responded, then I realised it was my Mexican delicacy.

'Do you mind if I ask you something?' I said to the manager once he'd set our food down.

'You can try,' he smiled.

'We noticed you don't have any Lawrence memorabilia on the walls.'

He looked puzzled. 'Lawrence who?'

'You know, D. H. Lawrence. *Women in Love*. *Lady Chatterley's Lover*.'

'Oh yeah. Did they film it round here then?'

'No, Lawrence used to walk through Newthorpe all the time while he lived in Eastwood. I just wondered if you'd ever thought of putting some pictures of him up in the bar.'

'No, we just do what the brewery tells us to do. Can I get you anything else, gents? Any ketchup, mustard? Salt and pepper's on the side-table.'

We tucked in, and moved on to other matters (football, trains, and how 'The Pig' alias the geography master had sneered at Keith Mills on learning he'd won a place at London University, and other stuff you wouldn't want to know about right now). Two hours later, we'd finished our Asian and Latino lunches, agreed to meet up again soon and gone our separate ways. I decided to wander round the village a bit more before heading back to Gloucestershire.

Newthorpe's a pleasant little place these days. The newish houses have well-kept front gardens and views from the back over open fields towards Greasley's fifteenth-century, eight-pinnacle church tower. I noticed the school was still there, where Bert and I both went. No shops though.

The terraced cottages where Sam and Mary Taylor and their neighbours once worked were painted up, and I could still see their extra-wide windows put in specially so the framework knitting machines could keep shuttling till the last flicker of sunlight had disappeared. A young woman came out of one of the cottages and got her twins settled in a double-buggy, while talking on her mobile at the same time. 'So what time do you think you'll get off work?' I heard her say. I guessed these cottages make starter-homes for people who work at Teknicolour or Touchable, or in shops and offices in Nottingham and Derby, or at IKEA near the motorway.

Ralph might say, 'Newthorpe is what it is.'

It doesn't have any pretensions.

The big difference between Newthorpe and Hogsthorpe – the village you remember where I spent my childhood summers – is that Newthorpe is not so isolated. It's only 4 miles from an M1 junction, so new businesses are more likely to set up here. Then too there's that tradition in Newthorpe of dealing with change and moving on. When the pits closed, people turned to any of a score of trades that they could practice in jobs that are easy to reach.

Of course, I'm not saying life's perfect in Newthorpe. For centuries, it's been hard here, in the damp vegetable fields, by the dark knitting machines, or at the choking coalface. Now in the twenty-first century, when the recession hits the east Midlands, unemployment goes up, in Newthorpe as much as anywhere else.

I walked on over to the Recker, short for recreation ground. The swings and slide had been upgraded. And the area was now surrounded by a 6-foot-high metal fence, to separate it from the world of dogs and paedophiles I suppose. And these days, each kid or set of kids was being watched over by a parent. You'd have been thought a 'reet mardy little bogger' in my day if your mum had to bring you.

To my joy, I saw the football pitch was still there. So Newthorpe still passed the football team test! But then when I walked over to the new sports hall, I saw on its noticeboard that – though there was a thriving Colts Club with four teams turning out every Saturday – there was no sign of a senior side. Still the more I thought about it, I wasn't sure there ever was, the reason being that nearby Eastwood always had a strong team. (My dad was a fan. He told me once that when, as a young man, he was offered a place at a Nottingham college to study to become a pharmacist, he turned it down. 'I'd have had to work Saturday afternoons,' he explained, then in a low voice, 'Never mention this in front of your mum.')

I strode a few paces along Dovecote Road to look for The Ram Inn. Almost every room and bench of it is described in *The White Peacock*. It's where George Saxton drank too late and too often. But it wasn't there any more. It was now a private house. There wasn't even a plaque.

As I got back in the car and drove off, I started wondering why Newthorpe neglects its literary past. Maybe there was a bit of Edwin Cresswell's opinion rife in the village still. Or perhaps nobody had time to think about anything so esoteric.

My route took me through Eastwood. At least there, I thought, they've made something out of the Lawrence link. The terraced house where he was born is now a museum, and there's a thriving Lawrence Society. But as I drove out of Eastwood on the Derby Road, the sign hit me. It said THE LAWRENCE SNACKERY (chips and a burger £2.49). And then, two doors up, across the front of a grey warehouse, the words PHOENIX CUE SPORTS ('We aim to provide the ultimate pool and snooker playing experience') sitting above a lurk of hoodies smoking in the doorway. And in case you thought 'Phoenix' had no connection with Lawrence's non-fiction writing published under that title, Lawrence's portrait, 3-metres high, was staring out – teeth no doubt gritted – from alongside the PHOENIX sign.

What kind of deranged mentality would lead anyone to associate burgers and cue-sports with a romantic-modernist author? How many Japanese literary tourists are lured to Eastwood by the prospect of sinking a few balls in a D. H. Lawrence snooker hall? Or conversely, how many hungry Eastwoodites say to themselves, 'I feel peckish. What would Bert Lawrence have done in my shoes? He'd have gone for a kebab and a Coke. I'll away to the snackery that bears his name.'

It's irony at its finest.

My recollections of that trip back to Newthorpe and Eastwood are interrupted. The sparrowhawk's back. He's sitting on an overhanging branch of the sycamore outside my window at Mill Cottage. I don't rush off for my camera this time. I sit and enjoy him. The breeze ruffles the barred feathers on his chest as he turns his head till I can see his hooked beak in profile. Then he flies off leaving behind a bouncing branch, its autumn leaves now all shed.

I turn back to the laptop and see that Ralph has replied. He says, 'You're behind the times with your thinking. It's neither class treachery nor escape from oppression. Both your father and your grandfather were trapped in a system that forced them onto different sides. Hey-ho, you'll be free of all that in Stow!!! Best – R.'

Life must be very comforting for Ralph. Everything's got its pigeonhole. There are never any untidy bits left over.

There's a book I need to find. So up I go into the third bedroom, where all the 'Not wanted on voyage' boxes are. Did we label them properly? The answer turns out to be 'up to a point', so it's forty minutes later before I come back down, if not in triumph, at least with a thin volume of essays on Lawrence.

Here's the bit I wanted to check. You may be surprised to learn that in-between lyricising about corn waiting to be *kissed* and shocking with graphic descriptions of inter-class sex, Lawrence formulated his own theory of town and country planning.

'The real tragedy of England, as I see it,' he wrote, 'is the tragedy of ugliness. The country is so lovely: the man-made England is so vile.' He asked why the miner's houses 'could not have been modelled on an Italian village with a piazza to instil some focus of community.'

Hmm. You don't think sunny weather's got anything to do with it, do you, Bert? People sitting around outside most of the year, chatting together. And I suppose nineteenth-century Umbrian villagers all had safe jobs guaranteed by liberal-minded landowners.

Now I'm sounding cynical. I'm forgetting all those things I said about Bledington's village green and Stow's Market Square giving those villages a centre, a heart that people they can feel they belong to. Don't they do the same job as Bert Lawrence's Italian-style piazzas?

CHAPTER 21

A HORSE IN THE BATHROOM

It's a week later on Wednesday at 11 a.m. that the radon barrier manufacturers call Nik to say the new miracle membrane has been delivered to the local builders' merchant.

Wednesday, 11.06 a.m.: the merchant says nothing's arrived.

Wednesday, 12.04 p.m.: the manufacturers say they'll redeliver it at the start of the following week.

Monday, 3 p.m.: no sign of it.

Monday, 3.14 p.m.: the manufacturers say it's the courier's fault and, 'We're trying to match our records.'

Monday, 3.17 p.m.: I shout down the phone to Nik, *What are they using? Dating agency software?*

Thursday, 9.43 a.m.: the merchant calls Nik to say the stuff's turned up.

Thursday, 10.31 a.m.: I arrive on-site to celebrate the event, to be told by Nik that actually only part of the stuff has arrived. And, it's not the right part to make a start with.

'I'm going to give them a bight rollocking,' I spit, confusing consonants in my huff.

'Trust me,' advises Nik, 'You'll get them all so turned off' (as in 'as turned as a newt') 'that they'll do nothing for a week.' He's right. Lateral thinking's needed. So I suggest if it's not with us by Monday morning, I'll get in the car and drive the 300-mile round trip to Tredegar and collect it myself.

Same day, 2.05 p.m.: the builders' merchant calls to say the rest *has* arrived. Simon goes straight off to collect it.

Same day, 3.36 p.m.: Simon, back on-site, sees it has protective paper on each side. Should both lots be removed? He phones the merchant, who phones the manufacturer, who tells the merchant, who calls Simon back to say: 'Yes, strip both sides.' Simon then finds one side is stuck firm. Another string of phone calls brings news that we must have a 'dodgy batch' and there are no replacements available.

This last sequence I only learn later from Nik, who at this point decides that if he sees my number on an incoming call to his mobile, he'll go and hide. But before this happens, he makes one last attack on the manufacturers' technical department.

They chortle at our pathetic ineptitude. Of course only one side is supposed to come off.

Later, over mugs of tea, Nik, Simon and I speculate on how long before garrotting-for-real is added to the list of apps available on iPhone.

So Simon starts to lay the great radon barrier membrane, two weeks and two days after Nik first tracked the stuff down.

Meanwhile, two other tasks have shot to the top of my To-Do list.

First, I've got to try to sort out what we're going to do about the flagstones inside the house. We don't want any artificial factory tiles. We want something in keeping with the old feel of the place. My visit to the trade show has convinced us we should go for limestone. They have the same natural feel as our exposed stone wall, and they get that kind of parchment yellow tint to them as they age. There are problems though. The price is bad enough. You can pay up to £100 a square metre. But there's worse news, as a friend of ours found out. Natural limestone scratches. Now you might put up with that as a mark of individuality. But, if anyone then spills a glass of Malbec or a can of Coke on the floor, it soaks in – and permanent ruddy brown stains all over your floor are too much of a lived-in look for most people. So the offending slabs would have to be hacked up and replaced.

We've found another option in a trade mag, and the agent for the company that produces it is coming round to see us late that afternoon. He's waiting in his car when Maggie and I get back to Blockley, and follows us in with several samples under his arm.

He explains that his product was developed to answer the very difficulties we've heard about. A factory in northern Italy found a way of hardening limestone by compressing it at a temperature of 1,200°C. Our man takes out a fifty pence piece and scrapes it backwards and forwards over the surface of a square of his wonder rock with a noise that shows he's not pussyfooting. With justifiable pride, he holds up the stone slab and insists we examine it, each of us in turn. He could have been using a five-pound note it's stayed so smooth.

'I had a customer in Shropshire,' he goes on, 'who owns a fruit farm and she asked me if it would show blackberry stains. I told her it wouldn't, and she asked me to post her a sample. A week later, she phoned back and ordered 150 square metres. I said, "What about the fruit stains?" She said, "Oh, I boiled that sample of stone you sent me in blackberry jam for two hours, and it just came off under the cold tap.''

I'm a sucker for a good story. He's just made a sale, because Maggie's impressed too.

My second task is to go and see Emi Grise.

Now that the Big Back Wall has been fully exposed, we've found that there are three small niches towards the top. They must have been either block holes for ceiling beams or else small windows now screened off with stone. We've had the idea of opening them up again. It's just the sort of feature that appeals to me. And of course Maggie can never get her hands on enough light. But before we approach the assorted planning and conservation bureaucracy of Cirencester, we figure it would be good to have local support on our side, to wit the *éminence grise* himself. And there are a couple of other things I need to sort out with Mr Grise too.

So I head up Fleece Alley into the middle of Stow, and pop into his emporium to find him in his den. He looks up from his hide-encased ledger, and I detect from the slight forward motion of his head that he has acknowledged my presence.

Item one on the agenda. What sort of topping are we going to put on the pinnacle of the building? He has a fixation about this. Every time I see him, he presses the merits of chamfered coping stones, taking me on tours of his domain to illustrate his favourites. Maggie and I have no particular hang-ups about smooth-edged roof bricks. But the decision has now been taken out of our hands by the planners, who won't allow us to raise the roof height by a single thumb width, and copers would stick up proud by a good foot. I explain this to E. G., who says, 'I'll have to think about that.'

Why do I feel myself regress to childhood in front of this man? It's like being in my old headmaster's study.

So, on to the main item. Would it be permissible for the prefects to play table tennis in the school hall on Thursday nights? Or, as I put it, 'Maggie and I were wondering what you think about our opening up the niches in the top of the wall.' And as I go on to explain exactly what I'm talking about, I see his face change from impassivity to frown to the verge of explosion.

'No!' he blurts out. Gone are those whispery murmurings. This is a straight *Don't be ridiculous, boy, get on with your homework* tone of voice.

But I'm not put off so easily. '… would enhance the building's heritage…' I'm saying.

'No! No!' He's shaking his head to add a third negative.

'We realise this is a slight change from the previous plan but…'

'It's out of the question!'

We're talking at the same time now.

'… the niches are actually so high that it would be impossible to see *out* of them from our side. And in any event, there's nothing but an unused piece of land on the other side.'

'No! I said, "No!" It would undermine the historic nature of the building. Frankly, it's an impertinence even to suggest it. How could you dream of it? No! No!'

I keep going longer than him for one and a half words. But I know it's a hollow victory.

'OK, ok.' I hold up my hands in a gesture of concession. 'It's not worth falling out about.'

'Anything else?' he asks. I can tell I've been dismissed.

The following week, Maggie and I relieve our stress with a visit to rural Oxfordshire and Nigel's workshop. It's on the edge of a wood down a single track road that seems to go on for ever, partly because we can't find the place and keep having to backtrack. But eventually, we come to a collection of brick-built barn-like buildings. We know it's the right place because there's Nigel with a mug of something steaming in one hand and a ciggy in the other.

'Hi,' he smiles. 'Glad you found us.'

Our 10-metre-long green oak frame is laid out on trestles in the yard. It's massive and chunky.

Maggie looks worried. 'It's a bit formidable, isn't it?' she says. 'Don't you think it'll look out of proportion? After all we're not going to have a big house. Do we actually need such thick columns?'

'Don't worry,' says Nigel, 'The posts'll be fine like this. If they were any thinner, the whole thing would end up looking like a posh garage.' We murmur our understanding.

There's something liberating to our spirits about this escape into the wide-open countryside. We're like kids on a school outing. We skip around the oak frame as though it's an adventure playground, trying to lift a beam to test how heavy it is, clambering onto a wall to see what the assembled timber looks like from above, fiddling with the wooden pegs that hold each piece in place – no nails or screws, this is traditional craftsmanship. It's going to be the most significant part of the building. Aesthetically that is. It's going to mark the end of that six-year dispute. It's my character and Maggie's light. It'll be supporting 20 square metres of glass.

And then it's time for a lesson. Nigel stops shaving some curved oak braces and puts his plane on one side. He explains that they're modelled from tree trunks or thick branches specially chosen because their grain matches the angle we need in the wooden braces that will support the cross-beams. 'That's because if you cut across the grain,' he says, 'it'll eventually come apart. But if you have a brace the same shape as the branch – with the grain running along it – it'll be as strong as it was on the tree.'

'Sounds good to me,' I say, patting the brace that we're looking at.

And we learn the language of oak. We already know about 'green'. But there's loads we didn't know.

The cracks in the oak are called 'shakes', and we have to expect them. 'They're normal,' says Nigel. 'Nothing to worry about. That's what happens as the wood dries.'

The dark stains we've noticed and were worried about are called 'bluing'. It's caused by contact with metal, and we'll need to get those sand-blasted off.

And here's one to amaze your friends at parties: 'hearts of oak', as in, 'Hearts of oak are our ships, jolly tars are our men, steady boys steady.' I'd always assumed it was a heroic notion about the pumping lifeblood of Nelson's fighting frigates. But no. 'Hearts of oak' is a technical term for the weather-side of the tree, which has been left to dry for at least a year to get rid of the tension in the wood caused as it's felled. This drying process stops it twisting when it's propping up your bedroom. Anyway, this is what we're getting in our house. Hearts of oak. I can't wait.

As we drive home, a romantic aura circles our heads. And we decide to call in at the site. There's no business to be done. It's just to dream. To imagine how beautiful our oak beams and braces will be, exuding the purity of nature and reminding us of generations of craftsmanship. Unlike me, Maggie's not usually given to staring at things and travelling back in time. But today after our visit to Nigel's oak yard, a sense of history is warming her soul. She surveys the barren walls that were once a stable and will soon be our home and says, 'Just think what this place has seen over hundreds of years. All the people that have passed through it.'

It's a noble thought. We are but the temporary stewards of our place on this earth.

'And all the horses that have been stabled here,' she goes on. 'In the first stall, there'd be one with its front legs where the guest-room bed will be and its hindquarters over there, on the other side of that wall, near where we're going to put the loo.'

I wish she hadn't said this. I mean I'm all for understanding the details of our national heritage, and I don't think I'm overly romantic in my view of history. I don't shrink from a graphic account of the symptoms of bubonic plague or shudder at the diaries of Crimean War doctors sawing off legs without anaesthetic. But your own twenty-first-century loo. Well that's different. It's personal. And private. So later, when the house is finished, I can never sit ruminating in the bathroom without seeing just above my head that image of the wrong end of a horse, raising its tail in preparation.

CHAPTER 22

THE GYPSY
AND THE JAGMAN

There's a sudden, panicky neighing from the direction of Back Walls. It's followed by two raised voices. Then shouting: '… your damned horses… get out…' and 'we've as much bloody right…'

Nik and I have been heads down over Anthea's plans, spread out on a pile of rubble. We can just see, over the roadside wall, the curve of what looks like a large green cylinder, about 6-feet wide. But it's got a black stovepipe coming out of the top.

We head over to take a look, and as we come round the corner, our eyes are hit by the colours – burgundy reds with delicate traces of yellow flowers. The grill of a silver Jaguar is snarling at the shins of a piebald horse harnessed to a Romany caravan. The animal's still neighing, the brown patches on its flanks shivering. Its owner, a black-haired youth in an oily leather waistcoat, has it by the bridle, trying to calm it and edge it back.

The red face framed in the side window of the Jag turns to Nik, and shouts, 'Is that your damned lorry?'

Nik holds up his hand in apology, gets into his dusty pickup truck and backs it away down the road so there'll be room for the gypsy and the Jag-owning citizen of Stow to pass in peace.

The car and the horse snort at each other, as they disentangle themselves. Then one roars off up the hill, and the other's led clopping in the opposite direction. A small boy, who's been watching throughout from the front of the caravan, mouth wide open, bends his head round the side of the green curved arch and stares at me till we're out of each other's sight.

It's the start of Stow's twice yearly Gypsy Horse Fair.

Now if you happen to be studying sociology and the title of your doctoral thesis is 'Cultural conflict in twenty-first century rural Britain,' then check in to a B & B on Sheep Street any mid May or mid October.

What you'll see is gangs/happy groups of layabouts/young people, screaming/calling to each other, as they scare the life out of law-abiding Stow people with their fighting/as they enjoy a drink like everyone else. The boys are menacing/lively. The girls look like tarts with tiny skirts and bikini tops that hardly cover anything and wear too much make-up/look like any young women out with friends in any British city on a Saturday night.

When you conduct interviews, you will be told that the gypsies intimidate schoolchildren, drive away business from the shops, and defecate in front gardens. You will also be told that the Jag-owning side don't understand that the Roma gathering in Stow-on-the-Wold continues an ancient tradition dating back a thousand years, and that the disruption is exaggerated. It's not as if there's an outbreak of mass looting and drive-by shootings every May and October. That at any rate is what the two sides say.

Nik takes a practical approach.

'It's too much hassle,' he says. 'So we'll stop work for a couple of days till things get back to normal.'

So two days later on Fair Day, my journalistic spirit comes to the fore and I decide to check it out for myself. First, I head off into the Square to see what's happening there, and bump into Arch. He's one of our new neighbours in Back Walls. Has he seen any trouble?

'No, it's pretty quiet at the moment,' he says. 'The Bell's closed though.' The Bell Inn is the pub closest to the field where the fair's held and is usually the only one that stays open in Stow, though with the chunkier half of Stow's Rugby Club First XV as bouncers. 'There was a bit of a riot there last night,' Arch continues. 'Some gypsy lads were effing and blinding and getting rowdy, so the landlord asked them to calm down, and they started smashing the place up.'

'Crumbs!' I say, as I feel myself edged towards the Jag-owning side the battle line. 'Most of the shops are shut, I see. Maggie always closes on Fair Day.'

'Yes, well there was that incident a couple of years ago when a bunch of gypsy girls went into one of the dress shops in Talbot Court and threw ketchup all over the frocks then ran out.'

'Hmm, I'd forgotten about that.'

'I think that's a bit of an exception though. It's the lads really that are the problem. Apparently it's all a mating ritual. I saw it on Channel 4. All these gypsy families get together in Stow during Fair Week, and that's the time when the teenage kids pair up. So the girls all dress up to show off how attractive they are, and the boys have to show how tough they are.'

'Wow, that's interesting.'

'Yup, so long as you don't get caught in the middle, eh?' And off Arch goes down Digbeth Street.

At that moment, I look up the otherwise empty road to see a very large family approaching. By 'large', I mean both in numbers and size. When they're about fifteen yards away, the heavy-weight boxing champion who's leading them shouts a challenge to me: 'HOW YER DOIN'?' It's so loud, it seems to echo off the shop windows.

'I'm fine,' I squeak.

'HANGIN' EH? In eh? eh?' it echoes again.

'Yes,' I squeak again, assuming that he's not asking my opinion on capital punishment, but probably means 'hanging about' as in loitering, or even 'hanging on in there' as in managing to survive.

His wife is two steps behind him. I'm careful not to stare at her, but get a fleeting impression of broad shoulders, a broken nose and lots of tattoos. The kids are like the chorus from *Oliver!* but without the music. They're darting about, punching each other and kicking shop doors.

All's quiet in the Square. There appears to be what the BBC always call 'a strong police presence', though when I get closer to the officers, I decide against the word 'strong'. There are half a dozen WPCs, none of whom seems to top 5 feet and it sounds to me as I approach that they're discussing overtime rates. The half-dozen male PCs are all thin-looking, even in their stab-proof jackets, and their bobby helmets seem a size too big. One of them is advising a

Japanese couple, 'There's Huffkins Tea Rooms, that's open,' and he's pointing.

I know where my money would be in a dust-up between one of these law officers and that tattooed gypsy woman.

So I head off down to the fair itself. This is held in a huge field on the edge of Stow. As I get closer, I find myself among more and more people. Ordinary people, not prizefighters or ketchup throwers, but people who look like they're from my side of the battle line. And there are lots more police, and they're considerably beefier too. This is clearly where the action's expected. There's a 'Mobile Police Station', a 'Mobile Camera Surveillance Unit' and a 'Mobile Medical Treatment Centre', and by the entrance to the field, there are two of those police vans that have metal grills over the windscreen, the sort of vehicles that baton-wielding riot cops burst from in documentaries about police brutality.

I enter the field, aware that I'm crossing the line. There are no forces of law and order here.

I'm on my own.

Well, I'm not actually. There are, without exaggeration, thousands of people. Ahead of me between market stalls is an alleyway that drops down a slope in the field, so I can see for 200 yards, and the crowd is so packed it looks like no one's moving. I opt for another stream of humanity to the right, where I can at least make slow progress between CHIPS AND GRAVY on the one hand and LAMB OGGIE AND PIZZA on the other. Ten minutes and about 30 yards later, we're into the non-edible section. There's a stall selling the biggest garden gnomes I've ever seen. They're about a metre high, and as well as the usual Bashful and Grumpy fishing or cobbling shoes, there's a Betty Boop in iridescent red and black looking sheepish next to a Virgin Mary in blue and gold. I work my way over to the opposite side to look at a large tent which is laid out like a Louis XV dining room. Two Asian-looking guys are selling the kind of elaborate lacquered chairs, tables and sideboards you see in French provincial furniture shops.

'Excuse me,' I say to one of the salesmen, 'I don't mean to be rude, but are you travellers?'

'Oh no,' he replies with a smile. 'We're from King's Heath in Birmingham. We go round all the markets in the Midlands. We always come here.'

'So...' I look about. It's slowly dawning on me.

'Yes,' he says. 'Most of the stallholders here are regular market traders. But you'll see more gypsy things if you keep going further down. Excuse me, please, sir.' And he turns to do his job with a middle-aged couple who are running their hands over a gold ormolu clock with sour-faced cherubs on each side.

I take another look at the people around me, the buyers. They're not travellers either. There are so many of them, they've obviously not all come from Stow. I listen and detect Birmingham accents, Welsh and even the familiar tones of my own east Midlands. I hear one woman say to the chap with her, 'It's not as good this year. You can see better stuff on Stratford market any Friday.' On all sides people are carrying plastic buckets stuffed with T-shirts and are pushing baby buggies whose tops are sagging under the weight of everything from discount nappies to rolls of curtain material. Behind the stalls and in much of the middle of the field, I can see a mass of pickup trucks, four-by-fours and loads and loads of the biggest caravans you've ever seen. They're the modern white and silver ones. In the gap between IRISH AND RAP CDS and GENUINE ROMANY CRAFTS, I see a white door swing back, and a middle-aged woman, making tea, turns to survey the crowds, her underclothes framed by her open dressing gown.

I've just spotted a red and gold traditional Romany caravan perched up on a trailer and am thinking what a shame it is that it's not on the ground being pulled along like it's supposed to be, when suddenly, the crowd in front of me parts and I see a pony galloping full tilt straight at me. I dodge right but the snorting animal does the same, and as I swerve back to the left, the pony's nose whacks me on the shoulder. I glimpse a boy of about ten, riding bareback, hear a shout of 'Git out!' and bump hard against someone. A powerful grip on my elbow steadies me.

'Are you orlright there?' It's an Irish accent. 'Sure there's no harm done at all.' He's in a singlet and flat cap. I thank him, and he points behind me, 'Watch how you're going now.'

There's a horse and two-wheeled trap now careering through the crowds. The driver, in a battered old straw hat, is laughing and shouting, 'Mind yer backs there!' And he keeps cracking the end of his whip over the top of the horse's head so the animal's fairly bouncing along, every fibre in its body sparking with life.

'So what's going on?' I splutter to my big Irish friend.

'John there. He wants to sell the mare. And he's showing her off.'

At which point, there's another crack, another 'Mind yer backs!' and the mare and John, still laughing, hurtle back the other way.

There are no stalls at the sides now. It's mainly horseboxes with ponies tethered to their sides. Now I don't know much about horses and their like – I took riding lessons in my late twenties and got sniggered at so often by know-it-all teenage girls that I stopped. But I do have a reasonably extensive knowledge of children's toys. And these animals look exactly like living, life-size replicas of 'My Little Pony'. Their manes, tails and fetlocks (I confess I looked up the word when I got home) are as fine and wispy as the down on a duckling's back. Their coats are smooth and gleaming, and the coy tuft of hair bobbing over their eyes seems to put a smile on their little faces. The fact that the nearest one to me suddenly shits, in a way that suggests it might have been overdoing the prunes and liquorice allsorts, does I admit cut short my musings on life imitating art. Nevertheless I'm captivated. And I watch while a young guy starts to size up one of the animals. It's a frisky creature. It keeps pulling at its tether and prancing in a way which, after my recent narrow escape from death by equine trampling, would tell me to keep well clear. But the man just picks up its foreleg so he can examine its hooves, then feels its ribs all over, before taking hold of its top lip and bending it over to look at its teeth.

Groups of men are standing around. The older ones favour long sticks, tweedie pork-pie hats and a muffler. The young guys go for singlets and mullet haircuts. I come across two men, a pork-pie and a mullet, standing in the middle of a circle. They're having an intense conversation, raising their voices every so often. I can't catch the words. Suddenly the pork-pie drags mullet over to one of the ponies, slaps its flank, then grabs mullet's right hand and tries to slap it too. But mullet's not having any. The two men's voices rise higher, then all of a sudden they both nod. Mullet puts out his palm and pork-pie slaps it. Mullet then pulls a crumpled clutch of banknotes from his back pocket, and the circle of watchers breaks out in a satisfied buzz of conversation.

'Mind yer backs!' Which we all do double quick. Seems to me John's having so much fun that if you offered him £5,000 in ten pound notes for the pony, he'd just say, 'Yeah, yeah, but later, later,' before belting off again with a demonic guffaw.

But it's not just horseflesh that's being traded. Two boys with what could be their grandfather pass me. One of the lads is cradling a cockerel in his arms, the other has a cardboard box with a bird's head poking out. The older man's saying, 'Now you gotta keep 'em separate or they'll fight like the Dickens.' And there are dogs for sale too. A pair of cuddly puppies snuggle together in a cage on the grass next to a wrinkled middle-aged woman with a roll-up hanging from her lips.

I spot two young women with RSPCA badges on their dark blue uniforms, and decide to see what they make of it all. Are they looking for cases of cruelty?

'No, there's not really much problem like that here,' says one of them. 'The animals are usually in superb condition. The owners want to sell them after all.'

'The main thing is to give advice,' says the other. 'The people here know a lot about horses, but they're not vets. So if a pony's got an ear infection or anything like that, we can show them how to treat it.'

'So it's a jolly for us,' grins the first.

'It's a lovely day out,' says her friend.

At this point, I'm nearly knocked over, not by flailing hooves this time, but by a quad bike. It's being driven by two extraordinarily good-looking young women. They ignore me, old fart that I am, and speed on.

It's the cue for me to report one of my other major discoveries at the fair.

The Carmen legend lives on.

There are significant numbers of stunningly beautiful girls here. There's a group of four walking towards me right now. The one in the lead looks like a seventeen-year-old Penelope Cruz. Her chums remind me of junior versions of other Cannes red carpeteers whose names I can't quite recall. Penelope's phone rings and the rest of them stop and gather round her, laughing. All four of them have hair that reaches just short of their waists – it looks like they've been brushing it for the last six hours – and wear flowered rosettes on the side of their heads. I could go on about the 6-inch heels (marvels of balance in themselves since this is a rutted field), the shortness of skirts and the more-than-glimpses of tanned midriffs, but I'll just say that none of these four young women would disgrace a Madrid catwalk in Fashion Week. If I'm being super-critical, I might observe that their make-up is a bit too much like that of the women you see behind the designer cosmetics counters at John Lewis. Of course, I'm not saying that all the traveller girls wandering round the fair look like this. There seems to be the same range of plumpness, squatness and acne that you'd find in the teenage population at large. I'm just saying the disproportionate incidence of downright beauties is a phenomenon worth reporting. Sociologically speaking.

Nearby there's a group of young men. And I detect some sly glances and smiles passing back and forth between them and the four female phenomena. The lads are pushing each other around in a puppy fight sort of way. Now I'd have thought the girls were a class or two up on the boys. But then who am I to judge? Nevertheless, I give the boys a wide berth, not wishing to end up the battered proof of some potential suitor's testosterone count.

'Mind yer backs!' This time he's got one hand on the reins, the other holding down his straw hat. Whoops! He nearly got that dandified looking bloke with the handlebar moustache. I join my fellow fair-goers in having a good laugh.

As I wander on for another hour or more among mares, foals and stallions, cut-price gnome vendors and dispensers of chips with gravy, I get to pondering. What kind of sorcerer's spell could transform these Carmens into the all-in wrestler I'd seen back in Digbeth Street?

As I walk past The Bell Inn, still shuttered and locked, and on back up towards the Square, two girls overtake me, perfectly steady on their stilettos. I hear one say to the other, 'Mi da won't even let me go on a bus. And mi mammy's the same. And I'm nearly sixteen.'

No difference there then.

It's two o'clock and I decide to drive back to Blockley, and soon find myself sitting behind what must be a fifteen-berth trailer home. The roads are always like this on Fair Day. Although the travellers drift into Stow in dribs for days ahead of the fair, they don't hang around once the crowds of buyers start to thin out. Romantics say it's the call of the open road. Cynics reckon it's because the sellers of horseflesh want to be well out of the way before the buyers have had a good look at their purchases and decide to demand their money back. Whichever version you go with, that's it for another six months. A retreat from tribal warfare, a cooling of mating instincts, and a line drawn under my investigation. I've had a grand day out.

I might go again.

I'll give The Bell a miss in Fair Week though.

CHAPTER 23

CULTURALLY DIVERSE MURDERS

Subject: Re: Invite to Stow
From Ralph Aardman [ralphaardman@internet.com]
Date: 14/11 19.23
To:<derekjtayl@internet.co.uk>
Cc:

Hi Derek,

Thanks for the invite. But I'm off to Cremona University for a few months to study Italian Communist Party influence in the Po Valley. Maybe I can get up to see you sometime later in the year, when your sheltered housing accommodation's been finished.

By the way, I see racism is alive and goose-stepping in the English village: http://www.news.co.uk/midsomer-murders-racerow

Best as ever
Ralph

My first thought is that he's read some Trotskyite twaddle in a left-wing blog about discrimination against gypsies at Stow's horse fair, and I'm all set to offer him a balanced, first-hand view of the matter. But when I click on the link, it turns out he's talking about the *Midsomer Murders* row. The series's executive producer has been suspended from his job after saying the ITV crime drama of that name has no place for non-white characters. The actual words that landed him in the soup were: 'We just don't have ethnic minorities involved, because it wouldn't be the English village with them.'

'Hang on, the opinion of one biased TV producer is hardly a fact-based sociological thesis,' I say out loud, stabbing the email REPLY button in irritation. But as soon as I've jabbed out, 'Deasr Rakph,' I realise I'd better get my arguments in unassailable bullet-point ranks first, if I'm not to hand him a win on a plate. So I open up a new Word document for some preliminary notes.

Point One. It's true the English village – as well as, falsely, representing some lost Golden Age of peace and perfection – is, for some, the model of quintessential Englishness. Remember John Major saying, 'There'll always be an England with postmistresses riding bicycles across village greens in the mist'? I suppose it's this idea that *Midsomer Murders'* Exec. Prod. is playing up to. For him Englishness

– he doesn't talk ever about Britishness – represents some kind of mythical, ancestral racial purity.

Point Two. So is there much cultural diversity in the average English village? What about Stow?

- Maggie's team of shop cleaners: one Hungarian (via Maryland, USA) + two Bulgarians.

- Cafe assistant where Maggie gets second coffee of day: Rumanian.

- About half the waiters and waitresses at The Unicorn: Polish.

- Maybe this is not much of a cross-section. Too non-professional, though they're all probably mathematics professors or award-winning post-modernist authors back home in Székesfehérvár and Cluj-Napoca.

- Ah, but there is Stow's postmistress, Gillian: South African. So that's one in the eye for John Major. And, what's more, I've never seen her on a bike, in or out of the mist. Gillian, it's worth noting, is universally regarded as super-efficient, courteous and an all-round nice person.

    The trouble is that, seen walking down Digbeth Street, all these people would be indistinguishable from card-carrying members of the Aga Owners' Club with pedigrees going back to Charles I. So is Stow short on non-white faces?

- Well, there's the extended family who own The Prince of India. Do they count? I'm not sure they all live in Stow. Some of them seem to arrive in cars at about 5 p.m. each day. Perhaps that doesn't matter.

- Then there's Sunny who sold us the burgage: Kenyan-Asian. Well-respected chiropractor. Hmm, but she doesn't live here any more. She's moved to Goa.

I'm still pondering over this next day when Mike calls to fix a date for a hike. He lives in Acton, west London, so I say to him, 'I'm curious Mike, what racial groups live in your part of the world?'

'Well, we've got lots of Poles,' he says, 'as well as other East Europeans...'

'Yeah, Stow's got those,' I pop in.

'... there are at least four Polish groceries in Acton, an Armenian social centre and the Ukrainians have even got their own cathedral...'

'I see.'

'... then there are significant numbers of Indians, Bangladeshis, Afghanis and Pakistanis...'

'We've got Indians.'

'... there's a mosque of course, not just for the Pakistanis. There's quite a famous Arab secondary school in Acton. Then as well, there are the Chinese and, perhaps surprisingly, lots of Japanese...'

'We get Japanese tourists in Stow.'

'... in fact there's even a Japanese school and a Japanese estate agent in Acton...'

'Hmmm, really.'

'... then there are groups from several different African countries...'

I get in quickly, 'We do have South Africans. Well, a South African.' But something tells me our valiant postmistress, kindly and helpful as she is, will be no match for the mustered masses of the sub-Sahara region.

'... the Somalis in particular,' continues Mike, 'they've got their own community centre. Funnily enough though, people from the West Indies haven't settled in Acton, not in any great numbers anyway.'

'Ah, ah,' I butt in, having just remembered, 'The chef at The Talbot's Caribbean. He does a fantastic goat curry. He gets the goat from that bloke on the BBC who does *Countryfile*, who's got a farm near here.' I immediately regret adding this last bit, which somehow seems to undermine Stow's multi-ethnic bona fides.

'I suspect one Jamaican might not make Stow a role model for racial diversity,' observes Mike. 'Just to put things in context,' he adds, 'what the census calls 'White British' make up just forty-five per cent of Acton's population, and the local high school has sixty-five per cent of students who don't have English as their first language.'

I concede the point, and we agree a date for our walk.

So Stow's not Acton. But then nor is it the fabled TV village of 'Midsomer Ethnicleansing' with border guards checking the blood purity of your English family tree for five generations. So let's cut the foreplay and put this to bed. Are villages in general racist?

This needs another expert answer, so I call Chris, my old school friend-cum-political scientist.

'That's a tricky one,' says Chris.

'Is it?' I challenge. 'It seems to me that if you take Stow for instance, there's no racism problem here.'

'Ah,' says Chris, 'that's exactly what people always say in villages all round the country.'

'So doesn't that prove villages don't have a race problem?'

'Not for sociologists, it doesn't. Faced with people saying "There's no problem", sociologists tend to say, "Well, there must be one, it's just a different sort of problem, so it gets overlooked". So, they say villages just have a different sort of racism compared with cities.'

'You mean we don't have racially motivated stabbings on tower block walkways, or fire-bombings of synagogues.'

'Exactly. Did you ever see the movie *Playing Away*, where a village cricket team meets a Brixton XI – all Jamaicans and Trinidadians – in an amateur cup final?'

'No, I missed that. I can imagine it though.'

'Right. The good old country gents treat the blacks like plantation workers or punkah wallahs, as though the sun still shone on the British Raj, and as though we true Englanders are doing these Johnnie Savages a favour by letting them play the hallowed game.'

'Yes I see. Mind you, when was this film made?'

'In the mid eighties.'

'Ah, well, I should have thought the number of times the West Indies, the Indians, the Pakistanis and the Sri Lankans have wiped the floor with England in the intervening years might have changed things a bit. I reckon any white English villager these days would have nothing but respect for a black face on a cricket pitch.'

'And in the pavilion? Over tea and watercress sandwiches?'

'Given the fearsomely competitive way that Stow's First XI play their cricket, there's always a bit of banter off the pitch, whether the other lot's from Adlestrop up the road or a touring team from Mumbai. And another thing, villages are sometimes suspicious of outsiders, you know. It's a tradition.'

'I'm afraid sociologists have seen through that excuse as well. It's a cover-up, they say, for something more sinister, like a more subtle form of racism. And believe me, Derek, I'm just telling you what some researchers argue. They're not my views.'

'No. Understood, Chris. I have to say it's all getting a bit too subtle for my simplistic brain. If I can't actually see racism in the countryside, I find it hard to believe in it.'

'I sympathise.'

I think for a moment and scratch my ear. 'But then, never having been on the receiving end of any discrimination myself, and having spent a lifetime inside a face as pallid as vanilla ice cream, maybe I'm not the best judge.'

'True,' says Chris. 'And of course, Stow-on-the-Wold isn't the same as some other villages. The answer to your original question – "Are villages racist?" – might be different if you lived in an east Kent village, say, where asylum-seekers regularly arrive on their way to London.'

I thank him, we agree to meet up for lunch, and I'm left with the job of drafting a counter-attack to Ralph. I fancy I do it with both wit and academic precision:

Subject: Re: re: Invite to Stow
From Derek Taylor [derekjtayl@internet.co.uk]
Date: 14/11 19.23
To: Ralph Aardman [ralphaardman@internet.com]
Cc:

Deasr Rakph,
   Hang on, the opinion of one biased *Midsomer Murders* producer is hardly a fact-based sociological thesis!!!
   Have fun in Berlusconiland, and see you when you get back.

   Best as ever
   Derek

With the concrete base that'll end up beneath the floor of The Old Stables now sealed against deadly gases, the next ten days see the shell of the building shoot up. And on a cold Wednesday morning, at 7.45, a flat-bed lorry arrives with our hearts of oak and curved braces strapped on the back. Nigel has brought his assistant, Bertrand. He's got a beard too, a ginger one. And a red bobble hat. Recalling my anti-stereotyping resolution, I do not sin in thought or word.

Nigel, picking up his coffee mug as a smiling Bertrand brings over a short oak joist slung over his shoulder, turns to me and says quietly, 'He looks just like Santa Claus Junior.'

But the peaceful assembly of oak frames, the gentle tap of pegs in holes, is soon shattered. Nik's man, Scott has started to drill one of the steel columns that Jeremy insisted on placing next to the higgledy-piggledy stone of the back wall. The towering column looks like it's wandered into the wrong building, like Sylvester Stallone on the set of *Shakespeare in Love*.

But the 5-metre high oak columns are going to be bolted to these steel pillars. Jeremy's taking no chances with any of this picturesque stone and wood. Champion of historical character I may be, but I'm not averse to a bit of twenty-first century steel and concrete when we're talking about whether the place will fall over. We won't see any of it, hidden behind the oak posts and boxed in by plaster board.

At the end of the second day, the frame has been pegged together and is standing four-square along the front of the building. And if you screw up your eyes, you can start to see what the house might look like finished. I wander out into the road to take in the whole scene and find Bertrand squaring up to Joanna next door.

'If you don't move it now, I shall call the police,' she says in a tone of voice that must, in her days as hospital matron, have let young heart surgeons know their place in life. It's the oaksmith's pickup parked in front of her driveway that's the problem. Bertrand turns to look over towards me with an expression that appeals for help, and I see Joanna send me a theatrical wink detectable at 50 metres.

'I should move it pronto if I were you,' I advise him. 'You don't want to mess with Mrs Neave.' As he hops up into the cab, she smiles at me and winks again.

Back on-site, Nigel's perched on a pile of yellow Cotswold stone, his fingers busy with a roll-up ciggy.

'So,' I say, thinking to be congratulatory, 'It all looks as solid as... well, oak.'

'Yep,' he nods. 'Remember though, it's going to shrink, as the sap dries out. You work it out like this. You take the number of inches across the post, add one, and that's how many years it'll take to settle. So for the big ones here, that's nine years.'

But I'm remembering what Nik said. 'So isn't there a worry that drafts will come in through the cracks?'

'Not for me there isn't,' he grins, 'I won't be here'.

Is it just me? Or do our craftsmen like winding up all their customers? 'Don't worry,' he says. 'The shakes won't go all the way through.'

We're moving at a clip now, and a team of carpenters arrives to put in the softwood rafters that will hold the roof in place. The chief chippy pauses to admire our oak now waiting for the several tons of glass to be fitted.

'Pity you don't have a view of the hills,' he says.

I'm defensive. 'Oh, we like the convenience of being close to the shops.'

'Yes,' he continues, patting the fat column by the gap that'll end up as Maggie's French windows. 'Wonderful thing, oak. A living being. We've just been working on a house with massive oak posts that'll take eighty years to dry out. They've got shakes in them already.' He laughs. 'The whole house creaks and moves in a storm like an old ship.'

Yes, but not ours, surely.

The thing about a roof is, if something goes wrong, you can fix it without much sweat. When you find a couple of broken tiles in the back garden after a stormy night, one call to the local handyman, and two hours and forty quid later, like the chief executive of an oil consortium once the leak's fixed, you've got your life back.

Floors are different. You might say, 'Yes, but there's not much can happen to a floor.'

Wrong.

Well, wrong in our case, anyway. Because we've agreed to go with Maggie's idea of underfloor heating. We've plumped for a company in Northern Ireland I'd found at the trade show in Birmingham. The people there seem helpful and so are their prices. This last point is a vital one, because we've got to look for savings wherever we can. The downside of using an Ulster company is we have to make all the arrangements by phone. I'd feel better if I could see the whites of the managing director's eyes now and again. It all seems a gamble too far. The hot water piping, hundreds of yards of it, will be stretched out on the concrete base of the building like giblets on a butcher's block. It'll then be entombed in thirteen tons of concrete screed, and on top of that will be laid our cleverly made, and quite expensive, limestone slabs.

'What if there were an earth tremor?' I muse to Maggie.

'Well, I reckon if there was an earthquake in Stow,' she answers, 'replacement heating pipes might be low on the schedule of our insurance claim.'

'No, I'm not saying a quake. I'm talking about a tremor, as when you wake up in the middle of the night with the mirror falling off the wall and the alarm clock dancing up and down, then when you get up, you find next door's chimney pot has landed in your fish pond.'

'Has that ever happened to you?' asks Maggie.

'No. Not as such.'

'What do you mean "not as such"?'

'Well, as a reporter I once covered an earthquake near Naples, and I felt the aftershocks.'

'Sure, but what about here in the UK?'

'No. But there was a tremor in Wolverhampton last year. One crack in the floor, and – Bingo! – your underfloor heating's pumping hot water round your ankles.'

'You don't think you're getting paranoid, do you?' says Maggie.

'All right then, what if one of the pipes gets a hole in it? It's always happening above ground. That's what plumbers do all day long, fix leaky pipes. So why wouldn't it happen down there?' Maggie frowns, and I press home the point. 'Or, what about if the pipes fur up? You'd have to use a pneumatic drill to smash up the limestone and the concrete to get at them.' And another, even greater terror grips me. 'And how would you know where the leak was?' My voice is getting shrill. 'You'd have to dig the whole *lot* up till you found it. And…' I'm panicking now. 'And… and then, you couldn't smash up the concrete without damaging all the pipes as well!'

Maggie's quiet. This pushes my derangement towards levels barely recognised by medical science. I'd been hoping my outburst would prompt some rational reassurance from her.

Next morning I ask Nik. He's bound to have useful experience.

'Well,' he says, 'Underfloor heating is standard in a lot of Scandinavian countries. People in Britain are confused about it. Normal central heating pipes, between the radiators, usually go under the floor, so if they go wrong, you still have to rip up tiles and concrete.'

This is not quite the answer I'm looking for.

I phone Portadown in Northern Ireland, to tell the manager of our underfloor heating company that we're having second thoughts, and I explain our worries.

'We've been in this business for fourteen years,' he explains, 'and we've not yet had a single problem. I can give you testimonials.'

This is more like it. We do fancy the idea of no radiators in the house, and heating bills are supposed to be lower.

We're still dithering when two weeks later, our son Dan and his fiancée Jo come to visit us in Blockley, and they get taken on the obligatory tour of the building site. There's a lot going on. Plumbers are linking up drains and installing water supplies, electricians are starting to pull cables, Simon's laying blocks for the kitchen wall. As usual though, for me, it's like visiting someone else's house. It's not ours yet. It belongs to the builders. And I keep thinking if they spoke their minds, they'd tell me I was in the way.

But this time, Mark the plumber calls out, 'Ahh, just the chap we need. We've got a problem. We can't put the toilet there.' He points to the right. 'Because the pipework won't fit. It could go there.' He points to the left. 'And the basin there.' He points to the right again. 'So we need you to decide.'

He needs me! I get on the phone to Maggie, and the deal's done. I announce the decision to Mark. Swap them over. Basin on the right.

The rest of the tour has an upbeat tone to it, as I explain to Dan and Jo how we have had to overcome setbacks at every twist in the project. What man doesn't crave to be a hero in the eyes of his son?

CHAPTER 24

OK, ETHEL, BACK OFF!

I wake early to an eerie white light filling the bedroom. It's odd because the front of the radio says '7.09AM NOV 29'. Yesterday about this time, the thin bedroom curtains had the rippled greyness of the River Mersey. Today they're shining silver. The clock must be wrong and we've overslept. After fumbling my watch onto the floor, I make it over to the window.

Snow.

Thick snow. At least a foot deep. And it's still falling.

A billion words have already been written about why quite normal adults (ones who don't do drugs and can read a newspaper inside their heads without moving their lips) adore scenes like the one now visible through the French windows of Mill Cottage, despite the fact that it doubles commuting times, balloons heating bills and then turns into grey sludge. I turn off the Breakfast News after hearing the phrase 'Winter Wonderland' forty-three times in the first two minutes, then Maggie and I permit ourselves a dose of such adoration.

'Oh, the ducks are having a hard time of it,' observes Maggie. 'The stream's frozen over.' She opens the window a slit and throws out some pieces of my best home-baked ciabatta. I don't begrudge it though, as we watch the powdered snow tossed around while a pair of mallards tussle over a large slice.

'Look at the weeping willow,' I say. 'Its branches are encased in ice. It looks like a glass model. There must have been an ice storm over night.'

'What's an ice storm?' asks Maggie.

'Well. I don't know really. The total sum of my knowledge on the subject comes from the film of that name with Sigourney Weaver. The characters all get marooned when the roads and railway are iced up.'

And so we go on, chattering away about everything snowy and icy for half an hour over our breakfast, or rather over my breakfast, while Maggie savours the Spanish-blended roast torrefacto *mezcla* coffee which, as usual, she has prepared with the care and precision of a Nobel Prize-winning chemist. After her second cup, she's ready.

'Right, let's go for it,' I say.

We pull on our wellies, brush the snow off the car and crunch it along the village road at ten miles an hour. Blockley is in a hollow. Stow is, as you know, on a hill. Thirty seconds after passing the last of the village's twelve mills, the car – with an elegance seen otherwise only in *Dumbo on Ice* – slides, with its rear offside wheel leading the way, back down as far as the neat front wall of that same last mill.

Blockley is cut off from the rest of humanity; for those without tractors or experience of Antarctic treks that is.

Back at Mill Cottage, I phone Nik. The road between Cheltenham and Stow is blocked by toppled lorries. 'And even if we could get through,' he says, 'there wouldn't be much point. You can't mix muck at minus six.' (Translation: when the thermometer shows six degrees below 0°C, mortar does not set.)

Even in Mill Cottage, we need two sweaters on. While Maggie checks her emails, I set about lighting a log fire to boost the efforts of the radiators. There's one thing about these old houses, you can't ignore the seasons. They seep in beneath the doors and whistle through the cracks in the eaves.

We're getting short on basics, like milk, bread, eggs. And tapenade. So I volunteer to walk back into Blockley and stock up.

It's a slow plod, and on two occasions between Mill Cottage and the village green, my feet fly up in front of my face in that comical fashion that would normally result in multiple fractures of the lower vertebrae. But today the laws of nature are suspended – it's the feast day when the jester can get away with anything – and the cushion of snow is so thick that, in order to recover, I have to do no more than check nobody is watching and get up.

At the village shop-cum-PO, there's a shock Blu-tacked to the inside of the window.

**As of January Blockley Post Office and Shop
will be closing down.
We would like to take this opportunity of thanking
all our customers for their support over the years.
-The Proprietor.**

'It's an absolute disgrace.' I turn to see a red-faced, elderly chap in trench coat and Cossack hat. 'The man should be ashamed of himself. Some people have got no sense of social responsibility.'

'It's terrible.' This is a woman on my other side. 'No sense of community, some people.'

And the two of them head off in opposite directions.

Inside, Doris, one of the regulars behind the counter is saying, 'Please don't shout at me. The boss isn't here right now. I'm as upset about it as you are.'

'I'm sorry, I'm sorry. You're right,' says a fur-clad woman putting down her basket brimful of bread, parsnips and tinned salmon.

'I live in the village too, and this is my job,' says Doris. 'It's awful for all of us.'

'There must be something we can do,' says a middle-aged fellow, thumping his mittened hands together. But nobody answers.

Back outside, my rucksack now stuffed with life-preserving nutrients, I see a figure stomping across from the churchyard and raising a duvet-jacketed arm in a wave.

'Hi Derek.'

It's Chris from the cafe.

'Hi Chris. I've just seen the news. About the shop.'

'Hi Margaret. Hi James. I know. It's hitting people badly. Hi Oliver.' This is the thing about having a conversation with Chris in the street, everyone knows him.

'It's been the death of some villages,' I observe. 'The shop and the post office closing. And of course, your cafe's gone now as well.' As I say this, I realise it sounds like I'm accusing him of helping destroy Blockley, and add, 'Sorry, I didn't mean...'

'It's OK, it's OK. Look I'll tell you what's going on.' He pulls me over by the arm out of the way of the crunching wheels of a Range Rover, and smiling and nodding to other passing Blockleyites, he says, 'We're going to open up a new community shop. Well, in fact, it'll be a shop, post office and cafe all in one. That's the plan.'

'Wow, that's fantastic.'

'I've got to go and meet someone at The Crown. Do you want to walk with me?'

On the way, he starts to explain. A group of them have been forming plans for well over a year, ever since they'd got wind of the possibility of the present shop shutting.

'It's all been a bit hush-hush. We haven't wanted to raise hopes. But news is leaking out now, and we're ready to go public. – Hi, how's it going? Yeah, see you tonight. – That's Chris Jury, by the way, who started it all. We're really lucky here in Blockley, the talent at our disposal. The committee includes a journalist, an accountant, a solicitor, a guy who's run a big business, and others. All with skills that they're giving to the project. I'm going to be managing it'

'Congratulations! That's all great news.'

'Yes. That's why I moved out of Murray's Cafe. The plan is to get the new place up and running by the spring.'

'Where's it going to be? In the same place as the shop now?'

'No, across the road in the Old Coach House. We've done all the research. We can get funding from a charity that's set up to encourage rural shops. They'll give us twenty grand, and lend us another twenty if we can raise twenty ourselves from local subscriptions.'

'Will you be able to do that?'

'I don't think it'll be a problem. You've seen how cross people are at losing the old shop. They don't want to go to the supermarket in Moreton every time they need a couple of rashers of bacon.' We've reached the door of The Crown. 'Oh, hi Pam. Yeah I won't be long. I'll be with you in a couple of minutes.' He draws me into the lobby.

'They seem to be getting more and more popular, village community shops,' I say. 'I saw an item on the local news the other night about one down in Oxfordshire. It was open for two or three hours a couple of days a week. They said it did wonders for the spirit in the village, with lots of people getting involved. They're usually staffed by volunteers, aren't they?'

'Right,' says Chris, 'what you're talking about is exactly and precisely,'... he's tapping my chest for emphasis... 'what we are *not* going to do in Blockley.'

'How so?'

'I've visited these places. Ethel with her wicker basket of home-made scones and watercolours of the parish church, set up in a garage, serving cups of coffee for one pound twenty that tastes of crap... crap...' He mouths the word with theatrical emphasis, glancing towards an elderly couple seated by the bar. 'And the village locals come and buy the stuff out of loyalty and listen to Ethel complain about volunteer fatigue. You can't run a business on guilt and duty. It won't last. It's like British Leyland telling us to "Buy British" when the cars were rubbish. And look where Leyland are now.'

'So what's the alternative?'

'Run it like a business. It's as simple as that. You *employ* the staff. You manage it professionally. – OK Alan, I'm on my way right now. – You aim to make a profit. It doesn't have to be a big profit. But to make this work, we've got to be quietly cut-throat. You need a Tesco mentality, but with all the local village friendliness.' As my mouth opens to form the next question, he adds, 'That, by the way, is going to mean a two and a half thousand pound coffee machine. Watch this space, Derek.' And he's gone.

It's stopped snowing and the road back to Mill Cottage has now got four flattened channels running its length along which cars are making nervous advances in both directions, but I choose the jester-friendly thick bits at the side. As I start my plod home, I'm on the verge of saying to myself that what Blockley's got, and what any village that wants to breathe life back into itself must have, is community spirit. But I don't say it, because whenever that word 'community' creeps into my brain, a spectre appears at my right shoulder. It's the spectre of Tony, an old university friend of mine. The merest sniff of the word 'community' prompts him to deliver a torrent of derision. Especially the phrase 'international community'. You notice, now I've mentioned it, how many times you hear it on the news.

'In what sense,' Tony will say, 'are South Korea, Italy and Canada a 'community'? They don't *do* anything together. Their interests are all so different and complex that there is absolutely nothing *communal* about them at all. It's just lazy journalism, and very misleading.' He's persuaded me over the years. Tony takes it a step further. He lives in North Carolina (where apparently they're just as sloppy in their language) and whenever he comes over to the UK, he always has a good chortle at the fact that we have a 'Secretary of State for Communities' in the Cabinet. 'It's the same nonsense,' he says. 'It just promotes the idea that thousands, maybe millions of people who've just got one thing in common – like their religion, say, or the fact that they live in Cornwall – somehow all have the same identical needs. It's dangerous baloney!' He's got a point, you can't deny it.

I brush the snow off my backside for a third time, calling out, 'No, I'm fine, I'm fine, honestly,' in the direction of an old lady at the wheel of a passing Morris Minor, and recall that I recently read that the world of sociology is coming round to Tony's view. Apparently one eminent member of the British Society of Sociologists has concluded that the word 'community' has ninety-four different definitions. Now, some of you may have suspected that I occasionally do exaggeration for comic effect. But not this time. Ninety-four definitions! The result, apparently, is that the word 'community' is regarded as useless for any kind of explanation of what's going on, for instance, in villages. So sociologists now resort to the word 'conviviality.' They don't mean 'conviviality' in the sense of Kev putting his arm round his mate in the pub and slurring, 'I love you, Jake, you're my best friend.' They use it to mean what-these-people-have-in-common-is-that-they-live-in-the-same-place-and-don't-necessarily-have-anything-else-in-common. I don't think somehow it's going to catch on. The Blockley Conviviality Shop and Cafe. Well maybe. I'll try it out on Chris.

However, the good thing about all this, on a freezing November morning in Blockley, is that the spectre of Tony makes me abandon my sloppy thinking and work out exactly what it is that Blockley's got going for it. And it's pretty obvious when you look at it like that. Blockley's got a couple of handfuls of people, Chris being one of them, who've got energy and talent and time, all of which they enjoy devoting to a project that'll make a lot of their neighbours happy. Blockley's lucky. Hogsthorpe didn't seem to have anybody like that, which was one of its many problems. Sociologists apparently have stuck a label on these get-up-and-goers as well. They call them 'fiery spirits'. Quite nice really. So long as they don't start to talk about a 'conviviality of fiery spirits.'

Mill Cottage hoves into view. There's a lot to tell Maggie. Especially about that coffee machine of Chris's.

CHAPTER 25

A HELPING HAND FROM A FAIRY

As the snow in Blockley shrinks, I sit for hours shifting numbers around on my spreadsheet. There's one thing about being a worrier. You're prepared to go to mind-torturing lengths of worry today on the off-chance it'll avoid an even worse worry tomorrow. The alternative would be not to fret today because the catastrophe's unlikely to happen tomorrow. I can't do that.

As far as I can make out, what's happening is the costs of building are outstripping our budget, but not in obvious ways. It's subtle. For instance, what we saved not having to underpin the walls got gobbled up by the oak. That was fine. But then, the odd bag of nails here, an incidental sack of cement there are up on forecast. Multiplied approximately ten thousand times.

My fussiness in getting the computer to total all the sums and organise the items in neat little categories, if not rearranging deckchairs on the *Titanic*, is akin to polishing a bucket that's got a hole in the bottom. The fact is – and as I sit watching the melt-water drip ever faster from the roof of Mill Cottage, I start to see it *is* a fact that has to be faced – we got a lot less from the sale of Maggie's old house than we'd budgeted. There's no point being a star juggler of the expenses, if the lion-tamer behind you has left the cage door open. And it's certainly a waste of time devising multiple elaborate metaphors instead of sorting out the finances.

Half a dozen letters plop onto the mat. Hiding beneath the *Reader's Digest* prize for Mill Cottage, South Street, and the cruise brochure for Mill Cottage, North Street is a letter stamped the 'Hang-Em-Hi Scaffold Co. Ltd' addressed to me. It's a bill for eight and a half thousand pounds. So, once again I prepare to nestle into the comfortable task of ticking off cost against budget on my spreadsheet.

I enter 'scaffold' into the FIND box and click OK.

Nothing.

So I try respectively 'Hang-Em-Hi', 'Hang-Em', 'Hang' and in desperation 'Hi'. All I get are those annoying little stickers that say, 'The search item was not found.'

I can't believe this. I've forgotten completely to put anything into the budget for all those steel poles and clamps that I've managed to bang my head against almost every day for the past four weeks.

What was I thinking?

That it was a little gift from the fairies?!

Well, that settles it. Maggie and I convene a summit in the kitchen.

'So how much do you forecast we're going to be overspent by the end of the project?' she asks, kicking off the debate.

'Hard to say exactly,' I mumble.

'Well, how much are we overspent right now?'

'Hard to say, really.'

She frowns.

I decide to resort to smoke and mirrors. 'Hold on,' I say, and leap over to the printer. After five minutes of keyboard poking and paper loading, the machine chugs out eighteen Excel landscape sheets, which I spread out on the table.

'So?' asks Maggie. And I launch into a line-by-line account of quarter-inch elbow drains and twenty kilo bags of sand brackets.

She listens for about twelve minutes, then jumping into the gap left by the eighth sheet fluttering onto the floor, asks, 'So do you reckon an extra fifty thousand would cover it?'

'Should do. With a bit to spare,' I call up from under the table. And that's decided. We'll take out a mortgage. And we agree the monthly interest won't be too bad. We'll soon pay it off. I've just done a deal to do a bit of part-time work as a consultant for the South Bank Centre in London, though I seem to be forgetting I hardly have time to do that as well as fret about The Old Stables conversion.

The next morning, when I arrive on-site, I make a point of glaring at the scaffolding. It had first gone up to carry the carpenters a month ago when they fitted the roof beams, felting and slats. And it's been loitering there ever since, like a hoody in a shopping mall. It should have been hounded out, or hugged off, to productive employment elsewhere ages ago. It's the problem of the roof tiles that's delayed things.

Maggie and I had found some Spanish slate that gets an aged look with the weather. It's indistinguishable from the

Welsh stuff, and costs only a third of the price. What's more, Queen Bee, Empress of Planning said, 'We approve.' But Nik has been informed by the building control department that the pitch of our roof is only eighteen degrees, whereas the building regs state that our slates need at least twenty-two point five degrees.

We are, it seems, to be battered by bureaucracy worthy of the Indian Civil Service.

'No,' says Nik. 'You'll be battered by the wind. It can get under the tiles with such a low-pitched roof.'

'So you're telling me,' I say, 'that the wind can distinguish between twenty-two point five degrees and twenty-three degrees?'

'No, I'm just telling you what the regulations are. I didn't make them. But at the end of the day, they're there for your benefit. I don't think Maggie and you are going to want to be sitting watching the telly one night, when the wind starts to rip your roof off because you've got the wrong tiles on.'

Fair enough, and I apologise to him for getting shirty.

Nik takes no offence, and he's already sniffed out an answer. He pulls from his pocket a sample of some artificial tiling with concealed drainage channels which will reroute any rain that gets blown under. The tile is shiny though, and Maggie and I don't like it. But we guess we're stuck. We need Queen Bella's approval, so we crave an audience. She's away on holiday and they're short-staffed.

So we wait. For a week and a half. During which time the work rate slows. There's a bit of desultory pointing of the back wall. But not much else. The roof's got to be made waterproof before we can get on with any of the more delicate jobs inside. Finally, rested from her hols, Queen Bee chucks Nik's tile back at us marked 'Rejected'. There shall be no artificial roofing in a conservation area.

'This is typical,' says Nik. 'Planning *and* Building Control both have to say "Yes", but they don't talk to each other, so you have to bounce back and forward between them till Bingo, the bell rings.'

He has a go at beating the system. The building control officer regularly drops by the site, and Nik knows him from a hundred past jobs. So on one such visit, Nik asks the guy which tiles we *are* permitted to use, so that we can then take that list to the Queen of Planning in order to find out which ones amuse or irritate her. But the BCO says, 'Oh no, I'm not here to act as your unpaid adviser.'

'But, come on Charlie,' says Nik, 'you must know the answer.'

'Yes, but I'm not allowed to say.'

Charlie then looks over each shoulder and slips Nik a shifty sheet of paper with a nine-digit code on it. Nik recognises it as a Birmingham phone number. I decide to accept the risk that the line's been tapped by the Roofing Regs Police, and tap out the digits on my mobile. An incomprehensible name answers. So, without knowing why I'm speaking to this person, I spill the story of our woes.

'Ah,' the voice replies, 'You'll be needing our double-'ook roof fixers. It's the nails Building Control don't like. The water goes through the 'oles.' And he finishes on a note of triumph, 'With our 'ooks, you don't need 'oles!'

The man has reliable intelligence, because both departments, BC and QB stamp our documentation 'Passed', and the Spanish tile solution, as originally favoured, is implemented with the hook modification.

A week later, I clamber up the scaffolding which Tinkerbelle had so thoughtfully provided, and Len, chief roofer shows me. The hooks clinch under the leading edge of each tile. Neither wind not water will shift it.

'Looks good, Len,' I say.

'Yeah, thanks,' he replies. Then putting down, or rather balancing his hammer on the equivalent of a rooftop knife edge, adds, 'By the way, some old bloke came by this morning and got really poncey with us.'

'What do you mean?'

'He said he was going to report us to Planning in Cirencester. Something about the roof height.'

Gawd, I think to myself, sounds like the Grise.

'Anyway, I told him to eff off, and got on with it.'

'You did what!'

'Just kidding. He said you'd know who he was.'

Pausing only to check my heart rate, I beetle off post-haste to the Grise emporium.

He's in his den as usual, stroking his chin. He doesn't respond to my cheery greeting.

'My roofing lads were just telling me you'd been round to have a quick shufti at the old work in progress.' My attempt to sound matey and matter-of-fact cuts no ice.

He erupts. 'It's an absolute disgrace! I don't know how you've got the gall to stand there and face me!'

I give a little laugh. I don't know what else to do.

He's wagging his finger now. 'You told me you would *not* be raising the height of the roof. But you have!'

'That's ridiculous,' I butt in. 'Of course I haven't.'

'You have broken your word to me, and I suspect broken the terms of your planning consent!'

'Em, you're mistaken. That's simply not correct.'

'Hah!' he says.

I turn and, giving the door a tug so the bell makes an extra loud clang, stomp out into the street, where – like Mole in *The Wind in the Willows* after his encounter with the weasels – I think of all the things I should have said. Especially that I have before-and-after photos that prove the roof's the same height as it started. Still, I console myself with the thought that if he does cut up rough with the Planners, I've got documentary evidence that should clinch the case in our favour, once it reaches the Supreme Court. And I suppose the Christmas card list will show a saving of £1.40.

CHAPTER 26

OF WALLS AND WIGMAKERS

Something's been bothering me whenever I go into the kitchen, or rather into the concrete cell with a pencil mark on the wall where the oven's going to be. I can't put my finger on it. But one evening when Maggie and I are doing a tour, trying to time travel to the days when the heap of planks will be transformed into a sofa and the ladder by the door into curtains, the suspicion jumps out of the shadows.

We've come to understand that rooms on a building site always look small. But that kitchen cell really does look impossibly small. I rush out to fetch the tape measure and Anthea's plan from their permanent home in the back of the car. Maggie holds one end of the measure while, brow crinkled, I peer at the numbers on the other. There's not enough light and I've got my wrong glasses on.

'Here, let me have a go,' says Maggie, and we swap ends. She can't see it either. She keeps her finger in place and takes the measure outside. But it's a gloomy night by the cement mixer, so that's no better.

'Don't move your finger,' I say, and we traipse out into Back Walls and over to the street light. Thus the awful truth is illuminated.

'The wall's in the wrong place!' I cry.

'It can't be,' says Maggie. 'Let's check again.' So three times we march in and out, taking it in turns to press a white finger against the dreadful little number on the metal measuring strip. There's no mistake. The kitchen is three inches narrower than it should be.

'This is terrible,' I squawk.

'Omigosh,' cries Maggie. 'The oven won't fit in!'

Now as you already know, this kitchen has been planned to be a miracle of design, with fridge, sink, hob, cupboards, fitting together as exactly as if they'd been welded into one piece as they came out of some kitchen parts factory. There's no margin for error. And now we've got an error, set in 8-foot-high concrete, mortared together and plastered over.

In disbelief, we examine the offensive piece of masonry from every angle. And then I see it.

'Shoot! Look at that,' I say, pointing up to the ceiling. 'It's supporting the roof. It's going to be too late to move it.'

So we look at Anthea's plan again and try to work out if there's any way we could swap around the fridge and the sink and the cupboards to make them fit. But it's hopeless.

At 7.45 next morning, after yet another night of pulling and knotting the bedclothes, I phone Nik. He's en route from Cheltenham to Stow.

'You're not going to like this,' I tell him.

'Try m…' The mobile signal's fading. He must be driving along the ridge-top near Cold Aston.

'The kitchen wall on the right-hand side,' I pause to make sure he can hear. 'It's three inches too far to the left.'

'Three inch... ... can't see... what can... completely impo...' And that's all I get from him before it cuts out. I call back half an hour later, by which time he should be in Stow. But his phone's busy, so I leave a message spelling out the problem again. I can't go straight off to see him because I've got an appointment with the bank to sort out that mortgage.

'So you're living in Blockley temporarily,' observes the bank manager, or rather community-based customer services interface facilitator, when he scans our application form. I nod, only half-listening as I wonder whether we could convert the kitchen into a bedroom and put the kitchen where the guest room was going to be. Guests would have to sleep on bunk beds. And they'd need to walk across the living room and through the kitchen when they wanted a shower. But maybe...

'I was brought up in Blockley,' he goes on. I raise my eyebrows in an automated 'That's interesting' signal. 'Do you know,' he asks, and I try to concentrate, in the belief that he's going to require information from me that may have nothing to do with mal-aligned kitchen walls. 'Do you know that when I was a kid in Blockley, it had fourteen shops?'

Now ordinarily, this would have me on the edge of my seat interviewing him about the cause and exact nature of Blockley's commercial decline. He's not eighty-nine. He can't be more than thirty-five, so what he's talking about isn't that long ago. But it's a measure of my distraction and anxiety that all I can manage is a not very expressive, 'Oh.'

'Yes,' he carries on, determined to forge a bond with the client just as he was taught on the training course. 'There was a butcher who specialised in pigs' cheeks, a wigmaker, a restorer of clavichords, a marble coffin seller, two military equipment dealers, and five second-hand dog shops.' I've made this list up of course, because my mind was back on whether it might be possible to put a very big hole in the rogue wall then build another wall immediately on the other side, so I didn't register the specifics of his mother's weekly purchases along Blockley High Street.

He tells me I'll have to go and see the bank's area Gauleiter in Evesham half an hour away, and I slope off.

It's gone eleven by the time I get to the site, and I'm afraid on reflection, that in my haste, I might have been brusque with Black Beauty and the vicar. Jason, who's stuffing muck between the stones on the Back Walls side of the stables itself, gives me a chirrupy 'Morning.' He can't have heard the news about the kitchen wall and our shattered dreams. There's no sign of Nik. I make my way towards the guilty corner of the building and bump into Simon.

'Hey, Derek,' he says. He's smiling. Nik's evidently not spoken to him yet. 'You look grim,' he adds. 'Something up?'

I'll have to break the news. 'We made a nasty discovery last night,' I say. 'About the kitchen wall.'

Simon taps out a cigarette from his pack and sticks it between his teeth. 'Oh that,' he says. 'Let's have a look. See what you reckon.'

He moves his vast bulk out of the way. And there before me, is a little heap of rubble where last night's 7-foot-tall pain had been. And right next to it is an adolescent wall of breeze blocks, wet mortar dripping from its sides.

'But you've just knocked it down!'

'Sure. No big deal.' I look up at the ceiling, expecting to see it flopping, ready to fall. Simon follows my thoughts. 'The roof'll be fine for a couple of hours,' he explains, 'just till the new wall's built up to the top.'

Simon's too big and ugly for me to kiss. Another job for Maggie.

Perhaps it's this tinge of anything's possible that colours my judgement, but that evening, I hear myself agreeing with Maggie as she presses the case for the underfloor heating. Her view is that on balance we should go ahead. So we sign the contract and pop it in the envelope. But the moment it leaves my fingers and disappears into the maw of the Sheep Street postbox, I feel a weight sag the bottom of my stomach again.

It's ten days later, the night before the installers arrive, and new terrors stalk my wakeful brain. What if they're inexperienced kids who don't care? Or worse, cowboys! I'm early at the site ready to let them in. After an hour, I'm still pacing the concrete floor. They've not arrived. *I knew it.*

Then along comes Ken. He apologises for being late, opens his toolbox and within ten minutes he's laid the first 40 or 50 yards of the piping in long narrow rows. In a soft Ulster accent he explains what he's doing. He's been installing it for twelve years. He's what you might call middle-aged. I know that's a politically incorrect thing to say. But right now I'm desperate for a shot of reassurance, and if I can only get my shot from a dirty source, so be it.

I share my we'll-have-to-dig-up-the-whole-floor worry with him. An old chestnut, you can see from his smile.

'Provided it's properly installed and run, you've nothing to worry about,' he soothes.

'And will ours be…? properly installed and run?' I ask, and I sit at his feet (or at least I would have done if it weren't for the pipes in the way).

'It will,' he promises. And he explains the four commandments of the underfloor heating Bible.

The first is: thou shalt install an automatic cut-out in case the pipes overheat.

The second is: thou shalt attach a made-for-purpose, non-ferrous pump to stop the system furring up.

The third is: thou shalt not drill holes in the floor.

The fourth and final commandment is: thou shalt cause thy manservant and thy odd-job man not to drill holes in the floor either.

Ken looks up towards the heavens. 'It'll be perfect for a place like this with a high ceiling,' he says. 'If you had conventional rad heaters, all the heat would rise up to the roof, then fill the room only gradually, so it would be warmest over your head. But with underfloor, it's hot down here straightaway where you need it.'

What a wise and virtuous man he is. When he's packed away his adjustable spanner, I thank him for his journey down the mountain, and promise that his tablets of stone will always sit in our hearts.

The peace which his presence exuded lasts the rest of that day. After that, my faith starts to leak away. I won't be a hundred per cent sure till we're sitting in a toasty house next January, congratulating ourselves. And meanwhile, Nik has to put the system through a pressure test a week later. Any sign of low pressure will mean there's some little crack or hole or loose joint somewhere in the system.

But when P-Day comes, I'm not there. Instead, I'm under the bed sheets on the fourth floor of London Bridge Hospital waiting to undergo a minor procedure on my heart. Nothing serious, it's just to try and correct that slight Morse code beat. I'll be out in twenty-four hours. The timing's not great though. And I can't help thinking as I lie there having my blood pressure taken that I'm breaking the first rule I was taught as a TV reporter. It came from Gerald Seymour who was then ITN's senior correspondent. 'If you're in the right place as a reporter,' he said, 'the story'll come to you. Go there and be patient.'

And as I lie on the operating table at London Bridge hospital, all I can think is, 'I'm in the wrong place.'

'I'm going to give you a sedative,' says the nurse, pumping the liquid into the drip on my wrist. She winks at me. 'You should feel a rush. It'd cost you 800 quid on the streets.' And I'm asleep while the crucial test takes place 110 miles away.

When I come round, Maggie phones.

'All clear,' she says.

'Is it? Oh thank goodness,' I reply. 'No loss of pressure then?'

'No, I mean you,' she says. 'I've just spoken on the phone to the doctor. He says you're fine.'

'Yeah, sure, but what about the heating pipes?'

'They're fine too. I watched the test myself.'

But our worries over them have hardly started. The company that was going to put in the concrete screed to encase the pipework can't come for another two weeks. I get on my knees over the phone to them. But their equipment is under repair and distraught customers are queuing outside their office. That means two weeks of those little red pipes huddled on the bare concrete, vulnerable to the hobnailed boots of every labourer who wanders in. I print off signs, and stick them on the walls, saying, 'These underfloor heating pipes are very delicate. Please do not tread on them. If they are damaged, we could have very serious problems.'

'Nobody's going to read that,' says Maggie. 'It's too long.' But she can't think how we could get the message over any shorter. She's right though. On a frosty morning, we arrive on-site just in time to see the apprentice chippy in the correctly proportioned kitchen throw a splintery piece of four-by-two in the direction of the floor. It bounces and bangs its nasty sharp edges against our little pipes.

'Can't you read?' I scream, arm jutting out at the notice taped to a dangling power cable. 'If the pipes get punctured and then buried under tons of screed and floor slabs, we are inconvenienced.' (That's from the verb 'to inconvenience' as used in the phrase "*Inconvenience off!*") 'I mean *seriously* inconvenienced!' The lad looks guilty.

Simon intervenes. 'The pipes have got water in them now, so we'd see if there's a puncture,' he says, 'and we'll do a pressure test before the screed's laid.' But I glare again at the apprentice, and am glad I made a fuss.

Maggie's left. She can't bear it.

But now I'm late. I've an appointment with the bank in Evesham 10 miles away, to plead for the mortgage. I'm still muttering to myself about the apprentice carpenter as I race a yellow Mini for a parking spot in the multi-storey. The sound of metal scraping against concrete jolts me into a curse. Then, pushing open the bank door, I realise I've also forgotten to get a parking ticket. So body repair *and* a £40 fine!

Are there such things as Bitterness Management Courses? £30 an hour? It could all go on the spreadsheet.

CHAPTER 27

HENGE, POUND, PUMP AND CROSS

The fifteen forms the bank person has sent me away
with do nothing to soothe my stress. I can feel the back
of my neck stiffening in a way that will have me shaking,
red-faced and screaming unless I take remedial action, and
quick. A walk, that's the thing. Fresh air. Wide open spaces.
Feet thumping up and down on solid earth.

I try to think of somewhere calming where I've not been
for a while. Condicote comes to mind. The perfect little
village, and I can park the car just outside Stow then walk
there along the old forgotten Roman road, Ryknild Street.

It's a bright, frosty January morning, something I hadn't
even noticed, rushing from crunched car to bank dungeon.
There's a lark singing what seems to be hundreds of feet
over my head. That's a rare thing at this time of year, so I
stop to watch it till it's almost too high to make out. Then
it descends and disappears behind thick elder bushes, where

a light breeze is skimming through bare branches. So by the time I'm half a mile along the ancient track, I feel a soothing release spread through my body.

Ryknild Street.

I love the irony of its name. 'Street' makes it sound like it should be in the middle of a town or a city, bustling with office workers. Instead it's a 2-metre-wide cart track bordered on each side by the dead remains of last year's thistle and purple loose-strife, then a low stone wall. There's nobody here but me. The channel made by the side walls is as straight as Stan Revel, my old history teacher, taught me a Roman road should be. But the track itself zigzags between the walls, just a couple of feet every now and then, like a snake in a tube. A chaos of hawthorn sometimes mobs its sides, but mostly you can see across ploughed fields to the far horizon in every direction.

Underfoot, rounded lumps of stone show through the half-frozen mud. And it strikes me that this is what roads used to be like before John Loudon McAdam gave his name to tarmac. Till then, carriage wheels juddered and jolted their way from pothole to jagged rock to hole again. So when characters in Jane Austen complain they're exhausted after a day's journey, they're not being girlie and feeble. It would have killed my back, I know it would.

After half an hour, Ryknild Street starts to drop from the ridge down towards Condicote. And the approach makes me realise just how isolated Condicote must have seemed for most of the past 2,000 years. Even today, if you're approaching it along the old Roman cart track, you can get within a few hundred yards of its first farmhouse before you feel asphalt beneath your feet as you join a narrow vehicle-friendly country lane.

I step to the side for a car to pass, and the elderly woman at its wheel returns my nod with the kind of enthusiastic wave and full-faced smile usually reserved for returning relatives at the airport.

In a field on the outskirts of Condicote, I peer over the hedge. You might think at first sight that the view is like any other Cotswold field with cows in it. 'Very nice,' you might say and stroll on. But you'd be missing something. Look very carefully and you can make out the long curve of an earth bank sweeping around the field in a vast circle. This is where archaeologists have discovered the remains of a henge – a mini-version of Stonehenge – built nearly 4,000 years ago for purposes no one's sure about. Although what makes Condicote special today is that most of its buildings are still much as they were, on the outside anyway, between two and four hundred years ago, it's a humbling thought that this is only the most recent 5 to 10 per cent of Condicote's long and mysterious history.

The place is really not much more than a hamlet. Two or three dozen dwellings at most. I stroll down the road past 1 AGRICULTURAL COTTAGE on the right, and half a dozen houses on the left, big enough to have not gardens at their rear, but acre-sized paddocks. A couple of healthy looking oldies – must be seventy-five if they're a day – doing some heavy digging, wish me a hearty 'Good morning.'

After a few steps more, I reach the heart of Condicote. This is the Pound. It's not like most village greens. It's a small field surrounded by a 2-foot-high wall, and it's where sheep were once penned. The little road runs right around it and separates it from the church on one side, a working farm, several houses, and a field containing two shaggy ponies on the others. A 500-year-old cross of lichen-encrusted stone sits on one side of the Pound, with the original village pump a few steps away over the little wall. The only sound is the wind swishing the top branches of the Pound's towering willow trees and the drone of a distant tractor.

No box of after-dinner chocs would be disappointed to have Condicote's picture on its lid. If your great-aunt from Nebraska asked you to show her an example of the classic English village just as it was before the Industrial Revolution and the Great Technological Page-turning of our own era, you could take her to Condicote. And you could guarantee that she'd drool and express the opinion that this little time warp of a village was a shining beacon of peace and kindness in a world that has been going to hell in a handcart ever since the invention of the internal combustion engine.

I'm just about to reflect on this from a sitting position on the time-eroded plinth of the wayside cross, when I hear a voice call, 'Hello there,' and I jump with a start wondering if I was on the verge of breaking some medieval sumptuary law by presenting my backside to the hallowed stone. But when I turn, I see a bearded smile approaching and saying, 'Hello, I thought I recognised a friendly figure.'

'Oh, Richard, hi,' I reply. 'How are you?'

Richard is chiropodist to half the feet in Gloucestershire, and is a well-known face around Stow where he practices. I'd forgotten that he lives in Condicote. I tell him how I was just admiring the place and marvelling at its history. After exchanging the usual pleasantries I tell him about my search for what makes a good English village and ask his thoughts. He beams with enthusiasm.

'It's not just that it's quiet and beautiful,' he explains. 'The people here are different.' This sounds like rich research material, so I give him an encouraging look. 'For example, when we moved to the village twenty years ago,' he continues, 'my wife was ill, and I was visiting her in hospital every day. When I came back here in the evening, there was a covered plate of food on the doorstep and a note that said, "For your dinner tonight."'

'Wow, I can't see that happening in Hampstead or Solihull,' I say. 'Sounds like a rural paradise here in Condicote.' Then I realise there could have been a tinge of disappointment in my voice. The thought flashes across my mind that I might be looking for what's *wrong* with village life rather than what's right.

'No, I wouldn't say Condicote's some sort of heaven on earth,' he replies. 'To tell you the truth, it's changing.' I raise my eyebrows in surprise.

'One or two bigger houses in the village are being bought by wealthy young couples. They don't take much part in village life.'

'What do these people do for a living?'

'Commute. Some work in the city.'

'What, you mean Cheltenham?'

'No I mean *the* City. As in City of London. It's making the village top-heavy.'

'How do you mean?'

'Years ago, Condicote was just agriculture, of course. Apart from the squire at the manor house, it was a place for poor people working on the land.'

'Sure, sure,' I say. 'That was the story everywhere in the country.'

'Well, although a few outsiders like me and my wife came in, there were still plenty of the old families here. But it's expensive living in a village. You have to go to Stow to shop. Petrol's ten pence a litre more expensive in the countryside, and public transport in Condicote means a bus out once a week on a Tuesday – if it arrives – and one back on a Saturday – if you ask it to stop here. The village has become an unfriendly place for old people without cars.'

'So what do they do?'

'A lot of them have had to move out. Their cottages are sold and done up and fetch a good price. Too much for an ordinary family to afford. There's one just over there,' – Richard points down the lane to the left of the church – 'that was sold for seventy thousand just a few years ago. It was on the market last year for four hundred thousand.'

'Hmm, so I guess there's no social housing – affordable homes – in the village.'

'Some of the old cottages are owned by the family at the manor house who deliberately keep the rents low, just to try and hold the balance of the village together.'

'You mean good old-fashioned Victorian philanthropy. The squire subsidising the rents of the less well-off in the village.'

'That's one way of putting it. It's a wonderful thing.'

But I'm curious about something. I've got Herbert Evans' *Highways and Byways* tucked away in my pocket, and I show him what it says about Condicote, that in 1905 it had 'a bleak poverty-stricken air.'

'Sounds about right,' he comments. 'Some of the old people here when we first arrived used to remember it like that.' Then he adds, 'But I don't want to give you the wrong impression about the place today. Changes are *starting* to happen in Condicote. But right now, for us this is *the* place. We wouldn't want to live anywhere else but Condicote.'

Richard's beaming again. I shake his hand, thank him, and begin my tramp back, up the same road the Roman legionaries trod before me. Only 1,800 years ago.

I'd quite forgotten about those fifteen pages of bank forms to be filled in. I'll do them tonight. A bore. But hardly the collapse of civilisation.

CHAPTER 28

A STILT-WALKER'S GUIDE TO HOPSCOTCH

When I was a kid, my parents used to take us to see the petrifying wells at Matlock in Derbyshire. For the price of the entry ticket, you went into a dark, dank cavern. There on shelves, spattered by water dripping from the rocky ceiling, you could see everything from car tyres to false teeth, all turned to stone. Magic. Or, as I learned in the third form, the action of very hard water, which left a mineral deposit on everything it touched.

On a murky afternoon in early March, our house-to-be in Stow looks like a Derbyshire petrifying cavern. Except that the main subject of the magic is a man. He's wading up and down in wall-to-wall sludge. His wellies are petrified. His long pole is petrified. So are his hands. Bits of his clothing peep through a stony covering. Gobbets of the stuff are sticking to his cheeks.

I stand on the outside of the oak-frame barrier to his world, and peer in. I introduce myself.

'Yis, men,' he says. 'This is a bested of a jowb, this wan.' In clipped South African tones he spits out the resented words. 'The mix wes tew liquid. Ah nearly fell into the staff. Jist saved maself in tam. It would hev bin a nahsty dayth. To drewn en cone-crete.' His face remains stony.

He has come to lay our concrete screed. It's what's called a 'floating floor.' It's been poured in from a lorry-mounted tank before I arrived, then it has to be thoroughly raked to get rid of any air pockets – which is what's happening right now. Then you leave it to set. That's the only way to get a flat surface, which is what we need for our Tuscan limestone flagstones to sit on.

'So is that going to be a problem for us? It being too liquid?'

He keeps on pacing as it slops around his boots, raking it this way and that. He says nothing for a while, offended perhaps that I'm more concerned with the quality of the floor than with his narrow escape.

'Should be OwKai, men. It's getting thicker all the tahm.'

But my real worry is more immediate.

'You will be careful won't you with that rake.' And I deliver my speech on the cataclysmic effects of spiking one of the heating pipes. Surgeons, it's said, bury their mistakes. This guy could do the same.

'No worries,' he says. 'These little besteds of pipes er es taff as a rhino's voors keen.'

I am about to point out to him the error in his imagery since procreation depends on sensitivity rather than invulnerability, when I'm joined by a small bearded chap in a cashmere sweater and orange-coloured cords.

'I'm sorry to interrupt,' he says, 'but I couldn't help noticing the name of your new house as I was passing.'

'Oh, terrific. Thank you,' I say, welcoming the interest of a fellow historian. I'd only stuck the temporary 'Old Stables' sign to Nik's mesh-gate the day before.

'It's going to be nightmare,' he says.

'Sorry?'

'For my friend. It'll be an absolute nightmare. His house in Stow is called The Old Stables already. I think you'll have to change it.'

'Sorry?'

'The mail will get mixed up all the time.'

'Will it?' I'm forgetting the Blockley Mill Cottages palaver, but then there are twelve of those, more or less. 'Well, I suppose it might. But we've got one of the most brilliant postmen in the whole of Gloucestershire, Michael. Not only does he *not* mess up the deliveries, he sorts it out when people have made a mistake writing the address. That's one of the joys of living in a little place like Stow.'

'I'm fully aware of the pleasures of living in Stow,' he answers with quiet persistence. 'I've been here many years.'

'I'm saying it's not like we're in the middle of London, where nobody gives a monkey's.'

'It's the sime in Pritoria,' intervenes the screed-layer, slurping by on his next circuit of the cavern. 'Ah used to git litters for pipple in the nixt strit.' This could be support for either side of the argument.

'Well, it would be so much easier for everyone if you were to call your house something else,' insists the visitor.

'I'm sorry,' I reply. 'That's what it is, an old stables. I've done all the research. And anyway, it's registered now with Royal Mail.'

The visitor tuts and leaves.

'Yew ivva bn to Sith Ifrica?' the screed-layer enquires in passing.

'Only once.' I reply. 'I used to be a TV reporter.' I'm addressing the last comment at his back as it disappears into the far bedroom.

Three minutes later he strides past me again and picks up the conversation, 'Wonderful country, marvellous wald laaf, lions, elephants...' before disappearing into the room at the opposite end. And this is how it proceeds for the next hour. Brief extract from a lecture on the Kruger National Park or the views from Table Mountain are delivered as he wades into sight to be followed by gaps of silence when he passes out of eye and ear range, during which I think up what I'm going to say to him on his next circuit but don't usually manage to do so because the screed-layer starts up his monologue just before he appears in one of the end doorways. I can't make an excuse and leave because I can never seem to get into the conversation. And anyway, thoughts of the Matlock petrifying cavern of my childhood fix me there entranced.

'That's it,' says the screed-layer suddenly, stepping out of the grey slush to stand beside me on the other side of the oak frame. 'The jawb's done. It'll go awff in a couple of days. But make sure now-body steps on it till then.'

I thank him.

'That's OwKai. It was a pleasure to mit a men who's visited ma lovely homeland,' he says, 'and who appreciates it so much.' He offers me his cement-studded hand, then trudges off, leaving a line of stony grey footprints on the black soil.

Three days later, Nik pronounces the screed set solid enough to walk on, and the building then starts to acquire things more associated with a house than with an upmarket garage. Eight door-sized pieces of extra-thick glass have now been fitted into the oak frame. The electricians turn up and run so much cable under the roof beams that you could imagine we won't need any other insulation. The plumber fits a boiler onto the end of those little pipes that have now disappeared for ever under 13 tons of concrete screed. We even have two giant boxes standing in the living room, one marked 'This way up. Refrigerator' and the other, 'Oven unit. Unpack before using.' But the task I'm really anxious to get done is the laying of the precious limestone slabs.

The supplier – the man who told us the story about his customer boiling stone in blackberry jam – keeps changing the price, then insisting we pay the whole lot upfront before we've taken delivery. He has a strange way of dealing with customers – or with me anyway. He doesn't *ask* for a cheque, or *enquire* when would be a suitable date for delivery. He *orders* me to pay now, and *instructs* me to prepare for its delivery on a date that's OK for him.

'It's probably you,' suggests Maggie. 'I expect you're getting worn down by the whole project. You're getting oversensitive.'

'No, I'm not!' I protest. 'He doesn't have to grovel. The occasional "please" would do. I just think it's a funny way for someone in business to behave. And we're paying him thousands of pounds for these earth-shatteringly miraculous – sorry – very special tiles. It makes you wonder if he's not a charlatan.'

'OK,' says Maggie, 'so why don't you do a bit of background research on him?'

Good idea. His website gives a number for a regional office. I decide to call it to see if it's real or not.

Me: 'May I speak to Archibald Loosetrap?'

Other end: 'Who is this?'

Me: 'Am I speaking to The Astonishing Floor Co?'

Other end: 'I'm no longer associated with that company.'

Me: 'May I ask why?'

Other end: 'No you may not. It's none of your business.'

Me: 'Is there any problem with the company?'

Other end: 'I didn't get on with Mr Loosetrap.'

Me: 'I'm a customer and about to pay to him a large amount of money. Would you advise me not to do so?'

Other end: 'No, no, not at all. Thank you. Goodbye.' Click.

So I suppose that's a good sign.

Then two minutes later I start to wonder. 'When he said "Not at all", do you think he meant, "No, don't give him your money on any account"?' I ask Maggie.

'I wouldn't have thought so,' she replies. 'If you ask someone, "Would you advise me not to do so?" and they reply, "Not at all," that means they wouldn't advise you not to do so.'

I scowl and say, 'I'm getting lost in all the negatives.'

'Well, what was his tone of voice?'

'What do you mean?'

'Did he say it sort of quickly and upbeat: "Not at all" breezily and cheerily. Or, did he say it sort of gloom-laden and shaking his head?'

'How do I know what he was doing with his head? It wasn't a webcam call.'

'You know what I mean. That kind of thumbs-down tone of voice. Anyway, what was your first reaction? That he was telling you it was OK? Or that he was warning you off?'

'The first. Definitely. I think.'

So that night Maggie and I hold a meeting to assess what alternatives there are. The kitchen table is wrist-deep in little squares of stone glued to bits of card, and brochures picturing Elizabethan mansions shot from the knee down. After a couple of hours of shuffling them around like a game of dominoes that can't get started, we call a halt to try and decide where we are.

'There's nothing else that'll go with the exposed stone wall and the oak like the Italian slabs from the dodgy bloke,' I say.

'And there's nothing else that won't scratch and stain and so have to be hacked up every time there's a spill,' Maggie adds.

So we decide to recognise it as a risk, go ahead anyway, and to sign a lifetime-binding pact which specifies that we'll still be nice to each other if it all goes wrong.

It's the turn of the plasterers next. Jonathan and Dave. I could watch them all day.

'It's a regression to your childhood,' says Maggie.

It's true. I loved the circus when I was a kid, and these two guys are one of the best acts I've seen since.

They're on stilts. Their boots are about 4 feet above the ground.

'It saves a lot of time,' says Jonathan, as he crouches, balancing, under the main oak cross-beam 8-feet high above the living room floor, 'given the height of this place.'

'We'd have to keep putting up scaffolding and ladders then taking them down again,' says Dave, addressing the words to the plasterboard over his head as he nails it in place.

Both of them are stamping backwards and forwards. That's the thing about stilts. If you stand still, you topple over like a felled tree. So you've got to keep moving. Not easy when the two of you are trying to work together to fix a 2-metre-square board up above you, so you can't look what's going on 10 feet below, around your stilt feet. And down there are all manner of wrenches and gash cable and buckets and bags of screws left on the floor by the electricians, the plumbers and the carpenters. For earth-bound walkers it's a game of hopscotch to get from one end of the living room to the other. For Jonathan and Dave, it means their stilt footwork has to be even fancier.

So they perform a surreal dance, rotating round each other, balancing the giant board over their heads with one hand, a drill or a bucket of wet plaster in the other, their bodies swaying from side to side in order to shift their centres of gravity, while their long stilted legs tramp in a peculiar sideways motion as though they've got dislocated hips. Time after time, one of them wobbles and looks like he's going to tumble as his stilt gets caught, or the two guys bump into each other. But at the last moment, they'll stab out a stilt in the direction of the drop and stay up in the air, the drilling, or nailing, or plastering uninterrupted.

By the end of the day, bits of mushy plaster have dripped from the ceiling, leaving Dave and Jonathan looking like they've come off worse in a custard-pie-throwing contest. But like all professional clowns of course, behind the funny faces and near prat-falls, are skilled, athletic performers. I never have any doubt that they're doing a good job.

CHAPTER 29

SAVING THE WHALE – OR THE HEDGEHOG AT ANY RATE

On a dull, unpromising morning in early March, I suddenly catch sight of two little green shoots heroically fighting their way up through the compacted rubble by the concrete mixer. I've no idea what they are. Must ask Maggie. But their appearance suddenly makes me look ahead to when this will be our courtyard garden. And I realise – the end of the whole project is… well, not exactly within sniffing distance. But it is just around half a dozen corners now. The problem is we've got to give a month's notice to the landlords at Mill Cottage in Blockley. We've already extended by two months, what with the snow and the roof and the rest of the delays. So we need some kind of estimate of when we might move in.

Move in! The words fill me with terror. I start to make a list of all the things still to be done. Things like take delivery of kitchen appliances, hang doors, paint inside of house, install both bathrooms, fit skirting boards. And we haven't even got these limestone slabs down yet. In fact they haven't been delivered. It goes on and on.

The bad news is that a lot of these jobs depend on other things having been done first. I try to draw a chart, with little blocks representing each job with dates when they could be finished. This shows us moving into The Old Stables in about two years' time. The not-quite such bad news is that there are some things which could be finished off while we're living here. Like painting the walls for instance, or putting in fitted wardrobes. I'm going to need Nik's help to get any kind of accurate picture.

When I catch him on-site next morning, he walks round the rooms and has a quick tot-up of what's outstanding.

'I could get the carpenters, plumber, decorator and electricians all working at the same time,' he suggests. 'So long as we don't get some unforeseen nasty coming out of nowhere, I reckon you'll be in by mid May.'

'Crumbs!' I exclaim. 'About four weeks' time.'

Nik nods. 'That's so long as Maggie doesn't mind Colin the carpenter and Michael the decorator sharing your bedroom for a few months.'

And there's me thinking he's joking.

'What yer goin' to do with them fences?' It's a thin, elderly chap, waving one of his two sticks at what for the last nine months we've been calling – with no sense of irony – 'the front gates'. "Cos if yer goin' to chuck 'em, I'll 'ave 'em.' Jason has just started to unscrew the hinges on which the two temporary panels swing open during the day. This is where the new roadside wall's going to go.

'No, I don't think we'll want them,' I say.

'Expect you've heard of me,' he shouts from under his flat cap, maybe not having registered my reply. 'I run The Stow Cat and Hedgehog Sanctuary.' He delivers each word separately, then pauses for the import of the announcement to sink in. 'See, if you don't want 'em...' He waves both sticks this time, and for a moment I think he might topple over. '... I can use 'em. For the cats.' But he's solid as a row of beans again. 'If your man here,' Jason's on the end of a stick now, 'could bring 'em over...' I raise a quizzical eyebrow at Jason, who nods. '... you'd be doing a service for the needy little animals of the community.'

'No problem,' I say.

'Shouldn't take him more than an hour to put 'em up,' he adds over his shoulder as he makes his way back down the road.

One of the several jobs we're getting on with while waiting for the screed to dry out, is building the perimeter wall. Here's a brainteaser. How much does a 1 metre length of drystone wall, 1.8 metres high, cost? In other words, a section about the size of a decent garden gate. Answer: (not counting the foundations, which would be extra, but which we dug out ready when the apprentice archaeologist came to call) 500 quid.

Why? Because the Cotswold stone is anything up to £90 a square metre (that's laid edgeways in a wall, not on the ground as crazy paving) and a drystone wall has a front and a back. Add to that, the labour of an expert stone-wall builder at around a further £50 a square metre. So that's £140 times two (for both sides) multiplied by 1.8. To save you reaching for a calculator, that's exactly £504. This is a shocker when Nik points it out to me, because we'll need something like a 35-metre run. That's £17,500. Just for a garden wall!

'Why fifty quid a metre for the labour?' I squeak.

'It's a skilled job,' Nik replies. 'And the other thing is, it's heavy work. The stones are a helluva weight. You're forever heaving them up, seeing whether each one fits, taking it down, trying another one. You need a strong, fit bloke to do it.' I get the point. 'One thing we could do though, is see if Bella...' – my shoulders droop at the sound of the planning officer's name – '... see if Bella would let us do block-work on the inside which you could have rendered in a light colour. That would save you some cost. It'd also give the courtyard inside a bit of a Mediterranean look.' And he adds, 'Maggie'd like that.'

Perceptive. She does. And remarkably, so does Bella. So that's the plan.

By the time I arrive on-site the following Monday, Simon has finished laying the block wall along the front, by the road. And there's another of these old geezers there, waiting to scrounge whatever's going begging. This one's small, no more than 5-feet tall in his dusty boots, with glasses and a grubby woollen cap of indeterminate hue. I'm determined this time that, although I'm happy to donate any unused blocks to the local badger reservation or sparrow clinic, we can't afford to keep stumping up for labour costs to erect the stuff as well.

'Good morning,' I say, businesslike.

''Ow do,' he replies.

'We might have a few breeze blocks left over,' I say, taking the initiative, 'which you could use to *build your own...*' – I stress the words – '... badger playpen or avian operating theatre.'

'Pardon?'

'This is Bill,' Simon interrupts. 'He's the waller.'

'The "whaler",' I repeat, half wondering if Simon in his Gloucestershire accent is telling me this man helps rescue large marine mammals.

'The drystone waller,' Simon amplifies.

'The drystone waller,' I'm repeating it to give my brain time to match what my eyes are showing me of the little chap in front of me, with the information it already holds on this subject.

''Ow do,' says Bill again, and pulls off a gigantic dusty glove to shake my hand.

'So you're the drystone waller.' I'm looking down onto the top of his head, as I take his bony grip in my hand.

He nods three times. 'So it's down 'ere and round the corner you want done,' he asks.

'Yes, it's quite a lot,' I say. 'Are you sure you've built a wall this size before?'

Bill puts his cap back on and prepares for a major announcement. 'The biggest job I ever did,' he declares, 'was down near Stroud. Round the outside of a big 'ouse. Do you know 'ow big that wall was?'

'No. How big?'

'One and a 'alf miles from end to end.' He pauses for effect, with justification.

'Strewth! How long did that take?'

'Just over nine years.'

'Crikey! Didn't it get a bit boring?'

'Ooh, no,' he comes back quickly. 'You see, every 500 yards or so…' – he pauses again – '… there was a right-angle bend.'

And he breaks into a cackle.

He wants to go to a nearby quarry to look at the quality of their stone before we place an order. So we arrange to go together that afternoon when Maggie can join us.

'Best take your car,' he says. 'You wouldn't want to go in my old trap.' He points across the road at what looks like the remains of a crash on the Kalahari Desert Rally. 'You can't get stone dust out, once it's got into the upholstery. So she's just for work. Then at home I've got my best car, as I keep for going out.' He does a little mock tap-dance to indicate his social life. 'Just hang on a minute,' he says, and he comes back a moment later with some cloudy grey plastic sheeting which must have started life transparent. He spreads it over our rear seat, climbs in and away we go.

'So, how old do you think I am?' he starts off.

Now, we've all been through this lots of times, so Maggie says, 'Ooooh. I don't know. Fifty?'

'I'm nearly seventy. Divorced. I've got twin sons. How old do you think they are?'

It's my turn. 'Ooooh. I don't know. Thirty-five?'

He can see I'm looking at him in the mirror. He winks.

'Fourteen.' He cackles, and I glance back in time to see a cloud of stone dust tumble from his hair. 'And they live with me, not their mother. My last job,' he goes on, 'was round some luxury flats, near where Princess Anne lives. Do you know how much they're asking for them flats?' This time he doesn't wait for our guess. 'Three-quarters of a million quid. Three-quarters of a million! I ask you. For a flat half the size of my cottage. But I tell you, if there'd been as much stone-laying work around when I were starting out years ago, as what there is now, I'd be buying a couple of them flats for my lads.' His cackle turns into a cough. It's the stone dust again.

At the quarry, he ferrets through bag after bag of rough hewn blocks before he pronounces them OK. We then spend ten minutes talking into a hole slightly larger than a letterbox in the side of a shed. The customer services manager, or whatever they're called at quarries, is on the inside. When *we're* speaking, we see one ear and an eye. When *he's* speaking, his nose and mouth come into view. Maybe they've discovered a way to gain a psychological advantage during price negotiations. It can't be entirely satisfactory for the quarry, because we come away with a deal which is a big improvement on Nik's first lot of figures.

'It depends on 'ow old the stone is,' Bill explains. 'If it's maggoty old cack from some rackety barn, it'll cost twice as much as the brand new stuff.' And he coughs and cackles till we can hardly see him for the stony plume of dust. The first load will be delivered that afternoon.

The next morning, I arrive around ten to find Bill explaining the obscurer techniques of drystone walling to two American tourists.

'Anyway,' I hear him tell them, 'I've got to get on. It's time for my coffee. I 'spect you want to take my photo.' He's not actually laid any stone yet, so they make do with one of him smiling in front of Simon's newly placed breeze blocks.

CHAPTER 30

KING PENGUINS AND MINIATURE VAMPIRES

'**H**ow's the village thesis coming along?' asks Maggie, carving her T-bone steak with enthusiasm. We've decided to treat ourselves to a meal out at The Talbot in Stow's Market Square. It's to celebrate not too many things going wrong this week.

'Confusingly,' I reply.

'How's that? I thought that ever since the deep depression of Hogsthorpe, you'd been to villages that are all perky and lovely.'

'Not really. Some of them are like Hogsthorpe, but posher.'

'You mean too many pensioners, and no football team.'

'That's right. But it's not as simple as that. Some manage to have a balance for instance between upmarket and cheaper houses and still look chocolate boxy.'

'Let me guess. Like Bledington.'

'Right. But it's not got a shop. And nowhere for locals to work.'

'I thought you'd decided that it's a mistake to think of villages as places where people work.'

'Partly true. But then the bigger ones like Stow or my own childhood home in Newthorpe *do* have businesses with jobs for locals.'

'So are they anachronisms? Villages. Or have they found a new role?'

'Well, that's the mammoth puzzle. One thing's sure. Whatever people believe who move home from cities to villages, there wasn't some golden age of rural life back in village history waiting now to be recaptured. The past of villages is a tale of struggle against starvation, death in childbirth, bubonic plague and similar man-made and natural atrocities. Life in villages has never been as comfortable as it is in the twenty-first century.'

'So there's no such thing as regenerating a village?'

'I don't know. Some need some sort of life putting into them. I can think of some that you'd call 'villages' for no other reason than that they're small.'

'Leafield, you mean.'

'Yes. If you could have a suburb without the 'urb', Leafield would be it.'

Maggie picks up the last double-fried chip from the communal bowl between us and pokes its end into the little pile of salt on her otherwise empty plate. 'I know a village that must be the last word in self-regeneration,' she declares, raising her eyebrows and waving the chip in front of me like a mini-flag at a royal wedding.

'Where's that then?' I ask, making a vain attempt to snaffle the triumphant chip for myself.

'Packingham.'

'Packingham. You mean Packingham in Norfolk?'

'No. Packingham-in-Stayle south of Bath.'

'Oh sure, a long way south I think.'

'So have you ever been there on a sunny Sunday afternoon?'

'No. Can't say I have.'

'We should go and take a look,' says Maggie. 'How about tomorrow?'

'It sounds an all-day trip to me, and I'd planned to go to the gym tomorrow.'

'The forecast is for temps in the twenties. You could maybe put off the weight-loss campaign for a day?'

'OK,' I nod and pick up the menu. 'Do you want to share a sticky toffee pudding?'

'There's one,' snaps Maggie, pointing at a camper van backing out 50 yards ahead to reveal its prized parking spot. We're on our third circuit of a car park which, if it were empty, would allow you to appreciate the curvature of the earth's surface. Eight coaches sit brooding side by side, their droop-eared wing mirrors ever alert.

'Have you got any pound coins?' I call over to Maggie. 'If you want to stay long enough for more than a cup of tea, it's £5.50.' Once she's scrabbled about in her bag, we join the river of humanity which is sliding past the green THIS WAY TO VILLAGE sign. We put our heads down and drive forward.

The first thing I notice is that the lower-body uniforms of our fellow visitors are either below-the-knee shorts with flip-flops, or brown support hose with orthopaedic shoes. Maggie and I feel intruders without a buggy or a walking stick between us. We move in a herd, by the same instinct that the management of Disney World exploits to keep its customers on the move, for a quarter of a mile down an alleyway between high stone walls before being disgorged into the teaming heart of Packingham-in-Stayle.

Packingham is one of 847 places on this earth which are referred to as 'The Venice of...' According to a colourful picture map we linger in front of, we're in THE VENICE OF THE SOUTH WEST. Through the crowds sauntering back and forth in front of us we can just make out the reason for this epithet. As far as I'm aware, Packingham does not have many frescoes by Tiepolo, nor a basilica overlooking a vast piazza where if you stay long enough you will meet everyone in the world, nor even gondoliers singing *Santa Lucia* on a network of canals. Maggie and I dodge through the surge of toddlers, dogs, grannies, mums and dads to take a look at what this Venice has: a very nice stream about 20-feet wide running right through the middle of the village with some pretty little bridges.

On each bank there are swathes of grass. I can tell it's grass because I can just make out some patches of green in between the picnic blankets and stretched-out support hose and white legs. In the water itself, which is only a couple of inches deep, hordes of kids, ranging from roughly two to eight years, are variously fishing with pink nets on canes, towing each other along on transparent mini-dinghies, kicking the water with their orange Crocs, or just paddling. If you screw up your eyes and fire up your imagination, you can see that the bridges, the stream and its banks, on a quiet day, would make a charming scene.

Maggie must have spotted some upward turning of my nose because she says, 'Oh come on. It's a wonderful place for families on a sunny day like this. I'd have loved it when I was a kid. Look what fun they're having. It's like going to the seaside.'

'Sure,' I say, convincing nobody.

It takes us about ten minutes to cross the nearest narrow footbridge. On the other side, we get swept sideways for a few paces by the dawdling masses, our ears filled by cries of 'Angelina/Brad/Claudia, watch where you're going!'

I look up at the signs on the old buildings beyond the ranks of packed cafe tables. LILLY'S RESTAURANT AND TEA ROOM, GIFTERAMA, THE RIVER RESTAURANT AND ICECREAM PARLOUR, THE I. OF MAN FLEA MARKET... 'The Isle of Man Flea Market!' I take a second look. Subtext: IN AID OF THE I.OF MAN DONKEY SANCTUARY.

We decide to take a look at one of the principal man-made lures of Packingham. This is about 500 yards away along the river. Our journey gets a little less slow as the people-density begins to drop to approximately two per square metre. There's also enough green appearing alongside for a dad to tap a red beach ball back and forth to his giggling toddler, and two small girls are able to skim pebbles across the stream without braining half a dozen other kids, and instead merely scatter a couple of dozy mallards.

ANIMAL WORLD. We've arrived and join the queue to pay. The accents around us are Welsh, Japanese, Brum and German. A sign informs us, RESERVÉ AUX ENFANTS SOUS SURVEILLANCE ADULTE PERMANENTE. The management of Animal World clearly knows which nation can't be trusted with the surveillance of children and, what's more, which nation's adults themselves might stop being adults at any moment and start demanding an ice cream or lapse into uncontrollable tantrums because they're tired. Bearing in mind this frightening prospect, we pay £14.50 for two and enter.

An ear-splitting screech makes us look up and see a macaque monkey swinging from a pole. We walk on. We read on a board that Animal World has fifty-three species of small wild animals and forty species of birds on display. The first we come across is a lapwing from Thailand. It's got a dull brown back, and is trying to attract attention by balancing on one leg, but nobody stops to look at it. The next exhibits might make you pause for a moment to see whether they're as exotic as their name suggests. *Phodopus sungorus*. There seem to be about twenty of the little creatures running about their enclosure and up and down ladders. They look like hamsters to me, which it turns out is what they are, all the way from Siberia. But the path in front of their little cage is empty too. The snowy owls have better luck at pulling in an audience. 'Come and see this one,' shouts a dad. 'It's Hedwig from *Harry Potter*!'

But the winning votes in the popularity poll by a fair margin go to the king penguins. There are about a dozen of them wandering about their enclosure with their flippers hanging away from their bodies, like multiple George W. Bushes walking out of the White House for a press conference. I suppose it's their humanoid characteristics that draw the crowds – that and the fact that king penguins manage to be comical without feeling the need to invade Iraq. One end of their enclosure appears to be in use as a rubbish dump.

There are two battered pub parasols and a heap of rusty metal there. I point this out to Maggie who says she thinks it may be a sculpture. Perhaps this is what the penguins do for therapy. Much of the enclosure is built high up which makes it difficult for the children to get a good view, so one mum helps her little girl clamber up the rocks next to the glass-sided pool so she can balance over an IT CAN BE DANGEROUS TO CLIMB ON THESE ROCKS notice. Admittedly the wording is hedging its bets with that 'can be'.

Back outside Animal World, we decide to go to another of Packingham's famous attractions, the Miniature Village. Both Maggie and I have vague memories of coming to see this as children. There are no signs to send us off in the right direction, and there doesn't seem much point in asking any of the German or Welsh ice-cream-eating buggy-pushers. But, as we pass the toilet block with an entry like a London underground station, we do spot a chap getting out of his car by the bottle bank to unload a clinking box from his boot.

I trot over and ask, 'Excuse me. Could you tell us the way to the Miniature Village please.'

'Hmm,' he replies. 'Well, I don't think it's that direction.' He points across the Animal World car park. 'I've lived here two and a half years, I should know.' I give him an encouraging smile. 'I can tell you where the village museum is. Or the model railway exhibition?' I switch to a slight headshake with intake of breath. 'You don't want the village museum. You want the Miniature Village.' I grunt, smile and nod. 'I get a feeling,' he says with deliberation, 'that it's that way.' He points across the road and down a bit.

'OK thanks,' I say. 'Do you mind if I ask you something?' It's his turn to nod, obviously keen to atone for his ignorance. 'Is it a nice place to live, Packingham?' Maggie's just arrived in time to hear this. She groans and backs away.

'Yes. We love south-west England,' he answers. 'It's not like this every day in Packingham, you know. All these crowds. It's only when the weather's nice. Well, I suppose if I'm honest, it's busy most of the summer. And on nice days in spring and autumn as well.'

'Is that a pain?'

'Not really. We live over there.' He gestures over his shoulder. 'On the edge of the village. It's like anywhere else there. We've got a little bungalow.' He's warming to his theme. 'The wife likes it. She's got a nice summer job in one of the gift shops. Keeps her busy, and the extra cash is always handy, eh?'

I thank him, and we head back in the direction we've come from, stumble on another coloured map that we'd walked straight past, and a minute later we're paying seven pounds for two to get into the Miniature Village.

'Have you been busy?' I ask the woman in the ticket booth.

'Very. As usual,' she answers in a cut-glass accent that sounds more used to addressing the WI than answering questions from the hoi polloi.

'Is it mainly families?'

'Yes, and older people who came here as children. And that can mean some *very* old people,' she adds with a note of pride, 'since the model first opened in 1935.'

'Wow,' I say believing that to be the dutiful response.

It is, there's no doubt, a wonder of patience and skill. All those little pieces of stone, bonsai maple trees and dolls house lace curtains beneath perfectly tiled cottage roofs, one of which brushes my bottom as I bow to a passing elderly Japanese couple. And it is such an exact model of the real village of Packingham-in-Stayle that there's even a miniature version of the miniature village in the Miniature Village, which of course provokes the question: is there also a miniature version of the miniature version of the miniature village in the Miniature Village?

Actually, Maggie and I discover, when we identify the centre of the village where the stream and bridges are, that it's an exact replica not of the village as it is today, but of the village as we might imagine it in that mythical golden age past. So there's no replica sprawl of cafe tables all along the riverside, no replica overflow of gift displays across the pavements, no replica Animal World, no replica earth-curved car park, no miniature cars – oh, except for one which is secured against thieves by what looks like a bath plug chain and small padlock – and most of all there are no hordes of replica people.

I'm not complaining. It's just that the Miniature Village, with its endless walls of dirty weathered stone, has a gloomy and deserted air. It's more like a haunted village in Transylvania than the vibrant jewel of regenerated villages in the English south-west. This impression is reinforced as we walk past the miniature parish church, through whose windows leak tape-recorded strains of what sounds like the most severe passage in Bach's *Easter Oratorio*, the sort of mood music Hammer House of Horror Films used to choose when the vampire's shadow stretched up the wall.

'Have you noticed something about our fellow visitors?' I ask Maggie.

She looks around. 'What's that?'

'No kids. They're all adults. Not a single child to be seen.'

'Could be a coincidence.'

'Could be. Or maybe today's kids are so used to exploring video game cities or watching cartoons of *Postman Pat* in Greendale Village, where everything's colour and fast movement, that this all just looks dead to them.'

Back outside in the land of toddlers, dogs, colour and fast movement, a woman screams as we draw level with her, pointing towards a clutch of five-year-olds pushing each other over in the water, 'Oy, Cameron, go back and get that bat! Now!' Obviously a Conservative supporter.

As we leave Packingham, driving past several car-packed fields advertising ALL DAY PARKING £2, Maggie asks, 'So, what do you think?'

'Well, I take your point that Packingham-in-Stayle is a brilliant place for all these millions of mums and dads and kids and grannies who visit it. And of course that means lots of jobs for the people who live here. But it just seems to be at the price of completely destroying what could be a charming village.'

'"Charming" huh? What would Ralph have to say about that? Wouldn't he say you're happy only if a village is turned into a tasteful little paradise for middle-class retirees? But if it's made into a paradise for ordinary working families, you don't like it.'

'I'm just saying it's not for me.'

'You've got to admire the commercial enterprise of the people of Packingham, though, haven't you?'

'Ah, there speaks a free-market capitalist businesswoman. Ralph would be on to you for that as well.' And as we pass a couple – Japanese probably – photographing some horses in a field by the main road, I add, 'I just think the place is OTT. If I'd wanted crowds, I'd have stayed living in London.'

CHAPTER 31

THE END IS NIGH...
BEWARE!

'Hmmmm.'

As a judgement, this is pretty damning. It comes from Tony, my old Oxford chum, the one with the strong views on the word 'community'. He's over from North Carolina and staying with us in Blockley for a few days. He's getting the VIP tour of the construction. We're standing in the living room next to a concrete mixer. Dave and Jonathan are slapping plaster on every visible bit of breeze block. And sludge and dust are sticking to our feet because Simon has been slicing the top off the concrete block, which one day will be a kitchen counter, with a super-sized circular saw that cools itself with water while it cuts. I've just told Tony we plan to move in here in three weeks' time. So, that 'Hmmmm' is an essay in scepticism.

But I'm not downhearted. I can dismiss Tony's comment, learned sage though he is, because 'Conversion of The Old

Stables' is a specialist subject on which I could do a Master's degree based on eighteen months' practical experience.

Behind the dirt and apparent chaos, I can recognise the positive in having all these craftsmen working alongside each other. Michael the decorator has even started painting the main bedroom ceiling. In fact, there's only one real hurdle now to be leaped, and that's getting the limestone floor laid. Once the screed has fully dried out, we'll be able to get that done. Then it's a quick downhill dash – fitting the kitchen and finishing the bathrooms – and we'll be in. You can almost touch the hope in the air. And as Tony and I leave, I give a cheery wave to Bill, who's just finishing off his lecture before an audience of three Australians – a couple and what looks like their elderly father. 'So, how old do you think I am?' I hear him ask as we get into the car.

The limestone slabs are to be laid by the first woman to work on the project since Anthea drew up the plans. 'About time,' says Maggie. And I point out the symmetry. Anthea started the project. Flora – that's her name – will be finishing it off.

'Well, not quite,' says Maggie.

'As good as,' I reply.

So, as the big day approaches, Nik and Simon clear all the muck and junk off the screed floor. And when I call in at the site around 4.30, Mark the plumber is fixing the pump onto the end of the underfloor heating pipes. The system's got to be tested before the slabs go down.

The chippy's hung the oak doors in both places that Maggie and I agreed on.

Nik says, 'Are you ready for this?'

'What's that?' I ask.

'Sime, drum roll please.' He turns to Simon, who does a quick riff with his screwdriver on the lid of a toolbox.

And Nik hands me a rusty bit of wire with three keys on it. 'There,' he says. 'That's official. It's now a house. Not a building site.'

It's an emotional moment. In my acceptance speech, I blend tears with thanks to everyone, from Maggie to the vicar's dog, which has demonstrated its support even in the darkest days. 'The yellow stain on the side wall should fade over time,' says Nik.

Eight a.m. the next morning I arrive ~~on site~~ *at the house*, to find Nik and Simon there already.

'I've just turned the heating on,' says Nik.

The three of us stare down, huddled, heads bowed and silent, like relatives gathered around the bed of a sick child in a Tolstoy novel. After five minutes, there's the first sign of life. Over in the far corner, I can just see the faint, dry outline of a heating pipe on the damp screed. Within a minute, the complete intestines of tubework are showing through like a primitive X-ray image.

I can't contain a little cheer.

'I told you it'd be all right,' says Nik and pats me on the back. 'We're good to go.'

'But no Flora,' says Simon.

She was supposed to be here first thing. Nik gives her a ring. 'OK, sure. We'll see you tomorrow then,' he ends, then turns to us. 'She's been on holiday in the States for the past two weeks. The plane only got in half an hour ago,' he explains. 'She's still waiting for her baggage. She's a good lass though. She's promised to get the job done in a week.'

'It's no bad thing,' says Simon. 'We can leave the heat on full blast now for twenty-four hours to get it nice and dry.'

So with nothing more for me to do here till tomorrow, I head off. Bill's struggling this morning. Standing round him are four French cyclists whose English is not up to a Gloucestershire stone mason's vocabulary. 'No, let me start again,' he's shouting. 'Me, seventy. My lads, fourteen. That's their age.'

That evening, Maggie and I go over the plan. If Flora sticks to her promise and gets it done in a week, we've got the kitchen units, oven, dishwasher and fridge-freezer all ready for Nik's lads to install them. And the company that does the marble kitchen worktop have said they only need a week from measuring up to fitting. We're due out of Mill Cottage in two and a half weeks, so all should be fine. We're prepared for decorators and carpenters to be working around us when we're in, and of course Bill will still be finishing the garden wall.

Still, we know by now there's usually some little hiccup along the way, so like the pro's we've now become, we make a Plan B. It runs like this. Instead of moving straight from Blockley to The Old Stables, we'd get the removals people to put the furniture into storage for a couple of days, and we could go and stay with our friends in Evesham or even at a local B & B.

That night we fall asleep still smiling, and dream long dreams of a perfect house in a pretty village.

Next morning, I'm up early and off to Stow. As I get out of the car in Back Walls, a green van pulls up in front of me. A young woman gets out and takes a toolbox from the back.

'Hello there,' I call out. 'You must be Flora.'

She gives me an empty look. 'No.' She shakes her head.

'So do you work with Flora?'

'No. Who's Flora?'

'Sorry, my mistake. Flora is our...' – the cogs of my brain can be heard engaging – '... floorer.'

'I'm Justine,' she says. 'I lay stone floors. Who are you?'

I apologise and explain. 'Did you have a nice time in the States?' I ask.

'Sensational,' she replies. And we're back on track.

The first I know that something's wrong is when we bump into Michael the decorator coming round the corner of the block wall.

'It's a disaster area,' he says. 'The whole place is awash. There's nothing I can do.' And he stamps past us, paint cans clanking in his fists.

I rush on ahead of Justine and there inside our house I see it for myself.

There's water everywhere.

The newly plastered walls look like someone's been hosing them down all night. The giant window panes are the same. Water's streaming down them and standing in deep puddles on the concrete screed. Where Michael had already painted the ceiling, there are brown swirls on buckled boarding. As for the oak columns, they look like the trunks of mangrove trees sticking out of a Florida swamp. The door frame is so swollen with the water it's sucked up that when I try to open the French windows to let some of the water wash out, they won't shift.

I utter one unwholesome word, and my mouth stays open.

Justine crouches down and puts her hand flat on the boggy floor. 'I think it's the heating,' she says.

I visualise a leak in the system, of domestic tsunami proportions. 'The screed must have a huge amount of water in it,' she adds, 'and with the temperature in the piping sky-high, it's all been evaporating.' She looks around. 'It was chilly last night. So, the moist air's been condensing on the glass and on the ceilings and walls, turning into water again. Then it's all streaming back down to the floor, and around it goes again.'

I can see what she means. It's a vicious cycle of flooding.

'So where's all this water coming from in the first place?' I plead. 'The screed's been drying out for the past two weeks.' She looks puzzled, and I go on, 'It can't be coming out of the underfloor heating pipes, can it? Can it?' Surely it can't.

At that moment, Nik arrives.

'Christ!' That's all he says, before paddling across the room.

Justine's left. Like Michael, there's nothing for her to do.

Nik's trying to look nonplussed, as he pulls away the loose, sopping plasterboard, puts his hand against the rivulets of water chasing down the glass, and stirs a puddle with his boot.

'It's terrible,' I say. 'How's this happened?'

Nik shakes his head, and walks into the end bedroom. 'It's the same in here,' he calls. I go into the other rooms. In our bedroom, the plaster has broken away from the wall in a 3-foot-long chunk, and in the bathroom there's a pond several inches deep. In the kitchen, the water's condensing on the ceiling then pouring onto Nigel's massive cross beam. From there it's spouting down to the floor, where I can make out steam rising.

Back in the living room, Nik takes a deep breath. 'First thing,' he says, 'is to do a pressure test on the heating system. See if it's losing water.' He phones Mark the plumber to get him to come over. He's working the other side of the county, so we'll have to wait two hours before he can get to us.

I call Maggie. I can hear she's as close to tears as I am, telling her. 'What about all the work we've done so far? I mean the plastering and painting. And the oak. What's going to happen to the oak? And all that heating stuff under the floor?'

'I don't know,' I say. 'I don't know.' She'll call in for an update on the way to the shop.

Meanwhile, Nik's got hold of a broom and he's attempting to swill some of the puddles out of the door. It's strange though. Within minutes of a patch being cleared, the water just appears again as though in some diabolic conjuring trick.

'I'm afraid it's not worth bothering to try and brush it out,' he says. 'And I've turned off the heating. But the concrete'll retain the heat for hours.' And with that, Nik too leaves saying, 'Mark'll be here in a couple of hours. I'll be back by then.'

Maggie arrives, takes one look at the flood, gives me a hug, and retreats to the shop. She can't do anything either.

I don't like to tell her the horrible thoughts I'm having. If it *is* the underfloor heating, there'll be months of delay and tens of thousands of pounds worth of cost. The whole floor will have to be dug up, and maybe the oak frame will have to be replaced. And could that be done with the roof on?

CHAPTER 32

LOTTERY WINNER FALLS OFF YACHT

I have seen Death.

And it is tinned mixed vegetables.

This is how it happened. Last night I watched a report on the *Ten O'clock News* about care homes for the elderly. It included, as such items usually do, what's known in the TV news business as 'wallpaper', that is video images which are vaguely relevant to what the reporter is saying, but often aren't and can even be distracting. This wallpaper showed a very frail, very old lady who was getting help eating her lunch. On her plate was a collection of small, almost colourless cubes, cylinders and balls. I was puzzled at first as to what they might be. Then I realised. They must have come from a tin labelled MIXED VEGETABLES.

So now I understand the truth. When – decades ahead I hope – I see in front of me a plate with tinned mixed vegetables on it, then I'll know. I'll know that this glorious thing called Life is over.

I think about that this morning as I wander, alone, round our building site. I want the thought of tinned mixed vegetables to help me get this flooding crisis into perspective.

It's drizzling now. But even being outside in the wet is better than standing inside, facing the disaster. And when it starts to rain in that sort of steady, determined way that makes you wonder if you'll ever see blue sky again, I go and sit in the car.

I mull over the varied consolatory aphorisms usually offered in such circumstances. They range from the true-but-useless ('It's not the end of the world') through the syrupy ('In every life a little rain must fall') to the downright fascist ('What hurts you makes you strong').

Maggie would say, 'You've got to be Buddhist about it.' Meaning you can never predict what's going to happen to you. Even a happy event can have disastrous consequences. In order to shoehorn myself into a Buddhist frame of mind, I try to think of an example. Lottery winner falls off back of yacht and drowns. Serves him right, I can't help thinking in a not very Buddhist way. What about the reverse? A disaster can be the prelude to something good, e.g. different man falls down manhole, suffers paralysing injury, but finds five pound note... OK, finds priceless jewels. My guess is he'd rather keep the use of his lower limbs than struggle on eBay to flog a tiara. I'm not doing very well at this.

There's an umbrella in the back of the car, so despite the rain, I decide to get out and go for a walk. At least the weather's not trying to con me into thinking all's right with the world.

As I head across the Square, the downpour suddenly delivers a force of water that wouldn't have been amiss 200 million years ago in the Mesozoic wet period. A gust rips my umbrella heavenward and I'm left holding a piece of conceptual sculpture. I splosh over to the nearest teashop, but there are so many people packed and dripping inside already I can't even get through the door. So I huddle in the porch, and am soon joined by a knee-length anorak with a very sensible hood.

A female voice from within it says, 'Hah, global warming, eh?'

'Yeah,' I reply, not having the enthusiasm to explain the difference between weather and climate. 'Wet, huh?'

Fortunately the anorak seems to think I'm being ironic, gives a little laugh, and asks, 'So how's the house building going?'

'Well, you know. Ups and downs,' I reply, then realising I'm not inviting much chumminess, add, 'Sorry, have we met before?'

'I live down the road from you,' comes the reply. 'And I know who you are.'

'Oh.'

'You're Mr Dress-Shop. There, I think it's easing off. Bye.' And anorak and hood scuttle away before I can pursue the discussion further.

Mr Dress-Shop. That's me. Well, I've been called worse. I'm just debating whether I mind having a bolt-on identity, when another deluged refugee hops onto the doorstep beside me.

'Hello Derek.' It's Jenni. She's the editor of *Stow Times* and a well-known figure around Stow. 'Phuuu,' she shivers, shaking the water off her own fully functioning brolly. 'You going in for a coffee?'

'Standing room only,' I explain.

'I bet there's room upstairs,' she says. 'Let's go and see.' She's right, and with no more than a few smiley 'excuse-me's and the odd 'I'm terribly sorry', we capture a leather sofa by the back window.

She asks about the building work. I give her a down-in-the-mouth summary. She sympathises, and I repay her thoughtfulness by enquiring how *Stow Times* is doing.

'Brilliantly,' she replies. 'We're now distributed to forty-one villages in the north Cotswolds.'

'What!' My bottom rises in shock from its black leather home. 'How many-one?'

'*Forty*-one.'

'Good God! That's extraordinary.' I should explain, so you can join in my astonishment, what and who *Stow Times* and Jenni are. She and her husband moved here eight or nine years ago wanting to join things, but found it near impossible to discover what clubs and societies were available. So they decided to do something about it. They produced a couple of sheets of listings, photocopied them 1,200 times, stapled the results together and personally delivered them around Stow. That's how it started. *Stow Times* is now a full colour, glossy design, fifty-two page magazine supported by high quality advertising. 'So what's been happening?' I ask. 'I knew you delivered to a couple of villages nearby, but forty-one!'

'Well,' she explains. 'If you think about it, Stow is a focus for thousands of people scattered in little settlements around the nearby countryside. They shop here, some come and work here, they might regularly drink and eat out in Stow. But at the same time they've got things going on in their own villages. So we thought, why not include them too?'

'But some of these villages must be quite a way away.'

'Sure. Some are even outside the county. But we've set up three 'regional editions' you could call them. One for Moreton, one for Bourton and one for Chipping Norton, each with special entries for the villages around them.'

'So how many copies per month?'

'We get pushed through 12,000 letterboxes.'

'Crikey! So how many readers is that?'

'Somewhere between thirty-six and forty-thousand.'

'Forty thousand readers! For *Stow Times*! But that's more than the number of people who buy *The Lady* magazine!' I happen to know this because I was recently condemned to leaf through a six-month old edition at the doctors when I'd forgotten my book, saw the circulation figure quoted, and I remember marvelling that there are still thirty thousand families looking for live-in nannies. Jenni beams and raises her eyebrows in confirmation, as I go on, 'Who delivers them all?'

'We've got seventy volunteers.'

'That's a small army,' I say, trying to calm my voice in case my repeated expressions of amazement come over as a slight on my perception of her organisational and editorial abilities rather than mouth-widening admiration. 'Why do they do it?'

'It's a trade-off. I put in their ads for the rural cinema, dog show or village fête and in return they deliver to their road. Oh, and by the way we've got some overseas subscribers now, in Canada and New Zealand. And a woman in Bermuda sends me £100 a year to have *Stow Times* posted to her.'

'So how do the finances work?'

'It breaks even. The advertising covers the cost of design and printing. But no one else gets paid.'

'Including you?'

'That's right. I just get my petrol expenses.'

'Well, what a success story!'

'Thank you. I think it's important because it helps make people feel a part of the place where they live.' She smiles. 'But I want to do so much more. I want to expand the magazine even further.' She stops for a moment while we both nod to a young couple – all grassy boots and soggy rucksacks – who are asking if they can share our table. She continues, 'One of the reasons why Stow is such a great place to live is not only because of its rich history, it's also a place with a future. You'll have to forgive me,' she goes on, 'I'm "banner-carrying", as my mother used to say.'

'So, do you reckon Stow's well-prepared for the future?'

'Yes, but we need more. Most of all we need a community centre. Somewhere that locals can hire for meetings, that the youth club could use for instance, and where there could be a museum. Can you believe that Stow – Civil War site, Iron Age fort and all the rest – doesn't have a museum!'

I'm nodding. 'Sure. You're absolutely right.'

She leans back. 'Well, if you'll excuse me, I need to make tracks, rain or no rain.' I thank her for her time, she wishes me lots of luck with The Old Stables, and we squeeze our way back downstairs through the packed wet ranks of coffee and hand-made-chocolate-cake consumers.

Something tells me that one way or another, Maggie's and my future is going to be here in Stow, and that one way or another it's going to be at The Old Stables. Flood or no flood. So I scamper through the rain, round the dog-leg of Church Street and along Fleece Alley before clambering back into the front seat of the car to wait for Mark the plumber.

By the time the wheels of his van shoot a muddy spray of water against my driver's side window, the air is so black that I can hardly make him out heading across the road. With his hoody up and a long piece of lead piping in his hands, he is the Grim Reaper of plumbers.

I scramble out and scuttle after him into the house. There's a further delay because he can't lay his hands on a certain spanner, so has to walk up to Stow Agricultural Services to buy one.

Nik arrives, nods, says nothing and potters round the place for want of anything else to do.

Mark returns and disappears into the boiler room. Nik does a running commentary. Mark is turning the boiler up to maximum, then taking readings at the point the heated water goes *into* the pipe network, and then where it comes *out* again. I hover at his shoulder.

'That's not going to speed him up, you know,' says Nik. In other words, it's slowing him down. So I slink away and sit on a stack of blocks where I soon feel the damp seeping up to my backside, and wait. It's fifteen years since I gave up smoking, and for the first time in at least thirteen, I might just have had one if it had been offered.

'Well,' says Mark, emerging at last from the boiler room and throwing back his Reaper's hoody, with nothing but a spanner in his hands, 'there's definitely no loss of pressure.'

'Hhmmhh,' I breathe again. 'So you're saying those little pipes buried under all that concrete screed are in mint condition?'

I study Mark's head for signs of affirmative inclination, and add, trying to encourage in him some sort of smile, however weak, 'Well that's something, isn't it?' Blank. I look over to Nik.

'Yeah, I suppose so,' he says. 'That doesn't help explain it though. We've just got to hope that for some reason this screed's got a lot, a *lot* of water in it.'

It's at this point I remember what the South African guy who laid it had told me. That he thought the slurry was extra runny at first. I now spill this news to Nik and Mark, my words a sloppy mix of excitement and apprehension.

'Well, that's probably it,' says Nik. 'It would make sense. But anyway, let's forget about what caused it for the minute. What we need to do now is get rid of all this water so it doesn't keep going round in circles. We need lots of heavy-duty dehumidifiers.'

So he goes off in his pickup to find some at the plant hire shop in Bourton-on-the-Water.

Mark hoods up again and trundles off back to wherever he was before, and I'm left alone once more, this time my brain embroidering an elaborate tapestry of solutions.

After thirty minutes of this, Nik's back and I'm helping him lug in a collection of weighty, battered steel boxes. By the time these dehumidifying monsters are all in top gear, the house is juddering with the combined din of eight motors sucking the moisture out of the air and sluicing it into eight knee-high buckets.

Nik and I review where we are over mugs of tea, leaning on the bonnet of his truck. The downpour's stopped.

'With the plaster and the paintwork, there's nothing permanent,' he says. 'They'll just have to be redone. Your heating system's probably fine. And we can only hope the floor will be as well, once it's thoroughly dried out. The oak looks a bit worse for wear right now. But my guess is it'll be OK. It'll just shrink again when it's dried. You might want to call Nigel, see what he reckons.' I nod and drink more tea. 'So really, at the end of the day, you've likely got two problems. Your costs are going to go up, because of stuff that's got to be done again. And you're not going to be able to move in when you thought you were.'

I phone Nigel, who commiserates, but says the oak should be no worse off than if it had been in a torrential thunderstorm, which is what the outside exposed columns and beams will have to put up with anyway. So that's a tick. I think.

I go round to Maggie's shop to give her the tidings.

She comes round from behind her counter and gives me a hug.

'Do you really think it's going to be OK?' she asks.

'Who knows? But it's for sure looking a helluva lot cheerier than it was first thing this morning. We've just got to let Nik and Simon get on with it, and hope there's no permanent damage.'

The shop's quiet, and we stand there speculating for the next half hour on why this has happened, how much it's going to cost us, how much longer it's going to take, but not whether the whole thing is a big mistake after all. I suppose we've invested too much hope and heartache in it to give up on it.

Then Maggie says, 'Maybe, this is a blessing in disguise. For the last few days before we move in, rather than drive some poor friends mad cluttering up their kitchen, or being miserable in a guest-house bedroom, why don't we clear off to the sunshine for a week or so? We'd be at the end of a phone if Nik needed to talk. And I think we might both go nuts unless we escape for a bit.'

Right again.

Like the tail of a comet, lesser setbacks follow in the wake of the main disaster.

When the dehumidifiers start rasping their throats and can find no more than an occasional mouthful to spit into their buckets, Justine comes back. But her water content gauge is the bearer of bad news. She shakes her head. 'Still too high,' she says. 'I don't want to trap any moisture underneath.' So we have to wait again.

Then the guys arrive with the slabs of granite for the kitchen worktops.

'It's wobbling,' says the foreman. I look quizzical. 'The kitchen units haven't been fixed properly.' He doesn't need to explain that sheets of rock weighing 200 kilos each probably need more than the odd 1-inch screw in the base units that will be holding them up. I phone Nik, who says he'll talk to the chippy. I then get a call from the outraged carpenter, who regards the accusation as a slight on his whole profession, and, in effect, condemns the kitchen worktoppers as Johnnie-come-latelies not worthy to lick the sawdust from the trainers of those that walk in the footsteps of Noah, Joseph and all the other great wood-joiners down the ages.

Ten minutes later, he calls back and explains that his apprentice has just confessed to having forgotten to tighten up the screws at the back of the kitchen units. I stop myself asking whether any of us would be here today if apprentices had been left to caulk the Ark without supervision. I settle instead for a disdainful 'Hah!'

When the kitchen bases have been made solid, the guys return to fit the granite. It's so heavy and cumbersome that it takes two men fifteen minutes and a pint of sweat to manoeuvre each of the three pieces into place. I keep out of the way. Then once the chaps are massaging their backs and pouring bottles of water down their throats, I go over to thank them and admire their work.

I shudder.

'I hate to tell you this,' I say, 'but the draining board channels are on the wrong side of the sink.' They take out the plans again, twisting them this way and that as though they're unfathomable works of modern art. The mistake was in the workshop. The middle piece has been cut wrongly. It'll have to go back, and because of the way they fit together, all three slabs have to come off again. The men's patience is up to Old Testament standards. Did Job come before or after Noah?

Then one sunny Friday morning, Justine pronounces the floor dry, and offers to work with her partner without stopping, through the weekend, to lay the limestone. We heap thanks on her, and a week later, we're able to shake her hand and coo over our long-yearned-for floor.

The effect is dramatic. For the past few weeks, since getting the doors on and the keys in our hands, I've felt a fraud calling this place 'the house'. Now, with the concrete gone, and with the creamy-butter-coloured, but rock-hard, faces of the slabs looking up at us, the words 'our home' now sit on my lips without blushing.

My suggestion that we should christen the place by smashing a bottle of Merlot on the floor, thus celebrating its invulnerability to scratch and stain, is rejected by Maggie, who instead shoves me into the car. We've got to finish clearing out Mill Cottage before we head for Birmingham Airport the next morning.

After three hours of mind-numbing duty, wrapping saucepans and dessert spoons in squares of white paper, we decide to reward ourselves with fish cakes, salad and sauté potatoes. Blockley's new community shop, cafe and post office has just officially opened.

'Hi guys, welcome,' says Chris from behind the counter. 'That's four pounds ninety, Mrs Stevens.' Then turning to us again, 'Grab somewhere to sit and have a look at the menu.'

The place is buzzing. There's only one table free. Doris, who used to work in the old shop across the road, greets us, takes our order, brings us drinks, and ten minutes later we're complementing her on the excellence of the food.

By the time we've finished my lemon meringue pie (Maggie doesn't eat puddings – well, not unless they're mine) the tables are starting to empty, and Chris, in maroon 'Blockley Village Shop and Café' apron, pulls up a chair and asks, 'Good?' indicating with a nod the clean plate and two spoons.

'Excellent meal,' we both say.

'How's it going?' asks Maggie.

'You've seen for yourself,' he replies. 'The cafe's overrun. And the shop too. People are telling us they do their main buy here rather go to the Moreton supermarket. And you remember we needed to raise £20,000 from local subscriptions. Well, we've got nearly £45,000.'

'That's brilliant!' I say. 'And are you sticking to your plan of no volunteers? Paid staff only?'

'You bet we are. We're employing sixteen local people. Part-timers on six-hour shifts. It's ideal for mums with kids at school.'

'And my guess is,' I say, 'that it's more than just a place to eat good food and buy your groceries.'

'You're dead on,' he answers. 'It's already becoming the hub of the village. There was a house broken into last week, and the police know we've got the emails of 400 households in the village – people who're on our mailing list – so the cops asked to send out a message to everyone telling them to take extra care locking up. Then the doctors' surgery have been in touch, asking if prescriptions could be left here when locals can't get into Moreton easily, when we get snow for example.'

We congratulate him, then explain this is our last day in the village before we move out. He hops up and shakes our hands, saying, 'Well, you don't have to live here to eat here.'

'Don't you worry,' says Maggie. 'You'll see us again.'

For ten days, in a *casita* with a south-facing view of mountains near Valencia, we manage not to call Nik. Then, on the eve of our return he rings us. All's fine. The water-damaged plasterwork has been repaired, the kitchen's finished with all its appliances plumbed and wired in, and the bathrooms are shiny white in all the places they should be. The furniture removers are delivering our stuff as he speaks.

We don't get much sleep that night with the thought that, this time tomorrow, we'll be in bed under the oak beams of The Old Stables for the first time.

CHAPTER 33

FIRST NIGHT NERVES – AGAIN

I wake with a jolt.

The bedroom door has opened and Maggie is sticky-taping her way out and into the living room of the The Old Stables. 'Uggh,' she says. 'What's wrong with this floor? And what on earth are you doing? It's five to six. How long have you been here?'

Too many questions. I'm still sitting on the packing case where I'd slumped after swilling the test patch of floor behind the TV, and as I straighten up, my back stabs where it's been draped sideways over something. A waist-high removals box, by the feel of it.

'Must've fallen asleep,' I mumble, coming back into the world. ''Sthebloodyflooragain,' I sigh. 'There's some sort of sticky mess coming up through it.' Maggie's bare feet back me up with delicate 'sick, sick, sick' noises each time they rise from the limestone slabs. 'It's never-ending,' I say. 'It's like a medieval curse, this floor.'

'How long have you been here?'

'I dunno. Since about three.'

'Oh,' she sympathises, walking over to put an arm on my shoulder. 'Come back to bed.'

I drop my gaze. 'Do that again.'

She strokes my head. 'Come back to bed and you can have a nice cuddle.'

'No. I mean, Yes. Just do that again. Walk away a couple of steps.'

She takes her hand from around my neck and moves backwards.

Nothing.

A lovely nothing.

Her feet leave the floor in unresisting silence.

'That's the bit I've just been swilling with hot water!' I cry. 'I did it three hours ago. The heat's been on all that time. And it's still OK!' I jump up, then stamp about on the test patch like a demented grape treader.

It's redemption. The floor has finally become a responsible member of society.

Three hours later, there's a knock at the door. I say to Maggie, 'There's a knock at the door.' The words have a warm and magical feel to them. 'There's a knock at the door' is what people say who have real houses. Like us.

It's Nik. He's carrying a huge bouquet of flowers. Maggie runs over and throws her arms round his neck. I pump his arm and clap him on the back. Not only has he brought flowers, he's got a glass vase as well to put them in.

'You are a genius, Nik,' I say. 'And not just for all this.' The sweep of my arm almost knocks the mop off the sideboard.

'Sorry we didn't get chance to finish the floor,' he says. 'Simon and me had just done mopping it over with some

318

cleaning stuff from the Co-op, when the removals blokes came. So we didn't get chance to swill it off with clean water.'

'That,' say Maggie and I almost in unison, 'is no problem.'

We spend the rest of the day hunting through the packing cases for saucepans and towels, and creating a little oasis of sofa, coffee table and TV. Our home is ours at last.

Well, for one day it is. Because Day Two sees the invasion.

By 0745 hours, Michael the decorator is whistling a merry jingle outside our bedroom door as he primes the skirting.

The carpenter's apprentice is measuring up for a wardrobe. I prepare to give him a headmasterly 'I'm-watching-you-Fosdyke-Minor' kind of a look, when he beats me to it with a jaunty, 'Y'orlright, Derek?' before putting his coffee mug on the ebony and mother-of-pearl chessboard that I brought back from Iran.

Simon, who's laying stone terracing in the courtyard, marches into the house and on into the guest bathroom. He leaves the door open, and Maggie and I look at each other while we listen to his manly tinkling followed by a flush, before he marches out again. We can't complain. Simon is one of the decorated heroes of the campaign. While he's still working here, it's his building site. We're squatters.

So these characters, plus the occasional electrician or plumber dropping by to fix a snag, are our housemates for the next three weeks. And that's not counting Bill, who spends all his coffee and meal breaks sitting just outside the door to avoid being mobbed by his fans. 'I 'ad some Austrian girls this morning,' he tells me as he munches his cheddar and pickle sandwich. 'There was eight of 'em. On a walking 'oliday.' He winks. 'They've all give me their phone numbers, and asked me to go and stay with 'em. Did I tell you about them flats near Princess Anne's place?'

I'm starting to get edgy. 'Look,' says Maggie. 'There are two choices. Either we have all the guys in at once and get the work done in two or three weeks, or we have them in one at a time, and it'll drag on for months and months.'

'OK, OK. I know. It's better to jump through a hoop of fire than walk over a mile of hot coals. It's just that this hoop seems to go on for a mile itself.'

'So find something productive to do.'

And, as it happens, I do have a nice little job up my sleeve that I've been looking forward to. Do you remember the old cart wheels my sister Anne spotted rusting half-hidden in a corner of the burgage about eighty years ago? (Eighteen months actually, but it seems like eighty years.) Well, I had the idea of turning them into a sculpture for the courtyard. It turned out there were three of these wheels (You could write a poem on what happened to the fourth. Pinched by an Edwardian spiv? Melted down to make the turret of a tank on the Western Front?) along with the iron end-pieces for the axles. The wooden wheels inside the iron rims, complete with all their spokes, collapsed into heaps of fine dust as soon as I went to pick them up. Still the rims will last for ever.

I assemble bits of cardboard and glue on the dining table, and come up with a sculptural design. It's a cross between a globe and a telescope (I can see it already: 'The pull of the stars and the drag of the earth create an unbearable tension in Taylor's work.' – Brian Sewell, *London Evening Standard*). Somehow the half-inch thick coat of prickly rust will need to come off, then the hoops will have to be welded together and painted.

So I scour the Internet for someone to execute the installation. I want a craftsman with experience of working with artists, not just any old wrought-iron gate-maker. The man Damien Hirst uses would do. But a quick google shows Hirst's got his own hundred-strong workshop. I find a company in Ayrshire. But 300 miles seem a bit far to go for the impromptu artistic consultations that'll be necessary. Then, when I've almost given up, I stumble on a welder's website that says, 'If you have a plan, a problem, or just an idea, large or small, one or one thousand, we are here to help you.' And what's more, this one's only half a mile from our old temporary home at Mill Cottage, Blockley.

I phone the guy: 'Is that Mick Keepence?'

'I'm afraid so,' comes the response in a Music Hall voice that I expect to add, 'I say, I say, I say, how does my dog smell…' or similar.

I drag the rusty rims – they're a yard in diameter and weigh about 70 pounds each – into the boot of the car, scraping the tailgate bodywork before they clunk in. It hardly matters. You could read much of the history of our stables conversion in the current condition of the car. There's the place where Jason 'touched' it with the JCB claw. The jagged lines on the top where I carried an oak brace without a roof rack. The multi-storey car park concrete embedded in the side where I was late for the bank manager. Not to mention the inch-thick skirt of caked mud from the hundred or so journeys back and forth between The Old Stables and Mill Cottage.

So off I go to find Mick.

Once in his yard, I open the boot, and he says, 'Ahh, tyres.' He strokes them, the rusty splinters sticking to his hands. 'Those old blacksmiths knew what they were doing,' he says, and he explains how the nineteenth-century wheelwrights used to weld these massive iron bands into a circle in the heat of the forge. Then while the metal was still red hot, they'd fit the wooden spoke-frame inside. When the iron cooled, it would contract and clamp tight round the wooden wheel. Perfect. Here's a man who'll love these bits of old iron while he turns them into our sculpture.

He tells me to come back a couple of days later when he'll have shot-blasted the pieces to get rid of the rust. And when I turn up on the Wednesday, there are the component parts of my sculpture in a corner of Mick's yard, gleaming in the sunlight as if they've just come out of a blacksmith's forge. He heaves them into his workshop, then, with a quick spot-weld, he 'tacks' them into the shape of my *Blue Peter* cardboard model. And when I think it's not quite right, he breaks them apart and tacks them again. His son then arrives and helps him hump the result down from the work bench. Back outside, his wife and daughter join us, half a dozen beagle puppies at their heels.

'So what colour do you want it powder-coated?' asks Mick. And I have to confess I don't know what this means. The two women explain it's a kind of long-lasting paint job carried out at a high temperature. Then they hold a debate on whether it should be gun-metal grey or rose red or sunset orange. They plump for the grey. And so do I.

Thus fortified, I return to The Old Stables. It's the end of the day, and Maggie and I have the place to ourselves. Or so we think. The front gate opens and in walk a dignified elderly gentleman and what could be his daughter.

'Oh, God,' says Maggie. 'They must have escaped from Bill's afternoon lecture. He had a whole busload of Japanese tourists spellbound for about two hours.'

'Yes?' I call through the open stable door. 'What is it you want?'

'Ee-eh,' says the frail old man, smiling and nodding. 'Ee-eh.' He moves his eyes along the whole length of The Old Stables, and adds, 'Ii desu yo.'

I return his smile, wondering if we should offer them tea.

Then the young woman says, 'My grandfather wishes to say to you that he admires your house. He believes it to be a very good house.'

'Oh thank you, thank you,' I simper, leaping to my feet. 'That's very kind.'

We all bow and smile to each other, and the granddaughter adds, 'It was also most generous of you to allow your servant to explain how to build such a wall as this,' – she touches Bill's stonework with the tips of her fingers – 'and to permit him to give such interesting insight into life of peasant in England.'

They bow once more and leave, shutting the gate behind them.

CHAPTER 34

PC JOBS' LOPSIDED HEART

'So remind me again which day he's coming.' says Maggie, her glass of Pinot Grigio balanced between forefinger and thumb.

'Next Friday,' I answer, sprinkling an extra tablespoon of flour into my mixing bowl. 'He says in his email that he'll be back from Cremona on Tuesday.'

'Remind me what he's been doing in Italy,' she asks.

'You know Ralph,' I reply, 'it was some study of Marxist social perfection in the Po Valley,' I reply, and give the pastry an extra hard pound with my knuckles.

It's noticeable that the output of expletives in the kitchen has fallen dramatically, now that things, e.g. garlic press, fish slice, that nifty bit in the food processor that grates cheese, can be relied upon to stay where they're supposed to be and not wander off. The incidence of swearing is now no more than you'd expect in the course of any creative cooking. The change has only been possible with the departure of Nik and Simon, of Mike the decorator, the carpenter's apprentice, and even Bill has said farewell to his last groupie. Autumn, signalled by the leaves from next door's sycamore blocking The Old Stables' gutter, has seen our siege and successful capture of the spare bedroom. The ceiling-high stacked boxes of unread novels, childhood photos and Great-auntie Phoebe's chipped potpourri urn, all the bits needed in humdrum life, are now suddenly available, and the spare bedroom has been liberated. We're all ready for our first staying guest: Ralph.

'He said before he left for Italy that he wanted to come and see us,' I remind Maggie, 'once we'd got settled into the new home.'

'I bet that's not exactly how he put it,' she says.

'No, you're right. He was rude about it in that all-English-villages-are-full-of-middle-class-retirees-trying-to-re-enact-*Lark-Rise-to-Candleford* sort of way that Ralph has.'

'Oh God, yes, I remember all that stuff now. It got under your skin.'

'Be fair. I've conducted an intellectual study of village life,' I say, gesturing with the rolling pin.

'Steady on,' says Maggie, as a spot or two of wine spills on the floor, 'I still don't know whether we should trust these floor slabs.' I ignore her concern – I've run out of worry for the likes of floor slabs – and start to clothe the salmon fillets in what will soon be croute. 'Go on then, tell me,' she challenges, 'how are you going to defeat him in this battle of intellects? What's the typical English village really like now? You've done enough research.'

I slide our supper into the bottom oven. 'Well, I think I've found out a few things that'll have him rattled. For a start there's no such thing as 'typical'. Hogsthorpe and Swinbrook, for instance are chalk and cheddar.'

'You mean hundreds of two-bed bungalows in parallel lines as against a cluster of exquisite eighteenth-century mansions.'

'Quite.'

'I don't think I'd want to set up home in either of those villages,' says Maggie.

'I know. I agree. Ouch!'

'I've told you to be careful with that fat-bladed chopping knife,' she warns.

I give my left thumb a quick suck, and attack the red peppers. 'OK, discovery number two. The idea of the English village as some eternal rural paradise, where all has for ever been right with the world, is about as accurate as *Jack and the Beanstalk*. If the history of Bledington is anything to go by, misery, poverty, starvation and the workhouse used to be just as common in agricultural villages as they were in the slums of the big cities.'

'And I guess what was true for Bledington was definitely true for the pit villages further north, like Newthorpe.'

'Yeah. Some Golden Age, huh, where Great-granddad Isaac Taylor celebrated his tenth birthday a mile underground, down a coal mine.'

'Hmm. But don't you think this'll provoke Ralph to rant on about the historical inevitability of the dictatorship of the proletariat?'

'Well, it might. But you've got to tell it how it was. The point is it's nonsense to talk about whether the English village can regenerate itself. The truth is most English villages in the twenty-first century are safer and more prosperous than they've ever been during the previous two and a half thousand years.' I shovel the pepper strips onto an ovenproof dish. 'What the English village is like these days is an altogether different question.'

'Did you know, by the way,' – Maggie reclines on a chair and puts her feet up on the adjoining one – 'that when Bill Bryson travelled through small town America, he invented the imaginary perfect town. He called it Amalgam. The question is, what does the English village Amalgam look like?'

'OK, now you're talking. Hang on a sec.' The rack above the baking salmon gives a clatter as I push in the dish brimming with red vegetables (you hardly notice the spots of blood) then chuck the oven gloves on top of the bread-maker, and join Maggie at the table. 'Well, I reckon you can draw up a list of things which will help a village along the road to perfection. By the way, I think Bill Bryson said that in his search along the back roads of the US, none of his little towns had got all the positive things. That's why he called the one where he'd like to live "Amalgam". It could exist only if you amalgamated bits from lots of different places.'

'OK, so it's pretty obvious, nowhere's perfect.'

'Sure. The thing is with the English village, some of those positive bits can't be acquired no matter how hard you try.'

'What, like thatched cottages or Victorian vicarages?'

'Exactly. Of course, not everybody wants to live in a cute zone. But a lot do. Personally, I'd rather look out on Cotswold stone cottages than concrete lockups in Liverpool Eight. And a pretty village can mean jobs – in the tourist business for a start – and jobs mean young people are more likely to stay rather than leaving the village to the oldies.'

'Packingham as opposed to Hogsthorpe you mean.'

'That's right. The good folk of Packingham-in-Stayle, as we know, have cashed in on their good looks. Though I have to say, for me, the place is like the young woman who realises her face and figure can be her fortune but then ends up as a spoilt brat of a supermodel.'

'That's a bit unfair to Packingham.'

'Possibly. For me, it's so commercialised that you have a job to make out the pretty, cute parts which are supposed to be its attraction in the first place.'

'OK, we agree to differ. So what's the next winning feature in the English village contest?'

'It's where they are geographically. For instance, Newthorpe's only four miles from an M1 junction, whereas it takes hours to reach poor old Hogsthorpe along zigzaggy narrow roads. Result, Newthorpe has got at least some jobs on tap, while the youth of Hogsthorpe leave as soon as they're old enough to buy a ticket for the weekly freedom bus to Scunthorpe and points south.'

'Hmm, that's sad.'

'It is.' I pause to top up my cranberry juice. 'Then, next on the list is a heart.'

Maggie prompts me: 'You said you thought that's something Condicote's got with its village green.'

'The famous Pound, yes. A village green, a market square, they're not just somewhere where people go and meet and talk, they're also somewhere you can take in at a single glance and say to yourself, "This is Condicote, this is what I belong to". Aston Magna or Hogsthorpe haven't got that kind of heart. They haven't got any kind of physical centre.'

'And Newthorpe?'

'It doesn't have anything like that...'

'What about that pub?'

'Not everybody goes to pubs. But Newthorpe could give itself a heart, a sense of its own identity if it looked to its Lawrence heritage.'

'So does that mean you think Swinbrook scores on this one?'

'Yes, I think it does. I suppose I'm saying that a bit of history can give a village something that people feel is theirs, that they all belong to, whether it's the history of Unity Valkyrie Mitford and her extraordinary sisters, or an Iron Age henge and a Roman road like Condicote's got.'

'So why don't either of us want to live in Swinbrook?'

'I think, because it's lopsided.'

'Now you've lost me.'

'Hang on, just got to check the croute's not turned to cinders.' Twenty seconds of clattering and delicate prodding show it hasn't, so I return and on we go. 'Lopsided. I mean it's too much of one thing. In Swinbrook's case, it's too precious. The village is like a museum occupied by millionaires. There's no variety. And how many villages in the whole country have got a philanthropic squire, like Condicote, turning down an income just to preserve the social balance of the village.'

Maggie nods. 'Leafield, I guess, is lopsided for different reasons.'

'It is, it is. You've got the point exactly. Leafield is a city suburb posing as a village. It seems to be end-to-end suburban houses and nothing else.'

'But at least you can say about Leafield that there's somewhere for people to work. It's not just a theme park for retirees, as Ralph might say.'

'True, though most people who live there don't work in the village itself.' I stop and ponder for a second or two. 'I'm always impressed by Newthorpe on that score. It lost its coal mine, but built an industrial estate on the old pit site.'

'OK, what about shops?'

'And post offices. Don't forget post offices. Yes, the death of the village shop cum PO is the story of the death of many an English village, or so it's commonly thought. Up springs Tesco and the dusty cornflakes packets next to the pensions counter are suddenly gone, and there instead is a chintz sofa in somebody's front room with only a picture window and a house name like "The Old Post Office" left to hint at what it used to be. And without the shop and John Major's postmistress biking into the mist, the village becomes just another estate of houses that happened to sit in the countryside. That's the theory on how villages die, anyway.'

'What do you mean, "the theory"?'

'You see, I don't think shops shutting actually *causes* a village to die. I suspect that in a lot of places, the last shop closing is just one more nail in the village's coffin. Or should I say, in some villages' coffins – the ones that were going to die anyway, because there were no jobs in remote parts of the countryside any more, or because in the less isolated villages the jobs are in a nearby town, and the village just becomes a dormitory.'

'But what about our friend Chris and the folk of Blockley?'

'Well, Blockley's not a dying village. It's got a lot going for it. It's pretty, it's got a heart, a village green. But Blockley certainly moves up the ideal village scale because of its shop-cafe-post office.'

'So you're not suggesting a shop or two aren't important to village life.'

'No. They obviously are. And this, of course, brings us on to one of the most important things a village can have.'

'A sense of community?'

'Ooh no, bad word. Censored. It doesn't mean anything. What Blockley's got is fiery spirits.'

'Paraffin!' she grins.

I ignore her. 'Fiery spirit, I'll have you know, is a technical term sociologists use for people living in villages who care about the place and who have the oomph and organisational ability – very important – to improve it and keep it thriving.'

'The food you get at that cafe of Chris's, it's something you want to keep going back for,' Maggie muses looking into the far distance. 'The whole place is... professional, it's the only word.'

'Chris would love to hear you say that. But of course not everywhere is as lucky as Blockley to have people living there with those sorts of talents.' Maggie nods. 'And there's another thing that's really important in deciding whether a village can make a go of it or not.'

'What's that?' asks Maggie. 'Let me guess. How big they are.'

'Exactly. Some villages are just too small to be able to score enough of these points. Take Condicote for example. It's got a solid ranking on the prettiness scale, heart coming out of its ears and a mix of people living there. But it's no more than a couple of dozen houses. So, in the first place, it couldn't support a shop or jobs. And, then, it only takes a few people to move there who don't muck in and the character of the whole place starts to shift. It's the little villages that are really vulnerable.'

'I can smell something... is it burning?'

'Jeeeees!' and I shoot into the kitchen, wrench open the oven door and snatch out our supper. 'S'OK,' I yell. 'Just caught it in time.'

Once we've both got outside a half-dozen forkfuls of croute, peppers and fish, Maggie asks, 'So you seem to have all the material here for your unarmed tussle with Ralph. But are you sure you'll be able to remember it and snap it out in the heat of combat?'

'Ahh, I thought I'd use my old exam technique. The key phrase is: "PC Jobs' heart is like a lopsided shop in Venice which is fiery and large."'

'What on earth are you drivelling on about?'

'The way to remember stuff in an exam is to have a single phrase or sentence that incorporates all your key ideas. "PC JOBS' HEART is like a LOPSIDED SHOP in VENICE which is FIERY and LARGE" is an easy way to remember the nine things which move a village along the scale from dump – zero score, to perfection – nine out of nine.'

'OK, OK. What's "PC"?'

'PRETTY and COMMUNICATIONS. Then the rest are JOBS, HEART...'

'And Venice?'

'Packingham, Venice of the south-west, example of over-the-top commercialisation.'

'Right. Got it. So let's do a practical test. How does Stow-on-the-Wold rate on this scale?'

'Great idea. I'll grab a bit of paper and mark them off.' I scoop in the last bite of salmon en croute and take up a ballpoint. 'The pastry was good wasn't it? OK, number one: is Stow-on-the-Wold pretty, i.e. are people attracted here by the look of its historic architecture?'

'A tick obviously. It's as easy on the eye as any village in England.'

'Yup. Two, does it have good communications or is it isolated?'

'Well, it's only ten minutes from Kingham Station on the Worcester to Paddington line, and it's on the tourist trail between Oxford and Shakespeare's Stratford.'

'Another tick. Three, does it have jobs locally?'

'I'd say yes. It's got hotels and pubs and shops and cafes. So that's got to be a tick.'

'Four. Does it have heart, a sense of its own identity? I'll answer that. It's got loads. It's got a physical centre, the Market Square, that everyone can stand in and say "This is my Stow-on-the-Wold", and as well, the place oozes history. Iron Age fort, the last battle of the Civil War fought here, centre of the medieval sheep trade...'

'You don't think you might be a little biased on this one, do you?'

'Absolutely. But I'm allowed to be. History's my bag. So I'm going to be a dictator and give it an extra big tick.'

Maggie gives a rascally giggle. 'I'm enjoying this. What's next?'

'Is it lopsided? Which would be bad.'

'Remind me again what we mean by that?'

'Well, is it all posh people, for instance? Or is it all commuters? Is it a ghetto?'

'I'd say definitely not. There are expensive eighteenth-century houses and there are affordable places to live in as well.'

'I think that's right. And if you like to join clubs, there's a big range too. From the British Legion to a thriving youth club, to the Women's Institute.' I pick up the serving spoon and divide up the last pepper strips, two and a half each. 'Hmm. Maybe more relevant though, there *are* a lot of oldies in Stow. Forty per cent retirees.'

'Is that enough to make it lopsided?'

I cluck and chew the end of the biro. 'Why don't we give it half a tick?'

'OK. Where are we up to?'

'Number six, shops. Well that's obviously a big fat tick. There's not a lot you can't buy here, whether you want a humane mousetrap, home-made sausages or the complete works of Dostoevsky.'

'And don't forget designer jeans!'

'Oops, sorry. I'll put a footnote to that effect.'

'Hang on though. Tesco came to the outskirts of Stow only five or six years ago, and didn't we reckon a supermarket usually kills off village shops?'

'You're right. The greengrocer's shut of course. But the little Co-op in the Square, and the two delis and Bob the Butcher's shop all carried on and do well.'

'So why do you reckon that was?'

'Well, I think it's because Stow's a thriving place anyway. It was strong enough to survive the competition. Next, number seven, is it *over*-commercialised?'

'Some might say too many teashops and gift shops.'

'Well, I'd make a strong case for a tick here. Stow has always been a place where people came to buy things. It's always been a market. And more important, Stow isn't just tourism. Its architecture doesn't get drowned in a sea of visitors.'

'Fair enough.'

'Next one: fiery spirits, that's people with get up and go to organise anything that's needed to improve the place. Like Jenni, founding editor of *Stow Times*, for instance.'

'And Joanna next door, she's a good example. She's on the Stow Council Planning Committee, the Committee of the Friends of Stow Surgery, sings in the church choir, as well as being in the Professional and Business Group, on the Civic Society Committee and in the Women's Institute. And there are plenty of others like her.'

'OK, tick. And finally, size.'

'Well, some people would say Stow isn't a village at all, that it's a town.'

'Look, this arrived through the post last week.' I get up and select a glossy pamphlet from the heap of papers on the desk. 'It's a flyer about a competition to find "the most vibrant village in Gloucestershire". Village is defined as a population under 3,500. Stow is under 3,000. So it's official, Stow is a village. But the point about size is that Stow has scored high on all the other points, partly because it is a bigger village. Big enough to have shops, lots of clubs, a mix of housing, etcetera, etcetera.'

'OK, so is that the lot?' I nod, but Maggie interrupts, 'Hang on, what about the football team test?'

'Cripes, yes. How could I forget that? Stow doesn't have a football team.' I scratch behind my ear and hmm. 'It doesn't feel right for it to fail the test though. Young people aren't deserting Stow like they are Hogsthorpe. There *is* a rugby team, of course. And some would say that rugby in Gloucestershire is like football on Merseyside. Rugby's not just a posh sport round here. So having a rugby club – and, what's more, one that has dances and barbecues and that kind of social stuff as well – is an indicator that young people tend to stick around in Stow, so I think it deserves a tick.'

'I agree. So what's Stow-on-the-Wold's score on the perfect village scale?'

I scan my list. '… nine and a half out of ten.'

'Bloody Hell!' exclaims Maggie. 'We live in paradise!'

CHAPTER 35

THE OLD STABLES INTO THE SUNSET

'**W**ell, now,' says Ralph settling himself in the middle of the sofa like a king on an overlarge throne, 'I've got an announcement to make.'

I gulp. I'm going to have to interrupt him. I've hardly spoken during lunch. This is for two reasons. First, I had a restless night, tormented by dreams about the imperfect village, full of policemen that all look like Wayne Rooney, and shops on fire, and where nobody could find work because the houses were leaning to one side and kept falling over. So I'm tired. Secondly, after this night of confusion, I'm no longer confident I can remember my key sentence, so all the time that Ralph has been telling us about the class solidarity at Cremona University and the ridiculous antics of the buffoon Berlusconi, I've been saying to myself, 'Is it PM JOBS has a SHOP-SOILED FIRE in his HEART and plays FOOTBALL badly? Or is it PC FIBS FIRES LOPSIDED SHOTS at the

SPIRIT SHOP?' However, returning from the kitchen to get the sugar for Ralph's coffee, I've had a crafty scrabble through the top drawer of the desk and taken a quick glance at my crib sheet, so I'm all set with my arguments, from PRETTY through to SIZE. Nothing can go wrong, so long as I recite it soon. The dust-up between me and Ralph on the worth of village life has got to be had now. I can't have him droning on for hours about the publication of his latest academic paper on Peruvian Marxism in the 1920s, or else I'll forget the ten bull's eye points again. So I interrupt.

'Can we just settle one thing first, Ralph,' I challenge him. 'You know Stow-on-the-Wold isn't *Lark Rise to Cranford*, I mean *Candleford to Downtown Abbey*.'

He gives me a nervous look as if he's being accosted by a man who a moment before was seen shouting at a lamp-post.

I seize the opportunity while he's on the back foot. 'Stow-on-the-Wold's got it all,' I bark. 'Nine and a half out of ten, it communicates well, it's got plenty of shops. *And* it used to have bubonic plague, but these days it's just pretty big. No football I admit. But best of all, Ralph, it's not very lopsided!' This isn't exactly what I say, but it's what it feels like to me.

Maggie seems to detect I'm drowning, and launches a small lifeboat. 'Derek's been thinking about what you said to him when you had lunch together last year, that living in a chocolate-box village like Stow is like setting up home in a theme park for old aged pensioners.'

'Is that what I said?' Ralph asks, cocking his head on one side.

'Yes, I remember it,' I barge in, grasping a flotation aid and flapping my arms a bit. 'You said you thought villages are just for old people who watch Sunday night rural nostalgia dramas.'

'Hmm, well, if you say so. I was probably just having a joke and trying to wind you up.'

'More coffee, Ralph?' says Maggie, sinking me with a pitiful look.

'Great, Maggie, it's good stuff,' he replies. 'Now then, for my big announcement.' He leans back on his throne. 'I've put 76 Rorkes Drift Gardens up for sale.' This is Ralph's terraced abode that's beset by wheelie bins and ASBO-shirkers in the East End of London.

'Oh,' says Maggie, cocking her head to indicate polite encouragement.

'Yes. And…' He pauses - it must be lecturing to first-year politics students that's developed his sense of timing. '… I'm in the process of buying an old farmhouse in a Tuscan village.'

'That's nice,' says Maggie.

'In Tuscany,' Ralph confirms. 'It's one of those beautiful villages that sits on top of a hill. I've been offered a research fellowship at Cremona. You'll love the village. It's called Santa Tomasina della Tranquillità.'

'Sounds lovely,' says Maggie.

'That's right,' Ralph continues. 'This village has got a bar with terrific views, and a little shop that sells local produce.'

'That's wonderful, Ralph,' says Maggie. 'How's your Italian?'

'Coming along. But actually a lot of the neighbours are English. It's a popular place for retirees.'

You may be wondering why I've not said anything so far. It's because it's difficult to speak when your mouth won't shut.

'Of course our mayor is a leading light in the local PCI,' he continues.

'PCI?' I manage to say in a croaky voice.

'Partito Comunista Italiano,' replies Ralph in a polished accent.

'Oh,' I say, 'Well, that's all right then.'

And when that evening we've watched Ralph's *deux chevaux* splutter off down Back Walls, I finally let myself erupt with a fiery burst of abuse and disdain.

Maggie waits till the bright puce in my cheeks has drained away and my language has subsided to an occasional spark. Then she laughs. I can't see the joke myself.

On the evening of the first of October, two years almost to the day since we first checked out Sunny's burgage, Maggie and I jointly prepare aromatic pork with couscous and a beetroot and feta starter without once infringing Rule 2B on non-interference with the other's cooking technique. It happens sometimes. Today is that sort of day.

I turn up the thermostat on the underfloor heating and pour two glasses – you should know by now what we both drink. Then, over the dining table, we congratulate each other on our culinary expertise, remark on the perfection of our kitchen design, savour the food, and when Maggie even says, 'You know, I think your new gym regime is starting to show results,' I pat my marginally less bulging stomach with satisfaction.

When the last morsel of pork has been appreciated, we sit down together on the sofa, and survey The Old Stables. Our home. Where we live. Where people come and visit us.

Thirty metres of oak-framed glass, a high back wall of exposed Cotswold stone, beams and braces carved from hearts-of-oak. Plus, of course, a floor of butter coloured limestone that would be happy to support the whole Stow Rugby Club First Fifteen still in their playing boots and celebrating a victory over archrivals Cheltenham Tigers, should we ever wish to invite them. What's more, it's a floor that exudes a gentle heat, with – now – neither puddle nor flood to disgrace it. And through the acres of glass, we look out onto a small floodlit courtyard designed by Maggie to be as calm and as exotic as a hideaway in the Alhambra Palace at Granada.

'Well,' says Maggie, 'we finally made it.'

'We really did,' I say. 'It's sort of slipped into a triumph without a fanfare.'

'So was it worth it?'

'Sure, it's got everything we wanted. Character, light and it's right in the middle of England's most perfect village, Stow-on-the-Wold.'

Maggie grins, sips her wine and looks up at the long living room. 'There must be something that hasn't worked though, mustn't there?'

'Well, the funny thing is that even some of the things that seemed to go wrong at the time have turned out OK. For instance, having to build a new wall for a metre up inside the Big Back Wall because of the radon gas. It's given us a long elegant shelf running the length of the room.'

'That's true. And those niches high up that we wanted to make into windows, but the Grise got shirty about. The little lights we've hidden inside them look magical right now.'

'Of course, it could be we've fooled ourselves a little bit along the way. When you see a place grow day by day, you tend to spot problems early, and either fix them or accept them. And you end up seeing it all as perfect.'

'Could be,' she says. 'The other thing is every bit of wall and roof and floor's got some near-disaster attached to it. It makes the whole place special.'

'You're spot on,' I say.

'What about the nasty vision of the wrong end of a horse in the bathroom? Is that still haunting you?'

'Well, I *was* starting to forget all about it. But now you've reminded me of it again, it'll be back to the psychotherapy for me.'

We both giggle.

'It's been a grand adventure,' says Maggie. 'But unlike any other adventure, it's a story we can keep reliving, just by looking around us.'

'And reliving without the stress this time,' I add.

We're quiet for a while.

'What do you think? Is there anything you'd want to change?' I ask.

Maggie looks around at the glass, the oak, the limestone floor and the Big Back Wall. 'No, I don't think so,' she replies.

We settle back into a comfortable fold of each other's arms and she adds, 'Well, I suppose the only thing I'd say is, perhaps next time we could try something a bit bigger.'

'*Next time!*' I cry, sitting up with a jump. 'What do you mean "Next time"?'

'Well,' replies Maggie, 'we might want to move some day, mightn't we?'

'What, go through all this lot again!'

'Not just yet, obviously. But we're still young, aren't we?'

'Yes,' I say, 'of course we're still young.'

'So we're still game for adventures together, aren't we?'

'Well, yes,' I reply, nodding now like a finely balanced metronome. 'More adventures. Together.'

Maggie puts her hand on my shoulder. She smiles.

And so do I.

THEN WHAT?

If you're standing up, getting ready to put the book back on the shelf, I think you'd better sit down again. You may be in for a shock.

A year after we moved in, Bill's wall fell down.

We were away on holiday when a neighbour phoned us. The council had been repairing the road and it seems the vibration from their equipment had the same impact as trumpet fanfares around Jericho. We resisted the temptation to fly home, and instead phoned Nik, and he and Simon, like the heroes they are, went straight to Stow, tidied up, and a few weeks later the wall was back in place.

But calamities didn't end there. You remember that bit about Ken the Underfloor guru and how indestructible his heating is? Yup, you're right. Six months ago, some flagstones by the door into the guest suite started to wobble when you trod on them, so we asked Justine the floorer to have a look for us. She found damp underneath. Half an hour and three phone calls later, I discovered that the company which had installed our heating system had gone out of business, that the pipes which they used aren't made anymore, and also that anyway they are – according to a local heating engineer I spoke to – 'rubbish.' The better news is that this engineer found the leak during a two hour house-call, with no more than a square foot of floor hacked up, and he did a repair. There was a little dent in the piping that looked suspiciously like something sharp had been dropped on it.

The other piece of news that made me gulp is that two of Stow's four bookshops have shut down. However, I'm glad to report that the Borzoi – in the words of the reviewer, Richard Osborne, 'As choice a small bookshop as any in the realm' – is still thriving.

Next, a Blockley Shop-Café-Post Office update. It's a raging hit, now selling over half a million pounds' worth of newspapers, stamps and fish cake lunches a year! Chris the manager reckons it's probably the most successful community enterprise of any village in the country. The Blockley Shop and Café is even cited in Conservative Party literature as a model for the Big Society. What's more, it's just won planning permission to expand to larger premises. This simple sentence however, masks a year-long struggle. The villagers' efforts to get their new shop were blocked at every turn. What villains would do such a thing? I hear you ask. Why, the planning authorities and the conservation officer, of course.

Then, there's an unalloyed piece of heart-warming news from Stow that shows how much its citizens cherish their heritage. A recent meeting of the Stow and District Civic Society was so well attended that there was standing room only inside St Edward's Hall with people outside having to be turned away. The meeting was to report the launch of a campaign for an investigation into whether the last battle of the Civil War was, in fact, fought much closer to Stow than previously thought. I'm hoping they might let me help with the archaeological survey.

THEN WHAT?

Finally, I can answer the question you might have been too polite to ask. Maggie and I still love Stow-on-the-Wold, and we still love The Old Stables. We intend to stay exactly where we are. Probably.

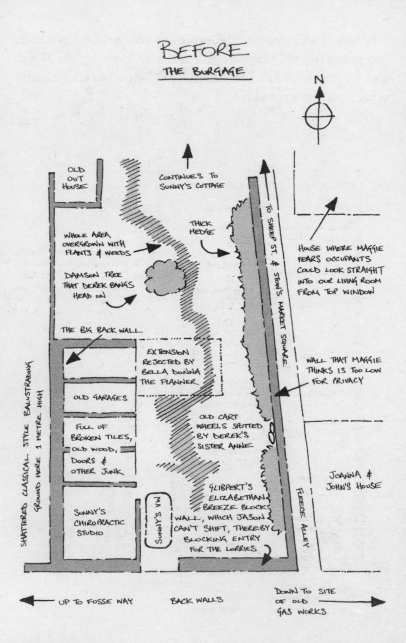

BEFORE
THE BURGAGE

N

OLD OUT HOUSE

CONTINUES TO SUNNY'S COTTAGE

THICK HEDGE

WHOLE AREA OVERGROWN WITH PLANTS & WEEDS

DAMSON TREE THAT DEREK BANGS HEAD ON

THE BIG BACK WALL

EXTENSION REJECTED BY BELLA DONNA THE PLANNER

OLD GARAGES

FULL OF BROKEN TILES, OLD WOOD, DOORS & OTHER JUNK

OLD CART WHEELS SPOTTED BY DEREK'S SISTER ANNE

SUNNY'S CHIROPRACTIC STUDIO

SUNNY'S VW

GLIBPERT'S ELIZABETHAN BREEZE BLOCK WALL, WHICH JASON CAN'T SHIFT, THEREBY BLOCKING ENTRY FOR THE LORRIES

SHATTERED CLASSICAL STYLE BALUSTRADING (GROUND HERE 1 METRE HIGH)

TO SHEEP ST. & STOW'S MARKET SQUARE

HOUSE WHERE MAGGIE FEARS OCCUPANTS COULD LOOK STRAIGHT INTO OUR LIVING ROOM FROM TOP WINDOW

WALL THAT MAGGIE THINKS IS TOO LOW FOR PRIVACY

JOANNA & JOHN'S HOUSE

FLEECE ALLEY

UP TO FOSSE WAY

BACK WALLS

DOWN TO SITE OF OLD GAS WORKS

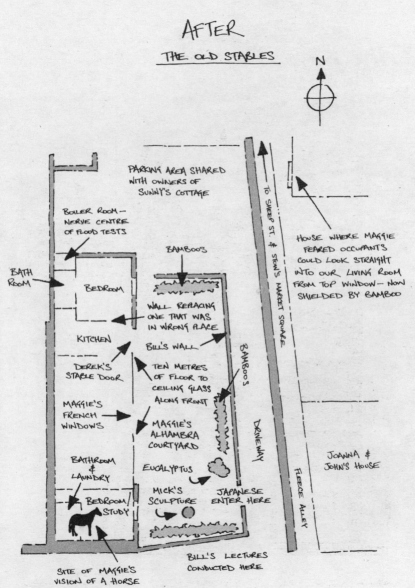

AFTER

THE OLD STABLES

N

PARKING AREA SHARED
WITH OWNERS OF
SUNNY'S COTTAGE

BOILER ROOM —
NERVE CENTRE
OF FLOOD TESTS

BAMBOOS

BATH
ROOM

BEDROOM

WALL REPLACING
ONE THAT WAS
IN WRONG PLACE

HOUSE WHERE MAGGIE
FEARED OCCUPANTS
COULD LOOK STRAIGHT
INTO OUR LIVING ROOM
FROM TOP WINDOW — NOW
SHIELDED BY BAMBOO

TO SHEEP ST. & STEW'S MARKET SQUARE

KITCHEN

BILL'S WALL

DEREK'S
STABLE DOOR

TEN METRES
OF FLOOR TO
CEILING GLASS
ALONG FRONT

MAGGIE'S
FRENCH
WINDOWS

MAGGIE'S
ALHAMBRA
COURTYARD

BAMBOOS

DRIVEWAY

BATHROOM
&
LAUNDRY

EUCALYPTUS

BEDROOM/
STUDY

MICK'S
SCULPTURE

JAPANESE
ENTER HERE

FLEECE ALLEY

JOANNA &
JOHN'S HOUSE

SITE OF MAGGIE'S
VISION OF A HORSE

BILL'S LECTURES
CONDUCTED HERE

BACK WALLS

ACKNOWLEDGEMENTS

I want to thank everyone who knew I was writing a book and who still risked talking to me, namely Richard Davis, Jeremy Drinkwater, Chris Elton, Chris Grimes, Mike Morris, Joanna Neave, Tim Norris, David Penman, Tony Percy, Geoff Richards, Jenni Turner, and especially Anthea Jackson (of AJ Architects) and Nik Weaver and Simon Townsend (of FDB Cheltenham Building Services).

My meagre knowledge of home conversion was built up by Ross Stokes, Editor of *SelfBuild & Design* magazine. For purposes of historical background, three reference books didn't leave my desk-top for months. They are: *Stow-on-the-Wold: Glimpses of the Past*, the excellent publication by the Stow and District Civic Society; *Highways and Byways in Oxford and the Cotswolds* by the tireless Edwardian cyclist, Herbert A. Evans; *The Changing English Village 1066-1914*, by M. K. Ashby who taught me about poverty through the ages in Bledington. The pages you have just read were also livened up by references to *Hons and Rebels* by Jessica Mitford as well as *The Phoenix, The White Peacock, Lady Chatterley's Lover* and the other Nottinghamshire novels of D. H. Lawrence. The Journals of the DHL Society were helpful here too. And I'm also grateful to A. A. Gill and his misguided views about Stow in *The Angry Island*, which provided several paragraphs of innocent amusement.

One of the great pleasures I've had writing *A Horse in the Bathroom* has been working with everyone at Summersdale Publishing, and especially with Jennifer Barclay, commissioning editor, who's been considerate, efficient, encouraging, astute in her criticism and constantly good-humoured.

And finally, my thanks to Maggie, who read all the drafts, and still had the energy to put squiggles in the margin wherever she unerringly identified that I was talking rubbish, as well as rewarding me with ticks where she approved or I made her laugh.

Have you enjoyed this book?
If so, why not write a review on your favourite website?

If you're interested in finding out more about our travel books
friend us on Facebook at **Summersdale Traveleditor**
and follow us on Twitter: **@SummersdaleGO**

Thanks very much for buying this Summersdale book.

www.summersdale.com